The Fall of Anne Boleyn

A Countdown

Claire Ridgway

The Fall of Anne Boleyn: A Countdown

Copyright © 2012 Claire Ridgway

ISBN-13: 978-84-944574-3-2

First Edition: April 2012
Second Edition: October 2015

M
MadeGlobal Publishing

For more information on
MadeGlobal Publishing, visit our website:
www.madeglobal.com

Front Cover Design by Tim Ridgway and David Leppenwell Includes background text from John Stow's "Annals of England to 1603" (Dated 1603) - Account of Anne Boleyn's Execution.

Image is © 2012 The Anne Boleyn Files and Claire Ridgway

Dedication

For Tim, Christian, Verity and Joel, always xx

In memory of Queen Anne Boleyn,
George Boleyn, Sir Henry Norris,
Sir Francis Weston, Sir William
Brereton and Mark Smeaton.

These bloody days have broken my heart.

Contents

Preface

Dressed in an ermine-trimmed, grey damask robe, with an English style gable hood and a crimson kirtle underneath, the slight, dark-haired woman took her final walk. She went out of the Queen's Lodgings, past the Great Hall, through Cole Harbour Gate, and along the western side of the White Tower to the black-draped scaffold. The Constable of the Tower of London, Sir William Kingston, helped her up the scaffold steps and she stepped forward to address the waiting crowd. Her coal-black eyes flitted over the crowd. As her gaze met those of her enemies - Thomas Cromwell, Charles Brandon, Henry Fitzroy and Thomas Audley – she didn't so much as flinch. The people fell silent as they gazed at their queen, Anne Boleyn, who one witness described as being "never so beautiful". The Queen took a deep breath and spoke:

> *"Good Christian people, I have not come here*
> *to preach a sermon; I have come here to die. For*
> *according to the law and by the law I am judged to*
> *die, and therefore I will speak nothing against it. I*
> *am come hither to accuse no man, nor to speak of*
> *that whereof I am accused and condemned to die,*
> *but I pray God save the King and send him long*
> *to reign over you, for a gentler nor a more merciful*
> *prince was there never, and to me he was ever a*
> *good, a gentle, and sovereign lord. And if any person*
> *will meddle of my cause, I require them to judge the*
> *best. And thus I take my leave of the world and of*
> *you all, and I heartily desire you all to pray for me."*

Her ladies stepped forward to remove Anne's mantle and Anne doffed her hood, loosening those famous lustrous dark locks before tucking them into a cloth cap to keep them off her neck - that "little neck". As her ladies sobbed silently, Anne paid the executioner, the famous Sword of Calais, who begged her forgiveness for the deed he was about to commit. Even he was moved by the dignity of the woman who stood before him. She showed no fear. Then the eyes that Anne had always used so powerfully were hidden by a blindfold and she knelt, in the straw, praying all the while:

> *"O Lord have mercy on me, to God I*
> *commend my soul. To Jesus Christ I commend*
> *my soul; Lord Jesu receive my soul."*

One by one, the crowd too sank to their knees out of respect for this woman whose courage and dignity spoke of her innocence. The Dukes of Suffolk and Richmond, stunned, watched the reaction of the crowd and refused to follow suit. Anne deserved this, in their opinion.

The silence was deafening as the crowd waited for the executioner to strike. The only sound was Anne whispering her prayers. The executioner, visibly shaken by the atmosphere and by Anne's courage, noticed that the Queen kept turning her head slightly, anticipating the blow, so he called out to his assistant to pass him his sword. As Anne moved her head to follow what the assistant was doing, the executioner came up behind her unnoticed and beheaded her with one stroke. Her ordeal was over. Her head may have been in the straw, her blood flowing freely across the scaffold, but Anne's soul was with her Father in Heaven.

Anne Boleyn was denied a proper burial with Christian service. Instead, her sobbing ladies gathered up her head and body, wrapped them in white cloth and took them to the Tower chapel, St Peter ad Vincula. Here, the Star of the Court was placed inside an old elm chest which had once contained bow staves. Anne Boleyn, the mother of the future Elizabeth I, was then laid to rest in an unmarked grave, buried as a traitor to the Crown.

It was the 19th May 1536 and a Queen of England had been executed.

Introduction

The fall of the Boleyns and the executions of Anne, George and members of the Boleyn faction cannot be put down to one single factor; the bloody events of 1536 can only be examined properly by looking at their context. A combination of factors all came into play that winter and spring.

In this guide to the fall of Anne Boleyn, I let the primary sources tell the story of spring 1536 because I believe that there is no better way to examine those events than through the eyes of people who were actually there. Obviously, we have to take into account the bias of those reporting the events and where they were getting their information from. Even so, they give us a unique insight into what was happening. This book is factual and is not a romantic retelling of Anne Boleyn's story. My mission has always been to get at the real truth about Anne Boleyn and to share it. This book is part of that mission. Full references are given, with guidance on how to find the sources named, so that you too can do further research if you wish. Warning: Digging into the 16th century is addictive!

I have chosen to look at the events chronologically and to take you through them a day at a time, so you can see exactly what led to Anne Boleyn's execution. Interspersed with some of the events are brief biographies of the people mentioned, so that you can see where they fit into Anne's story. I have also provided a "cast" list of those involved in the events. You will notice that the book is not written as a flowing biography or history book, but is written more like a journal or diary. My aim in writing it thus was to make it easy to find dates and events, and to allow you to follow Anne's final days, from start to brutal finish. It also makes it easier to digest.

The primary sources give us facts, but they do not give us the entire story. We do not know what Thomas Cromwell and Henry VIII were thinking; we only know their actions and some of what they said. We can infer, we can hypothesise, but we will never know for sure exactly what happened in 1536. We can argue that

Henry VIII was responsible for Anne's fall, we can argue that it was all down to Cromwell and that Henry was an innocent victim, we can argue that Anne was innocent, we can argue that she was guilty. We do not know the full story, merely partial truths. For this reason, I present here the evidence and my own thoughts based on MY reading of the evidence. You may think differently and I'm certainly not telling you what to think.

I hope you enjoy this journey back to 1536; hang on to your hats!

Note: In the Tudor times, there was no standardized spelling. All spellings in quotations are as they were in the contemporary sources.

The Cast 1535-1536

Henry VIII (1491-1547) – The King

Henry VIII was born on the 28th June 1491, the son of Henry VII and Elizabeth of York. Although the second son, he became King following Henry VII's death because his older brother, Prince Arthur, had died in 1502. Henry VIII married Arthur's widow, Catherine of Aragon, on 11th June 1509 but annulled his marriage to her in 1533. Henry VIII came to believe that their marriage was contrary to God's law because it was incestuous, in that she was his brother's widow, He believed that the lack of a living son was proof of this. Henry married his second wife, Anne Boleyn, in a secret ceremony on the 25th January 1533.

Henry is known for having six wives – Catherine of Aragon, Anne Boleyn, Jane Seymour, Anne of Cleves, Catherine Howard and Catherine Parr – and for executing two of them.

Catherine of Aragon (1485-1536)

Catherine of Aragon (Catalina de Aragón) was born on the night of 15th/16th December 1485. She was the daughter of Ferdinand II of Aragon and Isabel I of Castile, and was named after her maternal great-grandmother, Catalina de Castile or Catherine of Lancaster. On 14th November 1501, Catherine of Aragon married the heir to the English throne, Arthur, Prince of Wales, but was widowed just a few months later. She married Arthur's brother, Henry VIII, in June 1509 and the couple were married for over twenty-four years. Their only surviving child was a daughter, born in February 1516, who became Queen Mary I. It is thought that Catherine had at least five other pregnancies, which resulted in miscarriages, stillbirths or early infant death. Catherine died on 7th January 1536 at Kimbolton Castle.

Anne Boleyn (1501-1536)

Anne Boleyn was born in 1501 (some say 1507) and was the daughter of courtier and diplomat Thomas Boleyn and his wife Elizabeth Howard. Anne spent time at the courts of Margaret of Austria and Queen Claude of France before joining the English court in late 1521 to serve Catherine of Aragon as lady-in-waiting. It is thought that Henry VIII was in love with her by Shrovetide 1526 and in August 1527 he decided to ask the Pope for a dispensation to allow him to marry Anne. The King's Great Matter (Henry's struggle for an annulment of his marriage to Catherine of Aragon) ensued and Henry and Anne had to wait seven years to marry. Anne was crowned Queen on 1st June 1533 and gave birth to a daughter, the future Elizabeth I, on 7th September 1533. Anne experienced two other unsuccessful pregnancies. She was executed for treason on 19th May 1536, after being found guilty of adultery and plotting the King's death.

George Boleyn, Lord Rochford (c1504-1536)

George Boleyn was born around 1504 and was the younger brother of Anne Boleyn. He was a courtier, poet, diplomat, royal favourite and member of the King's privy chamber. He was married to Jane Parker, the daughter of Henry Parker, Lord Morley. George was influential in Parliament and carried out many important diplomatic missions on behalf of the King. His frequent mention in the privy purse expenses show that he regularly played dice, bowls and cards with Henry VIII and was a member of the King's circle of friends. He was also a zealous reformer and gifted poet.

George was executed on 17th May 1536 after being found guilty of treason and of incest with his sister, Queen Anne Boleyn. Popular fiction makes him out to be homosexual, but there is actually no evidence of this.

Thomas Boleyn, Earl of Wiltshire and Earl of Ormond (c.1477-1539)

Thomas was the eldest of ten children. His parents were Sir William Boleyn and Lady Margaret Butler. His paternal grandfather was Geoffrey Boleyn, the Lord Mayor of London, and his maternal grandfather was Thomas Butler, the 7th Earl of Ormond.

Margaret Butler was a descendant of Eleanor de Bohun and her first husband James Butler, 1st Earl of Ormond; interestingly, Eleanor de Bohun was the granddaughter of Edward I and his first wife, Eleanor of Castile.

In 1498 or 1499, Thomas Boleyn married Lady Elizabeth Howard, daughter of Thomas Howard, the Earl of Surrey (and later the 2nd Duke of Norfolk). The couple had at least five children: Mary, Anne, George, Thomas and Henry. Only Mary, Anne and George survived childhood. Thomas's flair for languages, his probable legal training and his intelligence made him indispensable at court and he served the King as an ambassador, privy councillor and Lord Privy Seal. Thomas was also a Reformer and supported his godson Thomas Tebold in the latter's travels around Europe in 1535 and 1536, spreading the news that Thomas Boleyn was a patron of the new learning and new religion.

Thomas Cromwell (1485-1540)

Thomas Cromwell was born in Putney circa 1485 and was the son of Walter Cromwell, blacksmith, cloth merchant and fuller. He studied law and was fluent in French, Italian and Latin, which helped him to become employed by Cardinal Wolsey in around 1514. After Wolsey's fall, and due partly to the patronage of Anne Boleyn, Cromwell quickly rose to be the King's right hand man. In this role, Cromwell assisted the King in his quest to have his marriage to Catherine of Aragon annulled as well as in the dissolution of the monasteries. He became the King's official principal secretary and chief minister in 1534. There is controversy concerning his actual role in the downfall of Anne Boleyn. It's unclear whether

Cromwell instigated the plot or whether he simply carried out the King's wishes.

Charles Brandon, Duke of Suffolk (c1484-1545)

Charles Brandon was one of Henry VIII's best friends. He was born circa 1484 to Sir William Brandon and Elizabeth Bruyn, and his father died carrying Henry VII's standard at the Battle of Bosworth in 1485. It is thought that Brandon grew up in the household of his uncle, Sir Thomas Brandon, a leading courtier in the reign of Henry VII. By 1507, Brandon himself was serving the King as an esquire of the body. Although he was seven years older than Henry VIII, Brandon became the King's lifelong friend, and was made Duke of Suffolk in 1514. He was forgiven for marrying the King's favourite sister, Mary Tudor, Queen of France, in 1515, without the King's permission. The couple had four children: Henry, Frances, Eleanor and a second Henry after the death of their first son. Mary died in June 1533 and their second son died in 1534. Brandon married for the fourth time in September 1534; his new wife was his 14 year old ward, Catherine Willoughby. Brandon had poor relations with Anne Boleyn, his sympathy being with Catherine of Aragon.

Thomas Audley, Lord Chancellor (1487/8-1544)

Thomas Audley was born around 1487/8 in Earls Colne, Essex. He came to the attention of Henry VIII in 1523 after taking Cardinal Wolsey's side in Parliament when Sir Thomas More defended the rights of the common people. He rose quickly from that point, and on 20th May 1532 he was knighted and made keeper of the great seal after Sir Thomas More resigned as Lord Chancellor. On 26th January 1533, he was officially named as Lord Chancellor. Audley is thought to have been responsible for smoothing the passage through Parliament of legislation regarding the King's break with Rome and the supremacy.

Henry Fitzroy, Duke of Richmond and Somerset (1519-1536)

Henry Fitzroy was the illegitimate son of Henry VIII by his mistress Elizabeth (Bessie) Blount. He was born at the priory of St Lawrence in Blackmore, Essex, around June 1519. In 1525, he was elected Knight of the Garter and made Earl of Nottingham and Duke of Richmond and Somerset. This was followed, by him being made Warden General of the Marches and Lord Admiral of England. In 1529 he became Lord Lieutenant of Ireland and in October 1532 he accompanied Henry VIII and Anne Boleyn to their meeting with Francis I in Calais. On 26th November 1533, he married Mary Howard, daughter of the Duke of Norfolk, but it is believed that the marriage was never consummated due to the couple's youth.

Eustace Chapuys, Imperial Ambassador (c1491-1556)

Eustace Chapuys was the second son of Louis Chapuys, a notary of Annecy in the duchy of Savoy, and of Guigone Dupuys. He became a doctor of civil and canon laws after studying at Turin University. By August 1526 he was the Duke of Bourbon's ambassador to Charles V's court in Granada. In the summer of 1527, after the death of the Duke of Bourbon in the sack of Rome, Chapuys joined the imperial service, working under Nicholas de Perrenot, seigneur de Granvelle. He arrived in England in September 1529 to begin working as Catherine of Aragon's adviser in negotiations regarding the annulment. He was her link to the Emperor and to Rome. He detested Anne Boleyn, never referring to her by name but as "the concubine" or "the putain" [whore].

Jane Seymour (c1508/09-1537)

Jane Seymour was born in 1508 or 1509, probably at the family seat, Wolf Hall in Wiltshire. She was the daughter of Sir John Seymour, soldier and courtier, and of Margery Wentworth. Like all of Henry VIII's wives, she was descended from Edward

III. It is thought that she arrived at court around 1529. She served Catherine of Aragon and then Anne Boleyn as a lady-in-waiting. Her brothers, Edward and Thomas Seymour, were on the rise in the 1530s and it is thought that they and Sir Nicholas Carew coached Jane to appeal to the King.

The Lady Mary, formerly Princess Mary (1516-1558)

Mary was born on 18th February 1516 at Greenwich Palace and was the only surviving child of the marriage of Catherine of Aragon and Henry VIII. She lost both her legitimacy and her title of Princess when her parents' marriage was annulled in 1533. She refused to recognise her father's second wife, Anne Boleyn, as queen, saying that she knew of no queen apart from her mother.

Princess Elizabeth (1533-1603)

Elizabeth was born on 7th September 1533 at Greenwich Palace, the only surviving child of the marriage of Anne Boleyn and Henry VIII. She was given her own household of staff at Hatfield, Hunsdon and then Eltham, and was put into the care of Lady Margaret Bryan. She was just two years old when her mother was executed in May 1536 and she was made illegitimate.

Charles V, Holy Roman Emperor (1500-1558)

Charles was born on 24th February 1500 to Joanna of Castile (Juana la Loca), sister of Catherine of Aragon, and to Philip I of Castile. His maternal grandparents were the Catholic Reyes, Isabella I of Castile and Ferdinand II of Aragon, and his paternal grandparents were Maximilian I, Holy Roman Emperor, and Mary of Burgundy. He became King of Spain in 1516 and Holy Roman Emperor in 1519.

In 1521 Charles became betrothed to five year old Princess Mary, daughter of Henry VIII and Catherine of Aragon. However, in 1525, he married Isabella of Portugal. The couple had seven children: Philip II of Spain, Maria of Spain, Isabella, Ferdinand,

Joan of Spain, John and Ferdinand.

Henry Courtenay, Marquis of Exeter (1498/9-1538)

Henry Courtenay was born circa 1498-9 and was the son of William Courtenay, Earl of Devon, and of Katherine, daughter of Edward IV and Elizabeth Woodville. In 1519 he married his second wife, Gertrude Blount, daughter of William Blount, fourth Baron Mountjoy, the Queen's chamberlain. Gertrude was a pious Catholic, associated with Elizabeth Barton, the Nun of Kent, and both Henry and Gertrude were religious conservatives whose sympathies lay with Catherine of Aragon.

Elizabeth Fitzgerald, Countess of Kildare (d.1548)

Elizabeth Fitzgerald (née Grey) was the daughter of Thomas Grey, first Marquess of Dorset, and of Cicely Bonville. She was the widow of Gerald Fitzgerald, ninth Earl of Kildare, who died in 1534. In 1536 she was a supporter of the Lady Mary.

Henry Pole, Baron Montagu (1492-1539)

Henry Pole was the eldest son of Sir Richard Pole and of Margaret Plantagenet, daughter of George, Duke of Clarence. His mother, Margaret Pole, was the Countess of Salisbury. She was a member of Catherine of Aragon's household and godmother and governess of the Lady Mary. His brother was Cardinal Reginald Pole. The family's sympathies lay with Catherine of Aragon.

John Skip (d.1552)

John Skip was a Norfolk man who studied at Gonville Hall, Cambridge, where he became a member of a group of Reformers who met at the White Horse tavern. He supported the King's annulment and became chaplain and almoner to Queen Anne Boleyn in 1535.

Sir Nicholas Carew (c.1496-1539)

Sir Nicholas Carew was born circa 1496 and was the eldest son of Sir Richard Carew of Beddington, Surrey, and of Maline Oxenbridge. Carew was brought up at court and was serving the King as a groom of the privy chamber by 1511. In 1515 he became an esquire of the body and in 1518 he became a gentleman of the privy chamber. His wife, Elizabeth, was the daughter of Sir Thomas Bryan, vice chamberlain of Catherine of Aragon, and of Lady Margaret Bryan who was governess to the Princess Mary and then to Princess Elizabeth.

Carew was best friends with his brother-in-law, Sir Francis Bryan. In 1535 he sheltered the King's fool who had angered the King by calling Anne Boleyn "a ribald" and the Princess Elizabeth "a bastard". He thus showed his clear sympathy with the Catholic conservatives, Catherine of Aragon and the Lady Mary.

Matthew Parker (1504-1575)

Matthew Parker was born in Norwich on 6th August 1504 and was educated at Corpus Christi College in Cambridge, where he became friends with a group of Reformers and was linked to Lutheran Thomas Bilney. He became one of Queen Anne Boleyn's chaplains in 1535, and Anne's patronage led to him being appointed Dean of the collegiate church of Stoke by Clare in Suffolk.

Sir Henry Norris (late 1490s-1536)

Sir Henry Norris was the son of Richard Norris. He married Mary Fiennes sometime before 1526 and the couple had three children before Mary's death circa 1530. Norris was Henry VIII's Groom of the Stool and was one of the King's best friends. By 1536, he was courting Anne Boleyn's cousin, Margaret Shelton.

Mark Smeaton (d.1536)

Mark was a talented musician who had been a member of Cardinal Wolsey's choir before joining the King's Chapel Royal. He became a Groom of the Privy Chamber in 1529 and was a member of the Boleyn circle.

Sir Francis Weston (c.1511-1536)

Sir Francis Weston was the son of Sir Richard Weston and Anne Sandys, a former lady-in-waiting to Catherine of Aragon. He became a Gentleman of the Privy Chamber in 1532 and was a popular courtier and member of the Boleyn circle.

Sir William Brereton (c.1487/1490-1536)

Sir William Brereton was the sixth son of a leading, landowning Cheshire family and himself became an important man in Cheshire and North Wales. He was married to Elizabeth Savage, daughter of Charles Somerset, 1st Earl of Worcester. He had a colourful reputation and was not a member of the Boleyn circle of friends.

Thomas Cranmer, Archbishop of Canterbury (1489-1556)

Thomas Cranmer was born in Nottinghamshire in 1489 to Thomas and Agnes Cranmer. At the age of 14 he attended Jesus College, Cambridge, where he studied for a Bachelor of Arts degree, followed by a Masters. He was then elected to a fellowship but had to relinquish this when he married. Unfortunately, his wife, Joan, died in childbirth. He married his second wife, Marguerite, in 1532.

In 1526, Cranmer was awarded a Doctorate of Divinity and from 1527 he was involved in the proceedings to get Henry VIII's first marriage to Catherine of Aragon annulled. He was consecrated as Archbishop of Canterbury on 30th March 1533 and opened a special court for the annulment proceedings on 10th May 1533. On

23rd May, Cranmer ruled that the marriage between Henry VIII and Catherine of Aragon was against the will of God, the marriage was declared null and void. Five days later, on 28th May, Cranmer declared the marriage between Henry VIII and Anne Boleyn valid and on the 1st June he crowned Anne Boleyn Queen of England. In September 1533, he had the pleasure of baptising the couple's daughter, Elizabeth, and becoming her godfather.

Sir Thomas Wyatt the Elder (1503-1542)

Sir Thomas Wyatt, "the Father of English Poetry", was born in 1503 at Allington Castle, Kent. He was the son of Sir Henry Wyatt and Anne Skinner. In 1520, Wyatt married Elizabeth Brooke, the daughter of Lord Cobham. In 1521, the couple had a son, Thomas Wyatt the Younger.

In 1524, Wyatt followed his father's example and started a career at court as Clerk of the King's jewels. In 1525 he was made Esquire of the Body and he went on to become an ambassador, undertaking many foreign missions for King Henry VIII. He served Anne Boleyn at her coronation in 1533 and was knighted in 1535.

Sir Richard Page (d.1548)

A gentleman of the privy chamber from 1516 and a man who started his court career in the employ of Cardinal Wolsey.

Sir Francis Bryan (c.1490-1550)

Sir Francis Bryan was born circa 1490 and was the first surviving son of Sir Thomas Bryan and Lady Margaret Bryan (née Bourchier). He was a cousin of Anne Boleyn, and had a reputation for liking rich clothing and for gambling. He was a popular courtier, skilled hunter and jouster, and lost an eye in a joust in 1526. Both Thomas Cromwell and the King referred to Bryan as "the Vicar of Hell".

Sir William Kingston (c.1476-1540)

Nothing is known of the early life of Sir William Kingston or of his first two marriages, but by 1534 he had married Mary Scrope, daughter of Richard Scrope and the widow of Edward Jerningham of Suffolk.[1] From 1497-1509, he served Henry VII as a yeoman of the chamber and was a gentleman usher at the King's funeral. In the early years of Henry VIII's reign he served as a soldier and was knighted for his part in the Battle of Flodden. He served on the jury at the trial of the Duke of Buckingham in 1521and benefited from his fall. He represented Gloucestershire in the Parliaments of 1529 and 1536, and accompanied the King and Anne Boleyn to Calais in 1532. He was Constable of the Tower of London from 28th May 1524 until his death.

William Latymer (1498/9-1583)

William Latymer (Latimer) was the second son of William Latymer of Freston, Suffolk, and of his wife, Anne Bokinge. Latymer read canon law and arts at Corpus Christi College, Cambridge, where he met Reformers like Matthew Parker. It is thought that Latymer was probably introduced to Anne Boleyn by Parker, who became one of Anne Boleyn's chaplains. In 1536 he was approached by Tristram Revell, a student of Cambridge, who wanted Anne's patronage for his translation of "Farrago rerum theologicarum". Latymer told Anne of the work but she refused to support it, probably because it was too radical for the vulnerable queen to be linked with at that time. In the spring of 1536, Latymer was in the Low Countries sourcing evangelical books for the Queen.

Henry Percy, 6th Earl of Northumberland (c.1502-1537)

Henry Percy was the eldest son of Henry Algernon Percy, fifth Earl of Northumberland, and of Katherine Spencer. He was brought up in Cardinal Wolsey's household and it was while he was there that he fell in love with Anne Boleyn on her return to the English court in late 1521. However, his father had already planned Percy's marriage to Mary Talbot, daughter of George Talbot, fourth Earl of Shrewsbury. In addition, Anne was meant to be marrying James Butler, son of Piers Butler of Ireland. As a consequence, Wolsey and Percy's father put a stop to the relationship between Percy and Anne Boleyn.

Percy married Mary Talbot in 1524 but the marriage was not happy. In 1532, Mary accused her husband of being pre-contracted to Anne Boleyn and Percy was examined by the Archbishops of York and Canterbury, He swore that there was no truth to the story.

Thomas Howard, 3rd Duke of Norfolk (1473-1554)

Thomas Howard was the eldest son of Thomas Howard, 2nd Duke of Norfolk, and of Elizabeth Tilney. He was the brother of Elizabeth Boleyn (née Howard) and so was uncle to Anne Boleyn. Howard's father and grandfather had fought on Richard III's side at the Battle of Bosworth but Howard was able to work his way back into royal favour by fighting for the Crown against both the Cornish rebels and the Scots in 1497. He was made a Knight of the Garter in 1510, was created Earl of Surrey in 1514 and succeeded his father as Duke of Norfolk in 1524. In September 1514 he was prominent in leading the English army in defeating the Scots at the Battle of Flodden.

In the 1520s, he clashed with Cardinal Wolsey over foreign policy – he preferred war and Wolsey preferred diplomacy – and was involved with the Duke of Suffolk's and the Boleyn family's push for Wolsey to be removed from power. In the 1530s, Norfolk carried out diplomatic missions and advised the King on the situation in Ireland. As Lord Steward of England, he presided over the trials of Anne and George Boleyn, his niece and nephew in May 1536.

Jane Boleyn (née Parker, d. 1542)

Jane was the daughter of Henry Parker, the 10th Baron Morley, and of his wife Alice St John, from Great Hallingbury in Essex. She married George Boleyn, Anne Boleyn's brother, in late 1524 or early 1525. Although some historians and authors view the marriage as loveless, there is no evidence of this. Jane accompanied her sister-in-law and the King on their visit to Calais in 1532 and served Anne as a lady-in-waiting. In October 1534, Jane was banished from court temporarily after helping Anne in her attempt to get rid of a "young lady" who had caught the King's eye. Jane was also the person in whom Anne confided regarding the King's lack of sexual prowess.

The Executioner

Known as the "Hangman of Calais", the executioner beheaded Anne Boleyn with his famous "sword of Calais". Mary of Hungary[2] referred to the executioner being from St Omer, as did The Spanish Chronicle,[3] but the disbursements in Letters and Papers refer to "the executioner of Calais" being paid "100 crs., 23l. 6s. 8D" for "his reward and apparel".[4] Sir William Kingston, Constable of the Tower of London, also referred to him as "the "executur" of Cales"[5] and The Chronicle of Calais referred to him as "the hangman of Caleis".[6]

Although, in his novel "The French Executioner", C C Humphrey named the executioner as Jean Rombaud, this is simply because a "Jean Rombaud" was listed as the executioner in St Omer in the 1530s. We do not know who executed Anne Boleyn.

The Spanish Chronicle noted that the executioner was ordered "a week before"[7] Anne's execution, so before a trial had even taken place.

Timeline of Anne Boleyn's Fall, 1536

7th January .... Death of Catherine of Aragon

8th January ...... Henry VIII, and possibly Anne Boleyn, celebrate news of Catherine's death by dressing in yellow.

24th January ..... Henry VIII's jousting accident at Greenwich

29th January ..... Burial of Catherine of Aragon. Anne Boleyn miscarries

10th February .. Record of Henry VIII showing favour to Jane Seymour

March 1536 ...... Act for the Suppression of the Lesser Monasteries

1st April .... Chapuys meets with Catholic Conservatives and hears of their plans for Jane Seymour and a breach between Anne Boleyn and Thomas Cromwell

2nd April .... John Skip preaches a controversial sermon

18th April .... Chapuys tricked into recognising Anne Boleyn as Queen

23rd April .... Sir Nicholas Carew elected to the Order of the Garter

24th April .... Commissions of oyer and terminer set up for offences committed in Middlesex and Kent

25th April .... King refers to Anne Boleyn as his "most dear and entirely beloved wife the Queen" and writes of his hope for a son

26th April .... Anne Boleyn charges her chaplain, Matthew Parker, with the spiritual care of her daughter, Elizabeth

27th April .... Writs issued summoning Parliament

28th April .... The King's Council recorded as meeting "every day"

29th April ....Chapuys records meetings between Cromwell
                 and Dr Richard Sampson, an expert on canon law.
                 Anne and Sir Henry Norris have an argument

30th April ....King and Queen's visit to Calais is cancelled.
                 Anne and Henry argue. Mark Smeaton is taken
                 to Cromwell's house to be interrogated. He
                 confesses to adultery with the Queen

1st May ....May Day joust. Henry VIII rushes off with Sir
                 Henry Norris and questions him

2nd May ....Sir Henry Norris taken to the Tower of London,
                 Smeaton is already there. Anne Boleyn is arrested
                 and taken to the Tower. George Boleyn arrested
                 at Whitehall and taken to the Tower

3rd May ....Archbishop Cranmer writes to Henry VIII
                 expressing his shock at finding out about Anne
                 Boleyn's arrest. Anne speaks to her attendants in
                 the Tower of her conversations with Norris and
                 Sir Francis Weston

4th May ....Arrests of Sir Francis Weston and Sir William
                 Brereton. Jane Boleyn, Lady Rochford, sends a
                 message to her husband

5th May ....Sir Thomas Wyatt and Sir Richard Page are
                 recorded as being imprisoned in the Tower.
                 Sir Francis Bryan is ordered to London for
                 questioning

6th May ....Date of a letter traditionally attributed to Anne
                 Boleyn and written to Henry VIII from her
                 prison in the Tower

7th May ....William Latymer, Anne Boleyn's chaplain,
                 searched on his arrival in England

9th May ....King had meetings with noblemen and gentlemen

10th May...........Middlesex indictment drawn up

11th May...........Kent indictment drawn up

12th May ....Trial of Norris, Smeaton, Weston and Brereton at special commission of oyer and terminer. Found guilty and sentenced to death

13th May...........Queen Anne Boleyn's household is broken up. Henry Percy, Earl of Northumberland, denies a pre-contract between himself and Anne Boleyn

14th May...........Sir Nicholas Carew moves Jane Seymour to Chelsea. Cromwell informs Wallop and Gardiner of the Queen's "incontinent living"

15th May...........Trials of Anne and George Boleyn. Both found guilty and sentenced to death

16th May...........Archbishop Cranmer visits Anne Boleyn

17th May...........Executions of Norris, Smeaton, Weston, Brereton and George Boleyn on Tower Hill. Cranmer declares the marriage between Henry VIII and Anne Boleyn null and void

18th May...........Anne Boleyn's execution is postponed

19th May...........Execution of Anne Boleyn within the Tower walls

20th May...........Betrothal of Henry VIII and Jane Seymour

30th May...........Marriage of Henry VIII and Jane Seymour

4th June.............Jane Seymour proclaimed Queen at Greenwich

Anne Boleyn: From Courtier's Daughter to Queen

Anne Boleyn was born in around 1501, probably at Blickling Hall in Norfolk. She was the daughter of courtier and diplomat Thomas Boleyn, and his wife, Elizabeth Howard. The family moved to Hever Castle in around 1505 and it is there that Anne would have received her education. This is likely to have been Humanist in character as her father was very much a Renaissance man.

Thomas Boleyn's friendship with Margaret of Austria, the most powerful woman in Europe, enabled him to secure a place for Anne at the Habsburg court in Mechelen in 1513. Margaret's court at Mechelen was known for its culture and was the perfect climate for the intelligent and precocious twelve year-old Anne Boleyn. It was to have a huge impact on her life and her later love of illuminated manuscripts, art, music and the courtly love tradition stemmed from this time. In 1514, Anne was appointed to serve Mary Tudor, Henry VIII's sister, as she travelled to France to marry King Louis XII.

It is likely that Anne met Mary in France in late 1514. Mary Tudor returned to England after the death of her husband in January 1515 and her subsequent secret marriage to Charles Brandon, the Duke of Suffolk, in March 1515. Anne Boleyn remained in France, moving on to serve the new French queen, Queen Claude, who spent considerable time in Amboise and Blois. Like Margaret of Austria, Claude was a patron of the arts and Anne would have soaked up the climate of culture at her court, a court that was visited by the likes of Leonardo da Vinci. In the seven years she spent with Claude, Anne would have been heavily influenced by her pious mistress. She would also have been impacted by the behaviour and beliefs of women like Louise of Savoy, Marguerite of Angoulême and Renée of France, as well as by the new evangelical religious ideas.

Anne was recalled to England by her father in 1521 to serve Queen Catherine of Aragon and to marry her Irish relation, James Butler. This marriage match aimed to unite the Butlers and Boleyns and to put an end to their squabbles over the Ormond lands and title. Anne's first mention in the records of the English court show her participation in the Chateau Vert pageant of Shrove Tuesday 1522, in which she played Perseverance. It is unlikely that the King paid her any attention because he had fallen head over heels in love with her sister, Mary.

As the Boleyn-Butler marriage plans stalled, Anne met and fell in love with courtier Henry Percy, the heir of the Earl of Northumberland. Unfortunately, Percy's father and Cardinal Wolsey put an end to the relationship and Percy was forced into marrying Mary Talbot.

Poet Thomas Wyatt, who was already married, also fell in love with Anne but his feelings were unrequited, as shown by his poetry. In 1526, it became apparent that Anne had a new admirer - the King – and Wyatt was forced to withdraw from his pursuit of Anne. An infatuated Henry VIII sent Wyatt abroad on a diplomatic mission and bombarded Anne with love letters. Seventeen of these still survive today and give us an unique insight into Henry's feelings for Anne and the challenges the couple faced; for example, when Anne nearly died of sweating sickness.

Anne's refusal to become his mistress led to Henry promising marriage, a promise which had multiple implications. It led to years of struggle with the "Great Matter", to Wolsey's fall from grace, to Henry breaking with Rome, and to the executions of Thomas More and Bishop Fisher.

It also caused the rise of the Boleyns as Anne became "queen in waiting" and changed the dynamics of the English court. Anne's mother acted as chaperone during her daughter's courtship with Henry VIII and Anne's father and brother were active in diplomatic assignments pertaining to the King's mission to annul his marriage to Catherine of Aragon. The failure of the Legatine Court was a huge blow for the Boleyns, as it delayed the annulment, but it did lead to the fall of Cardinal Wolsey, who had become a thorn in their side. When the King wanted to be recognised as the Supreme Head of the Church of England, it was Anne's brother, George, who was chosen to present his case to convocation.

1532 was the turning point for the Boleyns after the stalemate and frustration of the previous few years. On 1st September 1532, Anne Boleyn was made Marquis of Pembroke in her own right and a month later she accompanied the King on a visit to Calais, where she was recognised by Francis I as Henry's consort. In attendance were Thomas, George and his wife, Jane, as well as Sir James Boleyn and Sir Edward Boleyn. It was a moment of triumph. So sure of success were Henry and Anne with regards to Henry's annulment, that they slept together and started co-habiting on their arrival back in London. Even with the threat of excommunication hanging over the King, Anne was, to all intents and purposes, Henry VIII's Queen and consort.

Henry VIII married a now-pregnant Anne Boleyn in January 1533. Anne's pregnancy, and concerns over the legitimacy of the child she was carrying, made it imperative that their marriage be recognised as true and valid. Fortunately, the Boleyn faction now included Thomas Cromwell and Thomas Cranmer who worked tirelessly on "The Great Matter". Cromwell knew that there was no hope of bringing the Papacy round to Henry's way of thinking, so concentrated instead on getting convocation and Parliament to sort it all out. Cromwell's Act in Restraint of Appeals made Cranmer's judgement solid and unchallengeable with respect to the illegality of Henry's marriage to Catherine and the validity of Henry and Anne's marriage.

Easter 1533 saw a frantic series of events: Convocation's ruling on Henry VIII's marriage to Catherine of Aragon, Catherine of Aragon being demoted to Dowager Princess of Wales, the Royal Council being informed that Anne Boleyn was Queen and Anne Boleyn attending Easter Saturday mass as Queen, attended by 60 ladies-in-waiting. On 23rd May 1533, the new Archbishop of Canterbury, Thomas Cranmer, made the official declaration that

Henry VIII's marriage to Catherine of Aragon had been annulled. Just over a week later, on 1st June, a heavily pregnant Anne was finally crowned Queen at Westminster Abbey, following three days of lavish pageantry. George Boleyn's diplomatic duties meant that he was in France with the Duke of Norfolk and missed the coronation, but he would still have appreciated that moment of triumph which Anne shared with her mother and sister, who both attended on her that day, and with her father who escorted her both on the Thames procession on 29th May and on her actual coronation day. George returned to England at the end of June bearing a lavish gift from Francis I. The Boleyns had arrived and all they needed now was for Anne to produce a son and heir for Henry VIII.

The last few weeks of Anne's pregnancy were so difficult that Henry VIII feared for Anne's life.[1] Anne went into confinement on the 26th August 1533 and gave birth to a little girl just a couple of weeks later. A son had been predicted and the royal couple had even gone as far as preparing a birth announcement, which had to be changed from prince to princess. However, although the birth of Elizabeth was a disappointment, it was not the end of the world. On 10th September, Elizabeth's birth was celebrated with a lavish christening. Thomas Boleyn, as Elizabeth's grandfather, bore the child's long train.

It was a wonderful time for the Boleyns. Anne was queen, her successful pregnancy had shown her fertility and her ability to carry children successfully and there was hope for a future son and heir. Royal favour had also brought the family wealth. Although one historian writes of cracks appearing in the royal marriage as early as August 1533, there is actually no evidence of this. It is indisputable, however, that there were many pressures on the marriage – Anne's new role as queen/wife/mother, Henry's wandering eye, Mary's refusal to recognise her new stepmother as queen, Anne's unpopularity and the need for an heir. Furthermore, it was a very unusual royal marriage in that it was based on love and passion, rather than diplomacy. Volatile and passionate doesn't begin to describe it.

Anne was determined to succeed where her predecessor had failed, by providing Henry with a son and heir. She became pregnant again quickly after the birth of Elizabeth but unfortunately lost the baby late in the pregnancy.

Anne Boleyn was far more than just Henry's wife and consort; she was a patron of the Arts, a keen religious and social reformer and an influential woman in her own right. Henry shared his ideas for renovations and building campaigns with her, she had a close relationship with Thomas Cromwell, she acted as a patron to the likes of Hans Holbein and she used her power to help petitioners and to influence her husband.

In January 1536, everything was looking good for Queen Anne Boleyn. Her Nemesis, Catherine of Aragon, was dead, and she herself was pregnant again. Henry may have had a new flame, but that was to be expected, and Anne had no reason to fear a mere flirtation when she was carrying his heir. Storm clouds were gathering but the Boleyns had every reason to pin their hopes on a rosy future.

Summer 1535 -
The Royal Progress and Wolf Hall

In the summer of 1535, Henry VIII and Anne Boleyn carried out a royal progress (tour) to the west and south-west of England. It was traditional for the King and Queen to go on progress in the summer months as it was a chance for them to get out of the smelly city of London with its risk of plague and other diseases. This particular progress was also an opportunity for the couple to gain support for their marriage, to promote the Reformation and to visit the households of people seen as "pro-Reform".[1] It was a political and social progress, and far more than a chance for the couple to get away and have a break. The plan seemed to work; evidence for this can be found in a letter written by the imperial ambassador, Eustace Chapuys, on 10th August 1535:-

> "This King is still on the borders of Wales,
> hunting and visiting that principality with a
> view to gain popularity with his subjects. This
> he attempts by all possible means and ways, and
> it is reported that a large number of peasants in
> the villages through which he has passed, after
> hearing the preachers who follow the Court, have
> been so deceived as to believe that God inspired
> the King to repudiate his legitimate Queen owing
> to her having once been married to his brother."[2]

This royal progress led Henry VIII and Anne Boleyn from Windsor, to Reading, through Oxfordshire to Gloucestershire, through Wiltshire to Hampshire, and then back through Hampshire towards London.[3] Historian Eric Ives[4] writes of how the King was enjoying himself so much on this progress that the consecration of three new bishops (Edward Fox, John Hilsey and Hugh Latimer), planned for 19th September at Winchester, became a bit of a last minute panic. Eventually, Henry VIII signed the necessary documentation while staying at Wolf Hall, near Marlborough in Wiltshire.

Wolf Hall was the family home of the Seymour family. In fiction and on TV it is often the setting of Henry VIII's first meeting with Sir John Seymour's daughter, Jane Seymour. If we are to believe fiction, then Henry fell in love with the meek and mild blonde as soon as she walked into the room and that was the end of his love for Anne Boleyn. The facts do not support this. Henry VIII was on progress with his wife, Anne Boleyn, and Wolf Hall was one of the main stops on the progress, with the visit lasting from around the 4th to the 10th September.[5] He was not there alone. Plus Jane had served Catherine of Aragon and had been in Anne Boleyn's employ since at least early 1535, so it was hardly a first meeting. However, as Eric Ives points out, this visit did show that the Seymour family had risen at court, in that they were important enough to visit on this progress.

Anne Boleyn miscarried in January 1536 and it was reported that she had been around 15 weeks pregnant when she lost her baby. Therefore, Henry VIII was still sleeping with Anne in autumn 1535. He had not put her aside and moved on to Jane Seymour. In fact, there is no hint of Henry showing Jane any favour or attention until February 1536, when Chapuys reports Anne's miscarriage and writes of how Anne may have miscarried because of "a fear that the King would treat her like the late Queen, especially considering the treatment shown to a lady of the Court, named Mistress Semel, to whom, as many say, he has lately made great presents."[6] The Catholic recusant Nicholas Sander, writing in Elizabeth I's reign, recorded that Anne Boleyn's miscarriage was caused by her anger and sadness at finding Jane Seymour sitting on Henry VIII's lap.[7] However, we do not know if this is true. Furthermore, this incident was also in the January, four months after the couple's stay at Wolf Hall, rather than during the progress.

7th January 1536 –
Death of Catherine of Aragon

On the 7th January 1536, at two o'clock in the afternoon, Henry VIII's first wife, Catherine of Aragon, died at Kimbolton Castle. She had been ill for a few months but felt worse after drinking a draught of Welsh beer in December 1535. This, combined with the embalmer's report that all of her organs were healthy apart from her heart, "which was quite black and hideous to look at",[1] gave rise to rumours that Catherine had been poisoned. However, the embalmer, who was a chandler (candlemaker and wax worker) and not a medical expert,[2] also found a black body attached to Catherine's heart. It is thought that this was probably a secondary heart tumour caused by cancer in another part of the body.

On 29th December 1535 Catherine's doctor sent for Eustace Chapuys, the Imperial Ambassador and a friend of Catherine's, because Catherine had taken a turn for the worse. Chapuys sought permission from the King to visit Catherine and it was granted. Mary was not so lucky, Henry refused to let her see her mother in her last days, something which must have broken the hearts of both women. As Chapuys travelled to Kimbolton, Catherine received a surprise visitor on New Year's Day. It was her former lady-in-waiting and confidante, María de Salinas, now Lady Willoughby. Apparently, Maria begged entry to the castle by pretending that she'd been thrown from her horse and that her letter of permission to visit had been delayed.[3]

The Catherine that María saw on that day must have been a far cry from the Catherine she had once known, a shadow of her former self due to her weakness and lack of appetite. Chapuys arrived the next day and although the former queen was weak, she was still lucid enough to know that when she first spoke to him she needed witnesses in the room so that she could not be accused of plotting against the King. Later conversations, however, were in private. For four days, Chapuys visited Catherine every afternoon. He reported that Catherine was worried about her daughter, Mary, as well as concerned that the Pope and Emperor were not acting on her behalf.[4] Catherine was also worried that she might be to blame for the "heresies" and "scandals" that England was now suffering because of the battle over the divorce. She was haunted by the deaths that had resulted from Henry's Great Matter and by the fact that it had led to England breaking with Rome – were they down to her stubbornness, her refusal to go quietly? These were the questions preying on her mind during her last days.

Catherine's health seemed to rally in the first few days of January. She ate some meals without being sick, she was sleeping well and was chatting and laughing with visitors, so Chapuys was dispatched back to London. However, on the night of 6th January, Catherine became fidgety and in the early hours of the 7th she asked to take communion. It was unlawful for communion to be taken before daylight but Jorge de Athequa, Catherine's confessor and the Bishop of Llandaff, could see that his mistress did not have long to live. So he administered communion and listened to her confession. Catherine settled her affairs, giving instructions on what she wanted done with her worldly goods and her burial – she wanted to be buried in a chapel of Observant Friars (Franciscans). It is also said that she wrote a letter to her former husband, Henry VIII, although some historians doubt its authenticity:

"My most dear lord, king and husband,

The hour of my dear now drawing on, the tender
love I owe you forceth me, my case being such,
to commend myself to you, and to put you in
remembrance with a few words of the health
and safeguard of your soul which you ought to
prefer before all worldly matters, and before
the care and pampering of your body, for the
which you have cast me into many calamities

and yourself into many troubles. For my part I
pardon you everything and I wish to devoutly
pray to God that He will pardon you also. For
the rest, I commend unto you our daughter Mary,
beseeching you to be a good father unto her,
as I have heretofore desired. I entreat you also,
on behalf of my maids, to give them marriage
portions, which is not much, they being but
three. For all my other servants, I solicit the
wages due to them, and a year or more, lest
they be unprovided for. Lastly, I make this vow,
that mine eyes desire you above all things."[5]

Catherine then prayed, asking God's forgiveness for herself and
also for the King who had done her so much wrong. She continued
praying until the end, until her loving Father took her into Paradise.
Catalina de Aragón, daughter of the great Catholic Reyes, Isabel I
of Castile and Ferdinand II of Aragon, was dead. She had died not
in some sumptuous palace surrounded by her loved ones, but in a
small, dark, cold castle with her faithful staff in attendance. A sad
end for a woman who had once been Queen of England and who
had defeated the Scots as Regent.

Catherine of Aragon was laid to rest at Peterborough Abbey,
now Peterborough Cathedral, on 29th January 1536. She was, of
course, buried as the Dowager Princess of Wales, not as Queen,
but her grave is now marked with the words "Katharine Queen of
England".

Catherine of Aragon's will is recorded in Letters and Papers:

"Desires the King to let her have the goods she
holds of him in gold and silver and the money
due to her in time past; that her body may be
buried in a convent of Observant Friars; that 500
masses be said for her soul; that some personage
go to our Lady of Walsingham on pilgrimage
and distribute 20 nobles on the way. Bequests:

to Mrs. Darel 200l. for her marriage. To my
daughter, the collar of gold which I brought out
of Spain. To Mrs. Blanche 100l. To Mrs. Margery
and Mrs. [Whyller] 40l. each. To Mrs. Mary, my
physicians [wife, and] Mrs. Isabel, daughter to
Mr. Ma[rguerite], 40l. each. To ray physician the
year's coming [wages]. To Francisco Philippo
all that I owe him, and 40l. besides. To Master
John, my apothecary, [a year's wages] and all that
is due to him besides. That Mr. Whiller be paid
expenses about the making of my gown, and
20l. besides. To Philip, Anthony, and Bastian,
20l. each. To the little maidens 10l. each. That
my goldsmith be paid his wages for the year
coming and all that is due to him besides. That
my lavander be paid what is due to her and her
wages for the year coming. To Isabel of Vergas
20l. To my ghostly father his wages for the year
coming. That ornaments be made of my gowns
for the convent where I shall be [buried] "and
the furs of the same I give to my daughter."[6]

8th January 1536 –
Free from All Suspicion of War!

When a messenger arrived at Greenwich Palace with news of Catherine of Aragon's death, Henry VIII cried "God be praised that we are free from all suspicion of war!".[1] Catherine's death meant that Henry no longer had a quarrel with the Emperor, Catherine's nephew, and that the French would have to keep him happy or risk him making an alliance with the Empire.[2]

According to the imperial ambassador, Eustace Chapuys, Henry VIII celebrated the day after Catherine's death by dressing in "yellow, from top to toe, except the white feather he had in his bonnet".[3] He then paraded to mass with his two year old daughter, Elizabeth, "with trumpets and other great triumphs". The chronicler Edward Hall, however, puts Anne Boleyn in yellow, writing that "Quene Anne ware yelowe for the mournyng"[4] and making no mention of the King's attire.

The Catholic recusant Nicholas Sander, writing in Elizabeth I's reign, reported that "The king could not refrain from tears when he read the letter [Catherine's last letter to him], but Anne Boleyn, instead of putting on mourning on the day of Catherine's funeral, put on a yellow dress."[5]

But then Sander quotes Hall as his source, so he is certainly not a new source for this information.

Although some historians and authors have suggested that yellow was the colour of mourning in Spain, Catherine's homeland, I have never found any evidence of that being the case; white and black seemed to have been the only colours associated with mourning in Spain. In early Christian art,[6] yellow symbolized renewal, hope, light and purity, so perhaps Henry, and/or Anne, were simply expressing their hope for a new start now that Catherine was gone - war was averted and Anne was carrying a child.

As well as being good news for the King, Catherine's death

was also good news for Thomas Cromwell who was open to the idea of an English-Imperial alliance. Charles V's aunt, Catherine of Aragon, was now out of the way, so Charles could negotiate with Henry VIII without worrying about his aunt's opposition to Anne Boleyn. In a letter dated 8th January 1536, Cromwell wrote to Stephen Gardiner and John Wallop, the English ambassadors in Paris, to inform them of Catherine's death, adding the postscript:-

> "P.S.—As the King had seen this letter he desired Cromwell to write somewhat more at length, viz.:—Considering the death of the Lady Dowager, and that as the Emperor has now no occasion of quarrel, he will seek the friendship of Henry, Gardiner is to keep himself more aloof and less ready for any modification of the King's requests, showing what advantages he may now have at the Emperor's hands, and tell the Admiral it will be good for them to hasten to an agreement before the King is pressed by the Emperor."[7]

It is clear that Henry VIII and Cromwell were ready to play France and the Empire off against each other.

24th January 1536 –
Henry VIII's Jousting Accident

On the 24th January 1536, the 44 year-old King Henry VIII had a serious jousting accident at Greenwich Palace. Eustace Chapuys, the imperial ambassador, reported it in his dispatches, writing:

> "On the eve of the Conversion of St. Paul,
> the King being mounted on a great horse
> to run at the lists, both fell so heavily that
> every one thought it a miracle he was not
> killed, but he sustained no injury."[1]

It could easily have been a fatal accident. From Chapuys' report, we know that both horse and rider fell. The mailed horse, which would have been a large horse due to Henry's height and weight, could easily have rolled on to the King and crushed him.

Dr Ortiz also recorded the accident in a letter to the Empress:

> "The French king said that the king of
> England had fallen from his horse, and been
> for two hours without speaking. "La Ana"
> was so upset that she miscarried of a son."[2]

So, although the King survived the accident, it still may have had a major impact on him, his family and his reign. Dr Ortiz was of the opinion that the miscarriage Anne Boleyn suffered on 29th January 1536, just five days later, was due to the stress she suffered at hearing news of the King's accident. Chapuys concurs with this, writing that "the said concubine wished to lay the blame on the duke of Norfolk, whom she hates, saying he frightened her by bringing the news of the fall the King had six days before."[3] If you believe that Anne Boleyn's fall was a result of her failing to provide the King with a son, that she "miscarried of her saviour"[4] that day, then the jousting accident was definitely a factor in her fall.

An article in The Independent newspaper[5] put forward the theory that Henry's jousting accident caused Henry to undergo a personality change. This article was based on the findings of three people - historian Lucy Worsley, Henry VIII biographer Robert Hutchinson and medical doctor Catherine Hood - in the History Channel documentary "Inside the Body of Henry VIII". This programme looked at issues concerning the King's diet and lifestyle, and the medical problems which saw Henry change from the handsome, young, sporty King with a 32 inch waist and 39 inch chest in his 20s, to a man who probably weighed 28 stone by his death in 1547, at the age of 55, and whose waist measured 52 inches and his chest 53 inches. As his health deteriorated, leaving him unable to do the sporting activities he enjoyed, his personality also changed and he became "plagued with paranoia and melancholy".[6]

Although Henry had a few health issues by the time of the jousting accident in 1536 – malaria, contracted at the age of 30, and varicose ulcers which began on his left leg in around 1527 – the major decline in his health and personality seems to have started in 1536. Worsley, Hutchinson and Hood concluded that the accident caused his personality change from sporty, virtuous prince to monstrous tyrant. They noted that "from that date the turnover of the wives really speeds up", that negative perceptions of Henry increased and that being unconscious for two hours suggests "major trauma", a frontal lobe injury which can affect a person's personality.

However, it is more likely that it was a combination of factors that led to the King's decline, both physical and mental, and it cannot be blamed on that one accident.

29th January 1536 – Burial and Miscarriage

On 29th January 1536, the day of Catherine of Aragon's funeral, Anne Boleyn suffered her second and final miscarriage. It was her third pregnancy[1] – she had given birth to healthy baby girl, the future Elizabeth I, on the 7th September 1533, and then had suffered a late miscarriage in the summer of 1534 – and the loss of this baby must have been a devastating blow for both Anne and King Henry VIII.

Eustace Chapuys, the imperial ambassador, reported Anne Boleyn's miscarriage in a dispatch to Emperor Charles V:

> "On the day of the interment [Catherine of Aragon's funeral] the Concubine had an abortion which seemed to be a male child which she had not borne 3½ months, at which the King has shown great distress. The said concubine wished to lay the blame on the duke of Norfolk, whom she hates, saying he frightened her by bringing the news of the fall the King had six days before. But it is well known that is not the cause, for it was told her in a way that she should not be alarmed or attach much importance to it."[2]

Nearly a month later, Chapuys referred again to Anne's miscarriage in a report to Charles V, passing on gossip he had heard:

> "I learn from several persons of this Court that for more than three months this King has not spoken ten times to the Concubine, and that when she miscarried he scarcely said anything to her, except that he saw clearly that God did not wish to give him male children; and in leaving her

he told her, as if for spite, that he would speak to
her after she was "releuize." The said Concubine
attributed the misfortune to two causes: first,
the King's fall; and, secondly, that the love she
bore him was far greater than that of the late
Queen, so that her heart broke when she saw
that he loved others. At which remark the King
was much grieved, and has shown his feeling
by the fact that during these festive days he is
here, and has left the other at Greenwich, when
formerly he could not leave her for an hour."

Although Chapuys claims that the King had only spoken to
Anne ten times in the past three months,[3] this was more likely an
exaggeration because we know that they celebrated Catherine of
Aragon's death together. As for the King leaving Anne at Greenwich
during Shrovetide, Eric Ives points out that the King had business
(the Reformation Parliament) to deal with at Westminster and
that Anne was recuperating after her miscarriage. We just cannot
take Chapuys' words at face value, particularly when he disliked
Anne so much.

The chronicler Charles Wriothesley recorded:-

"This yeare also, three daies before Candlemas,
Queene Anne was brought a bedd and delivered
of a man child, as it was said, afore her tyme,
for she said that she had reckoned herself at that
tyme but fiftene weekes gonne with child; it
was said she tooke a fright, for the King ranne
that tyme at the ring and had a fall from his
horse, but he had no hurt; and she tooke such a
fright withall that it caused her to fall in travaile,
and so was delivered afore her full tyme, which
was a great discompfort to all this realme."[4]

So, it appears that Anne lost a son and not the "shapeless mass of flesh" that Nicholas Sander wrote of in 1585. This was a normal miscarriage, a heartbreaking tragedy, but something which was a common occurrence in Tudor times and is still common today. It is so sad that this pregnancy did not go to term; a healthy son would have made Anne secure in her position as queen. J E Neale, writes of how Anne "miscarried of her saviour".[5] Although this miscarriage is only one factor in her fall, it did make her vulnerable. Coming so quickly after the King's brush with death, it may also have panicked the King. He needed a son and heir to continue the Tudor line. Time was ticking, as was the 34 year old Anne's biological clock.

10th February 1536

Eustace Chapuys, the imperial ambassador, wrote to Charles V regarding Anne Boleyn's miscarriage, and regarding Catherine of Aragon's funeral and resting place, which he felt was not fitting for even "a simple baroness". The first mention of Jane Seymour is in this letter, in Chapuys' discussion of potential reasons for Anne's miscarriage:-

> "Some think it was owing to her own
> incapacity to bear children, others to a fear
> that the King would treat her like the late
> Queen, especially considering the treatment
> shown to a lady of the Court, named Mistress
> Semel [Seymour], to whom, as many say,
> he has lately made great presents."[1]

It is not known exactly when Henry VIII started showing Jane Seymour favour or how serious this was. It may have simply been part of the courtly love tradition, but it was enough for it to be court gossip and to have reached Chapuys. Although some historians[2] believe that Henry and Jane's relationship was "well-established" at this point and that Anne and Henry's marriage had irretrievably broken down, there is no evidence to support this theory. Anne had been pregnant up until the 29th January; in early February she would have been recovering from her miscarriage. It would have been typical of the time for Henry to have looked for a substitute, a flirtation, at this time. In fact, as Eric Ives[3] points out, as late as 1st April 1536 Chapuys described Jane Seymour as the lady "whom he serves".[4] This makes reference to the courtly love tradition of a knight serving a lady, and does not suggest a full-blown affair.

Jane Seymour

Jane Seymour was born around 1508/1509 probably at the family seat, Wolf Hall in Wiltshire. She was the daughter of Sir John Seymour, a soldier and courtier who served Henry VII at the Battle of Blackheath, and of his wife, Margery Wentworth, daughter of Sir Henry Wentworth of Nettlestead, Suffolk.

Through the Seymours, Jane was descended from Frenchman Guy de St Maur who is thought to have come from France to England with William the Conqueror. Obviously St Maur, pronounced San-Mawr, had become anglicised to Seymour over the centuries. Through her mother's family, the Wentworths, Jane was descended from Edward III, through Edward's great-granddaughter, Elizabeth Percy. The Seymours became members of the gentry class in the 14th century when Roger Seymour married Maud Esturmy[1] of Wolf Hall, Wiltshire; the house that became the Seymour family home.

Jane was related to Anne Boleyn through a mutual connection to the Howard family. Jane's mother's first cousins were Thomas Howard, 3rd Duke of Norfolk, and Elizabeth Howard, Anne Boleyn's mother. Jane and Anne were, therefore, second cousins.

Jane's exact birthdate is not known, but her biographer, Elizabeth Norton, points out that Jane had 29 ladies in her funeral procession in 1537[2] and that this was a traditional way of symbolising the age of the deceased. If this indeed was the case, then it indicates that Jane would have been born between October 1507 and October 1508.

Jane had nine siblings, although not all of them survived childhood. The most famous of her siblings was Edward Seymour, who went on to become Duke of Somerset and Lord Protector in Jane's son Edward VI's reign. Also well-known was Thomas Seymour, Lord Admiral and Baron Seymour of Sudeley, who married Henry VIII's final wife and widow, Catherine Parr. Both men were executed as traitors. Jane also had another brother

Henry, who died in 1578, and two sisters: Dorothy, who became the wife of Sir Clement Smith, and Elizabeth, who was married first to Sir Anthony Ughtred, then to Gregory Cromwell, son of Thomas Cromwell, and finally to administrator William Paulet, 1st Marquess of Winchester.

Chapuys described Jane as "of middle stature and no great beauty, so fair that one would call her rather pale than otherwise" and Hans Holbein's portrait of Jane is far from flattering. Jane was blonde, pale-skinned and rather chinless. However, this made her much closer to the Tudor ideal of beauty, the classic English Rose, than the dark-haired and sallow-skinned Anne Boleyn. We know nothing of Jane's early life and her education, although it appears that she could read and write, and had some knowledge of French and Latin.[3] She would have learned music and needlework, as well as the country pursuits of horse riding and hunting. Elizabeth Norton writes of how records show that in 1647, during the reign of Charles I, "a bed of needlework with a chair and cushions, said to be wrought by the queen, Lady Jane Seymour" was passed back to the Seymour family from the royal collection.[4]

It is not known exactly when Jane arrived at court but, taking into account her birthdate, she must have been appointed to Queen Catherine of Aragon's household between 1527 and 1529, the time when the King was courting Anne Boleyn and trying to annul his marriage to Catherine. The annulment finally went through in 1533. The King married Anne Boleyn this year and Catherine's household was disbanded in the August. Jane would have returned home to Wolf Hall. By this time, Jane's brother, Edward, had separated from his wife, Catherine Filiol, on the grounds of her infidelity. Edward went on to marry Anne Stanhope sometime before March 1535. On her arrival home, Jane's relative, Sir Francis Bryan, started trying to arrange a marriage between Jane and William Dormer, son of Sir Robert Dormer.[5] It seems that the Dormers were not keen on the idea as they quickly married off William to Mary Sidney, a much better match, in their eyes, than the 26ish year-old Jane, who didn't even have a dowry.

The failure of this potential marriage match must have been a huge blow to Jane and her family. Jane wasn't getting any younger and was now in the position where a good marriage looked unlikely, However, things looked up in early 1535; Jane was called back to court to serve Queen Anne Boleyn. This appointment was probably down to Bryan, who was also related to Anne Boleyn. Little did anyone know that this appointment would lead to Jane becoming Queen.

Jane has gone down in history as Henry VIII's true love, the woman he chose to be painted with in the Whitehall family portrait and the woman he chose to be laid to rest with, but this surely had little to do with true love and more to do with the fact that she gave him the ultimate gift, that of a son and heir. He didn't treat her particularly well when they were married, but Jane's death so soon after their wedding, after giving him a son, made him look back fondly on their union, regarding Jane as his only true wife.

Early 1536 – Foreign Policy

On 1st November 1535, Francesco II Sforza, Duke of Milan died childless. This caused trouble between Charles V, Holy Roman Emperor, and Francis I of France, and eventually sparked the Italian War of 1536-1538. The Duke's death put England into a tricky position. Either side may have dragged England in. Alternatively, as the Pope wanted, France and the Empire might actually join forces against England. Anne Boleyn was pro-French, which is understandable given her time at the French court, but Cromwell seemed to want to keep his options open. Anne was looking for an alliance with France, through a marriage match for her daughter, Elizabeth,[1] but, Cromwell[2] was open to negotiating with the Emperor.

Eustace Chapuys, the imperial ambassador, was firm in his negotiations with Cromwell and the King. When the latter pair made overtures to Chapuys in February 1536, after Catherine of Aragon's death in the January, Chapuys made it clear that he welcomed a restoration of the friendship between England and the Empire, but that there were conditions:-

1. A reconciliation between Henry VIII and Rome

2. The King's eldest daughter, Mary, must be made legitimate again and "reinstated in her rank".[3]

3. The formation of an Anglo-Imperial alliance against the 'Turk'.

4. If requested by the Emperor, Henry VIII would "make besides a defensive and offensive league against whomsoever might act wrongly towards one of the parties".[4]

If those points could be agreed upon, Chapuys was happy to go forward with a more general treaty.[5] According to Chapuys, Cromwell's answer to the fourth point was the his master, the King, "would do anything that might be desired" and he did not see that the third point would be a problem. As far as the second point was concerned:

> "With regard to the Princess, Cromwell observed
> this was the fit opportunity to treat of her
> prospects, and of the settlement of her affairs
> in future, in a manner to please Your Majesty;
> the door was already open for negotiation."[6]

The first point "was the most difficult of all", according to Cromwell, but he did say that "he thought the King, his master, would readily accede to what might be agreed upon between the deputies of both parties" and reminded Chapuys of the "wonderful things he had achieved ever since he had had the administration of the King's affairs". Cromwell was stalling, which was all he could do, but he appeared to be giving Chapuys hope of an agreement. What Chapuys didn't know was that Cromwell was also corresponding with Martin Luther[7] and Justus Jonas[8] in Germany, and negotiating a potential treaty between England and the Schmalkaldic League. Talk about keeping your options open!

March 1536 – Act for the Suppression of Lesser Monasteries

Brief Background

In 1534, Henry VIII broke with Rome and became the supreme head of the church in England via the Act of Supremacy. In the same year, the collection and payments of annates ('first fruits', or the first year's profits of a benefice) to Rome was abolished by the Act in Absolute Restraint of Annates (25 Hen. VIII c. 20). This was followed, in January 1535, by the appointing of a commission to conduct a survey of the income of ecclesiastical property in England and Wales. The commission was known as the Valor Ecclesiasticus and those under its employ were to:

> "examyn, serche, and enquyre, by all the
> wayes and meanes that they can by their
> dyscrecions, of and for the true and just, hole
> and entyere yerely values of all the manors,
> londes, tenements, hereditaments, rents, tythes,
> offerings, emoluments, and all other profittes
> as well spirituall as temporall apperteyninge
> or belonginge to any Archebushopricke, &c.
> within the lymyttes of their Commyssion."[1]

The commissioners collected this information and produced a financial statement for every religious community, which was given to the King's Exchequer.

Following on from the Valor, which was a financial audit of the religious institutions for tax purposes, a further series of visitations of the monasteries started in the summer of 1535 and was not completed until early 1536. The commissioners of this visitation were given a set of questions to ask each monk. The questions covered everything from their qualifications and information on daily life, to whether they were staying true to their vows and vocation.[2]

The Act for the Suppression of Lesser Monasteries

The results of the visitations and the reports of the commissioners were made into a report, the Compendium Compertorum (Comperta), and shared with Parliament when it convened on 4th February 1536. The abuses and corruption which had allegedly been uncovered in the smaller monasteries led to the passing of the Act for the Suppression (or Dissolution) of the Lesser Monasteries in March 1536. The preamble of the Act stated:

> "For as much as manifest sin, vicious, carnal and
> abominable living is daily used and committed
> among the little and small abbeys, priories, and
> other religious houses of monks, canons, and
> nuns, where the congregation of such religious
> persons is under the number of twelve persons,
> whereby the governors of such religious houses,
> and their convent, spoil, destroy, consume, and
> utterly waste, as well their churches, monasteries,
> priories, principal houses, farms, granges, lands,
> tenements, and hereditaments, as the ornaments
> of their churches, and their goods and chattels,
> to the high displeasure of Almighty God, slander
> of good religion, and to the great infamy of
> the king's highness and the realm, if redress
> should not be had thereof. And albeit that many
> continual visitations hath been heretofore had,
> by the space of two hundred years and more,
> for an honest and charitable reformation of
> such unthrifty, carnal, and abominable living,
> yet nevertheless little or none amendment is
> hitherto had, but their vicious living shamelessly
> increases and augments, and by a cursed custom

so rooted and infected, that a great multitude
of the religious persons in such small houses do
rather choose to rove abroad in apostasy, than
to conform themselves to the observation of
good religion; so that without such small houses
be utterly suppressed, and the religious persons
therein committed to great and honourable
monasteries of religion in this realm, where
they may be compelled to live religiously, for
reformation of their lives, there can else be
no redress nor reformation in that behalf."[3]

This Act affected the "lesser monasteries"; those with fewer than twelve members and those worth less than £200 per year. They were to be dissolved, their heads pensioned off and their members to become secularized or moved to larger monasteries "where they may be compelled to live religiously for reformation of their lives". The monasteries' possessions were to be given to the King and his heirs "to do and use therewith his and their own wills, to the pleasure of Almighty God, and to the honour and profit of this realm."

Historians are divided over the motives of Thomas Cromwell and Henry VIII in devising this statute. Some see its purpose as reform and a straightforward solution to the "incurable depravity"[4] in the smaller monasteries. Others see it as an excuse for the Crown to benefit from their wealth and lands[5] under the guise of reform. With hindsight, knowing about the later widespread dissolution of the monasteries, we can view this Act as nothing more than a first step in a money-making exercise. It could also be seen as a way of ridding the realm of the abuses and superstition that reformers associated with Rome.

6th March 1536

In a letter to the Empress, written on 6th March 1536, Dr Pedro Ortiz reported:

> "Anne Bolans is now in fear of the King deserting her one of these days, in order to marry another lady."[1]

The sentence comes after his report of Catherine of Aragon's burial and he does not elaborate in any way, apart from saying at the end of the letter that "At any rate, it must be owned that though the King himself was not converted like St. Paul after his fall, at least his adulterous wife has miscarried of a son."

It is safe to assume that Ortiz believed that Anne's miscarriage made Anne vulnerable, but any information he may have had regarding Anne's state of mind would be second-hand because Ortiz was in Rome at the time! It really cannot be used as evidence of a breakdown in Anne and Henry's relationship.

18th March 1536 – Jane in Favour

On the 18th March 1536, Chapuys reported:

> "The new amours of this King with the young
> lady of whom I have before written still go
> on, to the intense rage of the concubine;
> and the King 15 days ago put into his
> chamber the young lady's brother."[1]

Jane Seymour, and her brother Edward Seymour, who had been appointed to the privy chamber, were obviously rising in favour, and Anne Boleyn didn't like it one bit. Henry would have expected Anne to ignore his flirtation, as Catherine had done before her, but it would have been natural for Anne to have been jealous and to feel vulnerable. After all, her marriage depended on her keeping the King's love. Anne had set a dangerous precedent in rising from lady-in-waiting to Queen.

1st April 1536 -
Chapuys, Cromwell, Jane Seymour
and the Conservatives

On the 1st April 1536, Chapuys reported a meeting between himself, "the young marquis[Exeter], the widowed countess of Kildare, lord Montagu, and other gentlemen" where he was informed that Anne Boleyn and Cromwell were "on bad terms" and that there was talk of the King marrying another, "the daughter of France".[1] In the same report, Chapuys wrote of his concern for Cromwell regarding what Cromwell had told him of Anne's threat, namely "that she (Anne Boleyn) would like to see his head off his shoulders." Chapuys noted that his advice to Cromwell was that "He ought to take care not to offend or over-irritate her, or else he must renounce all hope of that perfect reconciliation we both were trying to bring about. I therefore begged and entreated him, in such an event, to guard against her attacks more effectually than the cardinal (Wolsey) had done, which I hoped his dexterity and prudence would be able to accomplish". Chapuys added that he hoped that Cromwell would soon have another royal mistress.

Later in the letter to Charles V, Chapuys described how he heard that the King had sent Jane Seymour a letter and "a purse full of sovereigns". According to Chapuys, Jane kissed the letter and begged the messenger to tell the King "that she was a gentlewoman of good and honorable parents, without reproach, and that she had no greater riches in the world than her honor, which she would not injure for a thousand deaths, and that if he wished to make her some present in money she begged it might be when God enabled her to make some honorable match." She had been coached well and there were definite echoes of Anne Boleyn in her reaction to the King. Of course, it could be that she was sincere in her words, wanting to protect her virtue, her reputation and honour.

Chapuys went on to write more of Jane Seymour and the King:

> "The said Marchioness has sent to me to say that
> by this the King's love and desire towards the
> said lady was wonderfully increased, and that he
> had said she had behaved most virtuously, and
> to show her that he only loved her honorably,
> he did not intend henceforth to speak with her
> except in presence of some of her kin; for which
> reason the King has caused Cromwell to remove
> from a chamber to which the King can go by
> certain galleries without being perceived, and has
> lodged there the eldest brother of the said lady
> with his wife, in order to bring thither the same
> young lady, who has been well taught for the
> most part by those intimate with the King, who
> hate the concubine, that she must by no means
> comply with the King's wishes except by way of
> marriage; in which she is quite firm. She is also
> advised to tell the King boldly how his marriage
> is detested by the people, and none consider it
> lawful; and on the occasion when she shall bring
> forward the subject, there ought to be present
> none but titled persons, who will say the same if
> the King put them upon their oath of fealty."

Chapuys was of the opinion that Jane was being coached to appeal to the King and to make him think that his people hated Anne and did not accept his marriage to her. This party of plotters – the Seymours and conservatives like the Exeters – then approached Chapuys for his assistance and that of the Emperor, explaining that their plan would help the Princess Mary, stop heresy in England and save the King from his "abominable and incestuous marriage". Chapuys passed all this information on to the Emperor, saying that he would "consult" with the plotters. Chapuys seemed convinced that Anne was out and Jane was in.

Jane and Anne

Thomas Fuller, the 17th century historian, gave an account of an altercation between Anne Boleyn and Jane Seymour when Jane first arrived at court:

> "It is currently traditioned, that at her first
> coming to court, queen Anne Boleyn, espying
> a jewel pendant about her neck, snatched
> thereat (desirous to see, the other unwilling to
> show it,) and casually hurt her hand with her
> own violence; but it grieved her heart more,
> when she perceived it the king's picture by
> himself bestowed upon her, who from this
> day forward dated her own declining, and the
> other's ascending, in her husband's affection."[2]

Fuller does not give a source for this story so it is impossible to know whether it really did happen; even he refers to it as a 'tradition'. Another legend, possibly based on the same source, is a story told in a book about Jane Dormer, Duchess of Feria and lady-in-waiting to Mary I. Henry Clifford, who transcribed an ancient manuscript on the life of Jane Dormer, reported "scratching and bye blows between the queen and her maid"[3] when Sir Francis Bryan took Jane to court and placed her with Anne Boleyn. However, Jane Dormer was not born until two years after Anne Boleyn's death, so could hardly have witnessed the event. Even if it was a family story passed down from Jane's grandmother, Jane Newdigate, it has to be taken with a pinch of salt. Chapuys never heard this story; he would have definitely reported it to the Emperor if he had.

2nd April 1536 –
A Controversial Passion
Sunday Sermon

On the 2nd April 1536, Anne Boleyn's almoner, John Skip, preached an incredibly controversial sermon on the Old Testament story of Queen Esther. This sermon did not help her already troubled relationship with Cromwell.

As well as serving as a clarification of Anne Boleyn's reformist religious stance, the sermon acted as "Anne's call to courtiers and counsellors alike to change the advice they were giving the king and to reject the lure of personal gain."[1] In this sermon, as Eric Ives[2] points out, Henry VIII was characterized as King Ahasuerus. The latter was deceived by his adviser, Haman (Cromwell) into ordering the killing of the Jews (the English clergy in this case). The Jews were saved when the King's mind was changed by his wife, the good Queen Esther (Anne Boleyn).

As Anne's almoner, John Skip must have had Anne's permission and blessing to preach this sermon, and it is likely that it was actually her idea. Anne had just quarrelled with Thomas Cromwell over the dissolution of the monasteries. It was not that she disagreed with this reform; she simply felt that the proceeds should be used on education and on charitable causes[3] rather than to make the King richer. There was no mistaking that this was a public attack on Thomas Cromwell, the King's main adviser.

John Skip did get into trouble for his words. Letters and Papers has records of his sermon and the following record:

> "A paper of singular moderation and ability,
> entitled "Interrogatories and articles to be
> administered to the preacher who preached the
> sermon in the Court on Passion Sunday," on
> these words: Quis ex vobis arguet me de peccato?

[which of you will convince me of sin?] for preaching seditious doctrines on these words, and slandering "the King's highness, his counsellors, his lords and nobles, and his whole Parliament."

Inc.: "First, whether this was his theme, Quis ex vobis arguet me de peccato?

Ends: "Item, finally, be it required of the preacher to bring forth and show his sermon in writing; and if he refuse so to do, or say he hath it not in writing, then be it inquired whether he did never write it, or never showed it to any man in writing before or since it was preached."[4]

Primary Source Reports on Skip's Sermon

"A sermon preached by Mr. Skyppe, in the King's chapel, upon Passion Sunday, in the year of Our Lord 1536, on the text Quis ex vobis arguet me de peccato? defending the clergy from their defamers and from the immoderate zeal of men in holding up to public reprobation the faults of any single clergyman as if it were the fault of all. He insisted upon the example of Ahasuerus, who was moved by a wicked minister to destroy the Jews. He urged that a King's councillor ought to take good heed what advice he gave in altering ancient things, and that no people wished to take away the ceremonies of the Church, such as holy water, holy bread, &c. That alterations ought not to be made except in cases of necessity. That in the present Parliament there were men of the greatest learning and ability, and perfect freedom and moderation in discussion. He described

2nd April 1536 –A Controversial Passion Sunday Sermon

the character of the debates in Parliament,
lamented the decay of the universities, and
insisted on the necessity of learning."[5]

"The preacher insisted on the strict following
of God's Word:—that Christ chose ignorant
followers, to teach men that nobility standeth
not in worth but grace; and he cited the
example of Solomon to show that he lost his
true nobility towards the end of his life, by
taking new wives and concubines. He insisted
on the need of a King being wise in himself, and
resisting evil counsellors who tempted him to
ignoble actions, by the history of Rehoboam;
observing that if a stranger visited this realm,
and saw those who were called noble, he would
conceive that all true nobility was banished from
England. He warned them against rebuking
the clergy, even if they were sinful, as rebukers
were often rebuked, like Nebuchadnezzar,
who was God's instrument to punish the Jews,
"and yet was damned for his labour." Against
evil councillors, who suggested alteration in
established customs, he instanced the history of
Haman and Ahasuerus. He then explained and
defended the ancient ceremonies of the Church
(as above). He concluded with a complaint on the
moderation of the High Court of Parliament."[6]

The full text of John Skip's sermon can be read in The National
Archives, reference SP6/1 "Folio 8 Sermon preached by John
Skip in the King's Chapel on Passion Sunday 1536", although the
handwriting is rather challenging!

Hugh Latimer's Sermon

John Skip was not the only chaplain Anne called on to preach about her views on the dissolution of the monasteries. She also asked Hugh Latimer to preach in front of the King. Latimer preached on Luke 20 verses 9-16, the parable of the vineyard. Here is a modern text of that parable from the New International Bible:

> "A man planted a vineyard, rented it to some farmers and went away for a long time. At harvest time he sent a servant to the tenants so they would give him some of the fruit of the vineyard. But the tenants beat him and sent him away empty-handed. He sent another servant, but that one also they beat and treated shamefully and sent away empty-handed. He sent still a third, and they wounded him and threw him out.
>
> Then the owner of the vineyard said, 'What shall I do? I will send my son, whom I love; perhaps they will respect him.' But when the tenants saw him, they talked the matter over. 'This is the heir,' they said. 'Let's kill him, and the inheritance will be ours.' So they threw him out of the vineyard and killed him.
>
> What then will the owner of the vineyard do to them? He will come and kill those tenants and give the vineyard to others." When the people heard this, they said, "God forbid!"'"

As you can see, it is a fitting text when you consider the first fruits and taxes that the monasteries had to pay. William Latymer wrote of this sermon in his "Cronickille of Anne Bulleyne". He explained that Hugh Latimer emphasised that the owner of the vineyard did not destroy the vineyard when the tenants could not pay him in fruit. Instead, he commanded it " to be fearmed and letton to others, whoo shoulde by their industroye and housebandrye amende the negligence of the other fearmers". In other words, the owner let it be used by others who would do the right thing. Latimer, and Anne through him, were saying that instead of dissolving the monasteries, the King could "converte the abbeys and prioryes to places of studye and goode letres and to the contynuall releve of the poore."[7] It was obviously something that Anne felt strongly about.

William Latymer also recorded that Latimer's sermon gave "the governors of the other religious houses" hope that the Queen may be able to help them if they petitioned her. They therefore sent a "brotherhood" to call on the Queen, who lectured them on their "detestable sleightes and frivelous ceremonyes" and made it plain that in her opinion the dissolution was "a deservid plague from almightie God", punishing them for their "lewdenes".[8] They had judged her incorrectly, she wasn't against the dissolution, she was against the Crown's plans for the monasteries' assets. That was Anne's stance: dissolution was necessary for reform but the money should go to education and to relief for the poor.

13th April – Maundy Thursday

On the 13th April 1536, Maundy Thursday, Anne Boleyn did her duty as Queen, distributing Maundy money (alms) and washing the feet of poor people.

It was traditional for the monarch and his consort to wash the feet of as many poor people as years they were old, as well as giving them purses of coins. In 1536, the court expenses show that the "costs of the Queen's maundy" were "31 l. 3s. 9 ½d."[1] Both William Latymer and John Foxe wrote of how the amount in the royal Maundy purses distributed to the poor increased significantly when Anne Boleyn was Queen, showing her passion for relief to the poor. Latymer recorded that one Maundy Thursday, Anne, after washing and kissing the feet of poor women, "commaunded to be put previlye into every poore womans purse one george noble, the which was vis viiid [6 shillings and 8 pence], over and besides the almes that wonted to be given."[2]

18th April 1536 –
The King Tricks Chapuys

On Tuesday18th April 1536, the imperial ambassador, Eustace Chapuys, was tricked into recognising as Queen the woman he called "the concubine".

Chapuys arrived at Greenwich Palace to meet with King Henry VIII and was greeted by George Boleyn and Thomas Cromwell, who brought him a message from the King. In the message, Henry VIII asked Chapuys to visit Anne Boleyn and kiss her hand. Chapuys excused himself because, as Eric Ives[1] points out, "that was going too far, too fast", and, in Chapuys's own words, it "would not be advisable".[2] He could not bring himself to kiss the hand of "the Concubine" and recognise her as Queen. So, George Boleyn, Lord Rochford, conducted Chapuys to mass, carefully placing the ambassador behind the door through which Anne would enter. Anne Boleyn, who was accompanying her husband to mass, knew exactly where Chapuys was and so stopped as she entered, swung round to him and bowed. Chapuys was forced to do reciprocate and bow to the Queen. Henry and Anne had got what they wanted, recognition of Anne's status, albeit in a rather underhand way.

It is clear that in mid April 1536, just two weeks before Anne's arrest, Henry VIII was still pushing for Anne to be recognised as his wife and rightful queen. Does this show that he was still committed to Anne? Why force Chapuys into recognising a woman you're going to discard? Is this evidence that Henry VIII was not involved in plotting against Anne Boleyn or is it just proof of his fickle nature? There is no way of knowing.

Chapuys, Henry VIII and Cromwell

Later that day, after dining with George Boleyn, Chapuys met privately with the King to discuss a potential alliance between the Emperor and England. This was a meeting which had been set up by Thomas Cromwell, who seems to have been intent on negotiating a twin alliance, allying England with both the Schmalkaldic League and with Charles V. [3] The only obstacle was Chapuys' condition that England should accept papal authority. Cromwell had worked on this, leading Chapuys to believe that Henry VIII might come to an agreement with France, instead of with the Empire, if Charles continued to be so demanding.

Unfortunately, at the meeting, Chapuys made it plain that for any alliance to go ahead, the Lady Mary would need to be restored to the succession. Although Cromwell had led Chapuys to believe that this would not be a problem, Henry VIII would not tolerate this idea. In his eyes, Mary was illegitimate and Elizabeth was his heir. Henry blew up, reacting "confusedly and in anger"[4] and "reproached" the Emperor with "great ingratitude". He made it clear that his relationship with the Pope and his daughter Mary's future were nobody's business but his, and that he would not be told what to do by Chapuys and the Emperor. According to Chapuys, Cromwell and Audley "appeared to regret these answers"[5] and when Chapuys spoke to Cromwell, the secretary was "mortified" by what had happened and was "hardly able to speak for sorrow". The stress of the situation led to him arguing with the King and then taking to his bed "from pure sorrow".[6] The King was ruining Cromwell's negotiations!

The next day, 19th April, the Bishop of Tarbes reported to his master, Francis I of France, that the Duke of Norfolk had told him "that what he had said the last time they met was true, and that whatever overture the Emperor might make things would not be other than they have been hitherto. Replied that he had no doubt of this, knowing that the friendship between the Kings cannot be affected by any practice or overture of the Emperor." The King was keeping the Emperor and the French king on tenterhooks.

Anne Boleyn: A Liability?

In Cromwell's eyes, Anne Boleyn must surely have been becoming a liability and a serious threat. Cardinal Wolsey had fallen, due in part to the influence of the Boleyns; and according to Cromwell, Anne had once said to him in an argument that "she would like to see his head cut off".[7] Although John Schofield points out that Anne's influence may not have been as strong at this time as it had been at Wolsey's fall, she was still a significant threat. Chapuys had commented on Anne's influence over the King in November 1535:

> "The concubine, who long ago conspired the
> death of the said ladies [Catherine and Mary]
> and thinks of nothing but getting rid of them,
> is the person who governs everything, and
> whom the King is unable to contradict."[8]

The King's marriage to her was also a stumbling block to any reconciliation with Rome and to the restoration of Mary. Anne was also pro-French, so if she did have any influence on the King with regards to foreign policy, then that would be the direction she'd be pushing him towards. Cromwell knew that Anne would never agree to Mary being restored; she had her own daughter's interests to look out for.

The King was obsessed with wanting a male heir; he was showing an interest in Jane Seymour; Anne was becoming a pain in the neck as well as a significant threat to Cromwell's foreign policy plans and, perhaps, even to his life. Perhaps it would be better if Anne just disappeared. Nobody knows for sure whether the plot against Anne started with the King or with Thomas Cromwell, but "on the third day of Easter, he [Cromwell] had set himself to arrange the plot (a fantasier et conspirer led. affaire)".[9]

It was, as historian Simon Schama says, "pure devilry, a finely measured brew: one part paranoia, one part pornography"[10] - a plot that would see a Queen, four courtiers and a musician brutally executed.

22nd April 1536 –
A Strange Letter from
Cranmer to Cromwell

On the 22nd April 1536, Archbishop Thomas Cranmer, who had been away from court staying at his country residence, Knole House, wrote the following letter to Thomas Cromwell:

> "Alas, Master Secretary, you forget Master Smyth
> of the Exchequer, who is near consumed with
> thought and pensiveness: even pity moveth me
> to rue the man (if I could) for his son's sake
> chiefly, and also for his own. I would give a great
> part of that I have to help him; and where I
> cannot myself, I make all my friends for him: so
> importune I am upon my friends from my friend
> his cause, I suppose more than I would be for
> mine own, or ever was: ruth and importunity
> of my friend maketh me so vehement against
> mine own nature. I have sent this bearer only to
> wait upon you until you have an answer of the
> King, and to put you in continual remembrance,
> for much business maketh you to forget many
> things, and yet I wonder that you remember so
> many things as you do. I was ever hitherto cold,
> but now I am in a heat with the cause of religion,
> which goeth all contrary to mine expectation, if
> it be as the fame goeth; wherein I would wonder
> fain break my mind unto you, and if you please,
> I will come to such place as you shall appoint for
> the same purpose. Thus He that made you, ever
> keep you. From Knol, the 22 day of April."[1]

The first part of the letter, referring to 'Master Smith', seems quite straightforward. Cranmer is simply reminding Cromwell of Mr Smith. Reverend Henry Jenkyns, the editor of Cranmer's correspondence, thinks this could have been "John Smith, father of the celebrated Sir Thomas Smith who about this time was distinguishing himself by his lectures on Greek at Cambridge."[2] However, the part of about religion seems rather odd. Historian John Schofield[3] puts forward the idea that what it may mean is that Cranmer had heard that Anne Boleyn was going to be set aside and replaced by the Catholic Jane Seymour. He may have feared that the cause of the new religion was under threat, as was his friend, Anne. Perhaps this is a coded message regarding Cranmer's concern and his need to talk to Cromwell urgently about it.

However, Eric Ives[4] believes that Anne Boleyn may have had words with the Archbishop regarding his Lent sermon supporting the dissolution of the monasteries, pointing out that the dissolution would not help the poor. Was Cranmer changing his mind about his support of Cromwell's policy? Cranmer's biographer, Diarmaid MacCulloch believes so, taking Cranmer's use of the word "religion" as referring to the monasteries.[5]

Unfortunately, there is no reply on record. We will never know exactly what Cranmer was trying to say.

23rd April 1536 – A Warning Sign?

On St George's Day (23rd April) 1536 the annual chapter meeting of the Order of the Garter took place at Greenwich. A record of this meeting can be found in Letters and Papers, Foreign and Domestic, Henry VIII, Volume 10:

> "On St. George's Day, 23 April 28 Hen. VIII., a chapter of the Order of the Garter was held at Greenwich, at which were present the King, the dukes of Richmond and Norfolk, the earls of Northumberland, Westmoreland, Wiltshire, Sussex, Rutland, and Oxford, lord Sandys, and Sir Wm. Fitzwilliam. It was determined to hold the feast on May 21, the earl of Northumberland taking the Sovereign's place, assisted by the earls of Rutland, Westmoreland, and Oxford, and Sir Wm. Fitzwilliam. Votes were taken for the election of a knight; and the next day, after mass for the dead, the King declared Sir Nic. Carew elected. He was installed when the feast was kept, on May 21. On this occasion the earl of Northumberland was seized with vertigo and weakness, so that it was feared he would not be able to take his part as deputy, but he recovered. The next day the hatchments of the deceased were offered up."[1]

As you can see, Sir Nicholas Carew was elected a Knight of the Garter at this chapter. His appointment was significant because Queen Anne Boleyn had put forward her brother George Boleyn, Lord Rochford, for the post. Her wish had been denied.

Was this a warning sign of the trouble to come? Maybe. Sir Nicholas Carew was an enemy of the Boleyn faction and he had also been mentoring Jane Seymour, Henry's new flame, in how to appeal to the King. The Imperial ambassador, Eustace Chapuys, wrote that "the Concubine has not had sufficient influence to get it for her brother",[2] seeing it as a sign that Anne Boleyn had lost her influence over the King. But perhaps Chapuys was reading too much into Carew's appointment. Henry VIII had promised the French King, Francis I, that Carew would be considered when a vacancy arose. Francis I's request to Henry VIII was made in May 1533[3] and was referred to in a letter from Palamedes Gontier to Admiral Chabot in February 1535:

> "Presented the letter in favor of the "Grand
> Escuyer" of England [Carew], to which he replied
> that the said place of the Chancellor of the Order
> was filled by the king of Scotland, and the number
> of 24 could not be exceeded. On the first vacancy
> he would remember the said Grand Escuyer."[4]

With the benefit of hindsight we see this as a warning sign of the events to come, as a sign that Anne had lost her influence with the King and as a sign that the Boleyn faction was losing favour. But perhaps we, like Chapuys, are reading too much into it. It is not known what Anne and George thought of this event.

Incidentally, Sir Nicholas Carew came to a sticky end. He was implicated in the 1538 Exeter Conspiracy, a plot to depose Henry VIII and to replace him with Henry Courtenay, 1st Marquess of Exeter and cousin of the King through his mother Katherine of York. Courtenay was executed on 9th January 1539 and Carew was executed on 3rd March 1539.

24th April 1536 – Legal Machinery

On 24th April 1536, Sir Thomas Audley, Henry VIII's Lord Chancellor and Thomas Cromwell's right hand man, set up two commissions of oyer and terminer at Westminster.

'Oyer and terminer' comes from the French 'to hear and to determine' and denotes a legal commission formed to investigate and prosecute serious criminal offences, such as treason, committed in a particular county. A grand jury in the county would first investigate the alleged offence and then approve a bill of indictment, if there was sufficient evidence. The case would then go on to the commission of oyer and terminer, the court with jurisdiction to try the offence(s).[1]

The two commissions of oyer and terminer set up by Audley were for offences committed in the counties of Middlesex and Kent and covered the crimes of misprision, treason, rebellion, felonies, murder, homicide, rioting, plotting, insurrection, extortion, oppression, contempt, concealment, ignorance, negligence, falsities, deception, conspiracy and being an accessory to these crimes.[2] The job of the commission was to investigate alleged crimes and to determine if there was indeed a case. These commissions were not common-place; in fact, there were only seventeen set up during the whole of Henry VIII's reign.[3] The fact that these commissions were so rare, combined with the fact that they were set up to judge offences in the counties of Middlesex and Kent – the counties of the grand juries which would later investigate the alleged offences of Anne Boleyn – suggest that the plot against Anne Boleyn was well underway at this time. These commissions surely could not have been a coincidence.[4]

Historian Eric Ives notes that Henry VIII's signature was not on the patent of the oyer and terminer. This may suggest that the commissions were ordered not by the King, but by Thomas Cromwell and Thomas Audley. Both Ives and Alison Weir explain how these commissions were usually only ordered after an arrest.

For example, in the case of Sir Thomas More, an oyer was only issued after he had been interrogated for eight weeks. Nobody had been arrested for treason in April 1536, so why the commissions? Could it be that Cromwell and Audley wanted to move quickly before the King could change his mind? Before Anne could talk him round?

Did the setting up of these commissions signal the end for Anne Boleyn? Was this event "virtually a death warrant for Anne"?[5] I believe so. I think it is too much of a coincidence; these commissions in 1536 were certainly only used in the case of the coup against the Boleyns. No other case of treason was investigated at this time. However, G W Bernard[6] believes that Henry VIII was fully committed to Anne Boleyn right up until her arrest and that the commissions need not have been set up to deal with Anne. He notes that as late as 25th April Henry VIII was sending instructions to Richard Pate, his ambassador in Rome, regarding his divorce from Catherine of Aragon. But was Henry just keeping up appearances or were Cromwell and Audley acting alone at this point? It's impossible to know, but something was amiss.

25th April 1536 –
Most Entirely Beloved Wife

On 25th April 1536, a day after the commissions of oyer and terminer had been appointed, King Henry VIII wrote letters to his ambassadors abroad: Richard Pate[1] in Rome, and Stephen Gardiner and John Wallop[2] in Paris. In these letters, the King referred to Anne Boleyn as "our most dear and most entirely beloved wife the Queen" and wrote of his hope for a son:

> "For as much as there is great likelihood
> and appearance that God will send
> unto Us heirs male to succeed Us."[3]

If we did not know with hindsight that trouble was brewing then we would think that all was rosy with the royal couple, that Henry had high hopes for the future and had no intention of setting Anne aside. What we will never know is whether these words were part of an act or whether Henry VIII was unaware of Cromwell's plans at this point. Henry still seemed to have been committed to Anne on 25th April 1536 and was still pushing for the rest of Europe to recognise her as his rightful wife and queen.

26th April 1536 –
Anne Boleyn and Matthew Parker

Around the 26th April 1536, Queen Anne Boleyn met with her chaplain of two years, her "countryman", 32 year old Matthew Parker. Parker[1] recorded later that Anne had asked him to watch over her daughter, the two year-old Princess Elizabeth, if anything happened to her.[2] She was entrusting him with her daughter's spiritual care.

Historian Eric Ives[3] writes that this was a request that Parker never forgot and something which stayed with him for ever. Parker obviously came to be important to Elizabeth because she made him her Archbishop of Canterbury in 1559. It was a post which Parker admitted to Lord Burghley, he would not have accepted if he "had not been so much bound to the mother".[4]

Matthew Parker was born on 6th August 1504 in Norwich and was educated at Corpus Christi College in Cambridge, where he became friends with a group of humanists and reformers. He arrived at court in March 1535 and was appointed as one of Queen Anne Boleyn's chaplains. He preached in front of both Princess Elizabeth and the King in 1535 and it was due to Anne's patronage that he was appointed Dean of the collegiate church of Stoke by Clare in Suffolk.

Matthew Parker is known for being Archbishop of Canterbury and also for being one of the men responsible for the Thirty-Nine Articles of Religion. These were established in 1563 and are seen today as "the historic defining statements of Anglican doctrine in relation to the controversies of the English Reformation".[5] He served as Elizabeth I's Archbishop of Canterbury until his death on 17th May 1575.

27th April 1536 –
Parliament Summoned

On 27th April 1536, writs were issued summoning Parliament, and a letter was sent to Thomas Cranmer, the Archbishop of Canterbury, asking him to attend Parliament. Here is the relevant section from the Letters and Papers, Foreign and Domestic, Henry VIII:

> "Summons to the archbishop of Canterbury to attend the Parliament which is to meet at Westminster, 8 June; and to warn the prior and chapter of his cathedral and the clergy of his province to be present, the former in person and the latter by two proctors. Westm., 27 April 28 Hen. VIII.
>
> ii. Similar writs to the different bishops, abbots, and lords; to the judges, serjeants-at-law, and the King's attorney, to give counsel; to the sheriffs to elect knights of the shires, citizens, and burgesses; also to the chancellor of the county palatine of Lancaster; to the deputy and council of Calais to elect one burgess, and to the mayor and burgesses to elect another."[1]

Although Anne Boleyn and the five men found guilty of adultery with her were all dead by the 8th June, these writs coming so soon after the setting up of the commissions of oyer and terminer suggests that Parliament was being called in order to deal with issues regarding the Queen, the King's marriage and the succession.

The King Thinks About Divorce

According to Chapuys, John Stokesley, Bishop of London, was approached on the 27th April to see if the King could "abandon" Anne Boleyn. Chapuys does not mention who consulted Stokesley, but he was told of it by Geoffrey Pole:

> "The brother of lord Montague told me yesterday at dinner that the day before the bishop of London had been asked if the King could abandon the said concubine, and he would not give any opinion to anyone but the King himself, and before doing so he would like to know the King's own inclination, meaning to intimate that the King might leave the said concubine, but that, knowing his fickleness, he would not put himself in danger. The said Bishop was the principal cause and instrument of the first divorce, of which he heartily repents, and would still more gladly promote this, the said concubine and all her race are such abominable Lutherans. London, 29 April 1536." [2]

Stokesley was not stupid, he was not going to endanger himself by working against the King and Anne.

28th and 29th April 1536

Something was definitely going on during April 1536. Commissions of oyer and terminer had been set up, writs for Parliament had been sent out and secret meetings were taking place.

On 28th April 1536, Thomas Warley wrote to Lord Lisle in Calais, informing him that the King's council had been meeting daily at Greenwich "upon certain letters brought by the French ambassador, who was at Court yesterday and divers other times."[1]

The imperial ambassador, Eustace Chapuys, also noticed the goings-on, reporting to Charles V on 29th April:

> "The day after the courier Gadaluppe left, the
> King sent for the French ambassador, and
> there was great consultation in Court. As I am
> told by one who is in the French ambassador's
> secrets, the King asked him to go in post to his
> master on certain affairs, which the ambassador
> agreed to do, and next day made preparations
> for leaving, then returned to Court on the
> day appointed, viz. Tuesday; but the Council,
> which was assembled in the morning till 9 or 10
> at night, could not agree to the dispatch, and
> the ambassador was put off till Thursday."[2]

Although both Warley and Chapuys refer to meetings regarding the French ambassador, the frequency of the meetings and the secrecy surrounding the subject matter may suggest that something else was going on too.

In this same letter to Charles V, Chapuys writes:

> "The Grand Ecuyer, Mr. Caro [Sir Nicholas
> Carew], had on St. George's day the Order of the
> Garter in the place of the deceased M. de Burgain
> (lord Abergavenny), to the great disappointment

of Rochford, who was seeking for it, and all
the more because the Concubine has not had
sufficient influence to get it for her brother;
and it will not be the fault of the said Ecuyer if
the Concubine, although his cousin (quelque,
qu. quoique? cousine) be not dismounted. He
continually counsels Mrs. Semel [Jane Seymour]
and other conspirators "pour luy faire une venue,"
and only four days ago he and some persons of
the chamber sent to tell the Princess to be of good
cheer, for shortly the opposite party would put
water in their wine, for the King was already as
sick and tired of the concubine as could be."[3]

It is hard to know whether Chapuys is simply repeating court
gossip or whether he does actually know the facts, but it appears
that Jane Seymour was being coached by the conservatives and that
they were hopeful of success.

In a letter written on the same day to Granvelle (Nicholas
Perronet, Seigneur de Granvelle, the Emperor's adviser), Chapuys
reports that "Dr. Sampson, dean of the chapel, has been for the
last four days continually with Cromwell."[4] Dr Richard Sampson
was a royal chaplain and was dean of Lichfield and also the
Chapel Royal. He had supported the King in his efforts to get his
marriage to Catherine of Aragon annulled, was a friend of Thomas
Cromwell and also an expert on canon law, having graduated BCL
at Cambridge. It is likely, therefore, that Cromwell was picking his
brains about a possible annulment of the marriage of Henry VIII
and Anne Boleyn. He did act as the King's proctor against Anne
Boleyn in the annulment proceedings.[5]

Again, with hindsight, it is easy for us to see these meetings as
suspicious and as the beginning of the end for Anne Boleyn, but
they may have been about other matters. We may also be reading
far too much into the events as well as into the words of Chapuys,
a notorious gossip. What we do know is that there were moves

against the Queen from 30th April and that just over three weeks later a Queen was dead, along with five members of the Boleyn faction.

29th April 1536 -
Sir Henry Norris and Dead Men's Shoes

Also on the 29th April 1536, Anne Boleyn argued with Sir
Henry Norris, an argument which led her to instruct him to go to
her almoner on Sunday 30th April and take an oath that Anne "was
a good woman".[1] It was an argument which caused gossip around
the court and which may also have led to cross words between
Anne and her husband the King.

Sir Henry Norris was Henry VIII's groom of the stool, a
member of the Boleyn faction and a man who was courting Anne's
cousin and lady-in-waiting, Madge Shelton. Anne asked Norris
why he was taking so long to marry Madge and when he gave her a
non-committal answer she rebuked him, saying, "You look for dead
men's shoes, for if aught came to the King but good, you would
look to have me"[2], thus accusing Norris of delaying his marriage to
Madge because he fancied her. A horrified Norris replied that "if he
[should have any such thought] he would his head were off".

Anne's anger had caused her to speak recklessly. Not only had
she said something very inappropriate for a married woman, let
alone Queen; she had also broken the rules of courtly love and
spoken of the King's death. The courtier was meant to proposition
the lady; however, in this argument Anne had been the 'aggressor'.
She had turned the courtly love tradition on its head and had also
spoken words which could be construed as treason. That is why
Norris was so horrified. It is also why Anne suddenly ordered him
to go to her almoner and swear an oath about her character. This
argument would haunt Anne in the Tower; her words were used
against her by the Crown, not only to provide evidence of some
kind of relationship between her and Norris, but also as proof that
she was plotting the King's death with Norris and others.

Sir Henry Norris

Sir Henry Norris was born sometime in the late 1490s and was the son of Richard Norris and grandson of Sir William Norris of Yattendon and his wife, Jane de Vere, daughter of John de Vere, twelfth Earl of Oxford.[1] Norris's family had a long history of serving the monarch – his great-grandfather, Sir John Norris, had been Keeper of the Great Wardrobe to Henry VI and his grandfather, Sir William Norris, had been Knight of the Body to Edward IV. Sir William Norris had been attainted after being involved in the Duke of Buckingham's rebellion against Richard III and had been forced to flee to Brittany, where he joined the forces of Henry Tudor and may even have fought at the Battle of Bosworth. Sir William had a command in June 1487 at Stoke and went on to become the Lieutenant of Windsor Castle.[2]

Sometime prior to 1526, Sir Henry Norris married Mary Fiennes, daughter of Thomas Fiennes, eighth Baron Dacre. The couple had three children. Mary, their daughter, grew up to marry Sir George Carew, Captain of the Mary Rose which sank in 1545 along with its captain and many of its crew. Henry was born around 1525 and educated in a reformist manner alongside Mary Boleyn's son Henry Carey. Edward did not survive infancy, dying sometime around 1529. Norris was left a widower in circa 1530.

A Royal Career

Sir Henry Norris received his first royal grant as a young man in 1515 and by 1517 we know that he was serving in the King's Privy Chamber. By 1518, he had obviously proved himself enough to be handling money for the King and he was probably made a Gentleman of the Privy Chamber in September 1518.[3] Just a few months later, in January 1519, there is record of Norris receiving a annuity of 50 marks. This shows the high regard that the King must have had for him. Norris was definitely on the rise and a royal favourite.

Norris's popularity and his loyalty to the King meant that he survived as Gentleman of the Privy Chamber when Cardinal Wolsey "weeded out" some of Henry's men in May 1519. We know that he attended the Field of the Cloth of Gold in 1520. Like the King, Norris was a sportsman, excelling at jousting, and was an attractive and popular courtier.

Sometime before 1529, Norris became Groom of the Stool, the man whose job was to "preside over the office of royal excretion".[4] In other words, wiping the royal bottom! Although this sounds an appalling job, it was a position of high esteem and it did make Norris and the King very close friends. It was also a position of influence, in that the Groom of the Stool was often approached by petitioners who wanted him to influence the King on their behalf.

Sir Henry Norris was one of the King's closest companions and he controlled access to the King's private chambers, and the King himself. No wonder Cromwell included Norris in his coup against Anne!

Sir Henry Norris also held the position of Keeper of the Privy Purse. This involved him looking after gifts that the King had been given, such as jewellery. Norris's high favour was also shown by the fact that he was appointed keeper of the manor of Placentia (Greenwich) and also of East Greenwich Park and Tower. When Sir William Compton died in 1528, Sir Henry Norris took his place as royal favourite. A popular and trustworthy man, he deserved this position. The King obviously trusted Norris because he gave him very important, and rather "delicate" jobs. For example, it was Norris who carried the King's secret letters and messages to Wolsey after the Cardinal's fall from Grace. The fact that Wolsey rewarded him with a precious cross containing a piece of the true cross of Christ, and a cross that Wolsey always wore next to his skin, shows that Norris must have treated the Cardinal with much respect, courtesy and kindness.

Other posts that Sir Henry Norris held include Chamberlain of North Wales (appointed in 1531), Master of the Hart Hounds and of the Hawks, Black Rod in the Parliament House, Graver of the Tower of London, Weigher of the Goods at the port of Southampton, Collector of Subsidy in the City of London, High Steward of the University of Oxford and steward or keeper of various parks, manors and castles. These positions, offices and lands meant that Norris was "wealthier than many leading nobles".[5] Eric Ives writes of how Norris's annuities from the Crown added up to £542, his fees of offices to £328 12s. 3d. And earnings from farms and grants to £370 10s. This made a total of £1241 2s. 3d. which was then boosted to £1327 15s. 7d. from private sources!

Sir Henry Norris and the Boleyns

It is thought that Norris had been a member of the Boleyn faction since at least 1530, around the time that he was widowed. He had much in common with Anne Boleyn and her circle, being of a reformist persuasion. His servant George Constantine was described as "an active instrument in the hands of the early promoters of the Reformation"[6] and in 1530[7] was actually apprehended for heresy by Sir Thomas More because of his "connection with Tindall, Joye, and other reformers, in translating and printing the New Testament abroad."[8] When Constantine was questioned by More regarding the smuggling of heretical books and where funding for the operation was coming from, Constantine replied that the Bishop of London was their best supporter, "having expended large sums of money in the purchase of their Testaments, for the purpose of burning them"! The amused More ordered Constantine to be put in the stocks, rather than burned, but Constantine managed to escape the stocks and fled abroad. It was Sir Henry Norris who brought him back to the English court, along with a copy of Miles Coverdale's English Bible for Anne Boleyn.

Norris's favour with both the King and Anne Boleyn led to him accompanying them to inspect York Place, after it was surrendered to the Crown by Cardinal Wolsey. He accompanied them to Calais in autumn 1532 and was probably one of the witnesses at their secret marriage in January 1533. Eric Ives[9] points out that Norris's son was educated by the French reformist scholar Nicholas Bourbon in the company of Anne Boleyn's nephew and ward Henry Carey. This fact shows that Norris shared the Queen's reformist sympathies and that he was close to the Queen.

It was in the 1530s that Norris started courting 'Mistress Shelton'. Margaret Shelton was the daughter of Sir Thomas Boleyn's sister, Anne, and of her husband Sir John Shelton. This courtship came to nothing. Anne teased Norris about his lack of commitment to Margaret. She also reprimanded Sir Francis Weston for his interest in Margaret. Both these conversations were subsequently used against Anne in Cromwell's plot to oust the Queen and her circle.

30th April 1536
– A Royal Argument
and the First Arrest

At 11 o'clock on the night of Sunday 30th April 1536, the King and Queen's upcoming visit to Calais was cancelled and arrangements made for the King to journey alone a week later. We know about this from a letter written by Thomas Warley to Lady Lisle in Calais:

> "I wrote by Collins that the King would have been at Rochester tonight, but he has changed his mind, which was not known till Sunday at 11 o'clock, and will go to Dover next week."[1]

No reason is given for the change in the King's travel arrangements.

Furthermore, on that same Sunday, Scottish theologian Alexander Alesius witnessed an argument between Anne Boleyn and Henry VIII. This argument may well have been caused by the King hearing of Anne's words with Norris or by her trying to explain what happened:

> "Never shall I forget the sorrow which I felt when I saw the most serene queen, your most religious mother, carrying you, still a baby, in her arms and entreating the most serene king your father, in Greenwich Palace, from the open window of which he was looking into the courtyard, when she brought you to him. I did not perfectly understand what had been going on, but the faces and gestures of the speakers plainly showed that the king was angry, although he could conceal his anger wonderfully well. Yet from the

> protracted conference of the council (for whom
> the crowd was waiting until it was quite dark,
> expecting that they would return to London),
> it was most obvious to everyone that some deep
> and difficult question was being discussed."[2]

The mention of a "protracted" council meeting sounds ominous and it is clear that Alesius's suspicions were aroused. Something was going on.

Also on 30th April, court musician and member of the Boleyn circle, Mark Smeaton, was taken to Thomas Cromwell's house in Stepney and interrogated. Within 24 hours he had confessed to making love three times to the Queen. It is likely that the note that Henry VIII received at the May Day joust, the next day, contained details of Smeaton's confession.

There is an intriguing story about Mark Smeaton and Anne Boleyn in The Spanish Chronicle (Cronica del Rey Enrico), also known as The Chronicle of King Henry VIII of England. This is a rather gossipy chronicle and one historical source to take with a rather large pinch of salt, but the story is interesting nonetheless.

It concerns a certain musician, a cupboard, a jar of jam, a bed and a certain queen. After reporting how Anne had fallen in love with Smeaton, the Chronicle goes on to say:

> "One night, whilst all the ladies were dancing,
> the old woman called Mark and said to him
> gently, so that none should overhear, "You must
> come with me;" and he, as he knew it was to
> the Queen's chamber he had to go, was nothing
> loth. So she took him to an ante-chamber, where
> she and another lady slept, next to the Queen's
> room, and in this ante-chamber there was a closet
> like a store-room, where she kept sweetmeats,
> candied fruits, and other preserves which the
> Queen sometimes asked for. To conceal him
> more perfectly the old woman put him into this

closet, and told him to stay there till she came for him, and to take great care he was not heard. Then she shut him up and returned to the great hall where they were dancing, and made signs to the Queen, who understood her, and, although it was not late, she pretended to be ill, and the dancing ceased. She then retired to her chamber with her ladies, whilst the old woman said to her, "Madam, when you are in bed and all the ladies are asleep, you can call me and ask for some preserves, which I will bring, and Mark shall come with me, for he is in the closet now."

"The Queen went to bed and ordered all her ladies to retire to their respective beds, which were in an adjoining gallery like a refectory, and when they were all gone but the old lady and the lady who slept with her, she sent them off too. When she thought they would all be asleep, she called the old woman, and said, "Margaret, bring me a little marmalade." She called it out very loudly, so that the ladies in the gallery might hear as well as Mark, who was in the closet. The old woman went to the closet and made Mark undress, and took the marmalade to the Queen, leading Mark by the hand. The lady who was in the old woman's bed did not see them when they went out of the closet, and the old woman left Mark behind the Queen's bed, and said out loud, "Here is the marmalade, my lady." Then Anne said to the old woman, "Go along; go to bed."

"As soon as the old woman had gone Anne went round to the back of the bed and grasped the youth's arm, who was all trembling, and made

him get into bed. He soon lost his bashfulness,
and remained that night and many others, so
that in a short time this Mark flaunted out to
such an extent that there was not a gentleman
at court who was so fine, and Anne never
dined without having Mark serve her."[3]

Now this story is quite hilarious until you stop and realise that
this was some of the propaganda which helped to blacken Anne
Boleyn's name. It is such a silly story and I cannot see that there is
any truth in it. There is certainly no other evidence to back it up,
unless you believe the poem by Lancelot de Carles, telling of the
alleged witness statement from the Countess of Worcester.[4]

Elizabeth Browne, the Countess of Worcester, was one of
Anne's ladies and she apparently told her brother, Sir Anthony
Browne, that her own offence (possible adultery) was nothing by
comparison to those of the Queen, who allowed members of the
court to come into her chamber at all hours. Browne continued
that if her brother did not believe her then he could find out more
from Mark Smeaton. She then accused George Boleyn of having
carnal knowledge of his sister, the Queen.

If this exchange between the Countess and her brother did
take place and was then fed back to Cromwell, we can see how
this, combined with Anne's ramblings in the Tower regarding
Smeaton and Norris, could well have made Anne look guilty or
have been enough ammunition and "evidence" for those conspiring
against her.

Smeaton Mooning Over Anne

When Mrs Stonor, one of the ladies chosen to attend Anne
Boleyn in the Tower, spoke to Anne about Smeaton being held in
the Tower and having to wear "irons", Anne was quick to comment
that "it was because he was no gentleman". She went on to tell of
Mark mooning over her:

"I never spake with him since, but upon Saturday

before May-day [29th April], and then I found
him standing in the round window in my
chamber of presence; and I asked why he was so
sad? And he answered and said it was no matter.
And then I said, You may not look to have me
speak to you as I should do to a noble man,
because ye be an inferior person. No, no, said he,
a look sufficeth me; and thus fare you well."[5]

Anne's account suggests that Mark had a crush on her but that
there was actually distance between them, and that she put him in
his place by pointing out his inferiority. Clergyman and historian,
John Strype, who published his "Ecclesiastical Memorials" in 1721
and who saw Kingston's letters and various records before they
got damaged in the Ashburnham House fire of 1731, wrote that
Smeaton was "some haughty person" who "thought the Queen
gave him not respect enough. And so might take this opportunity
to humble her; and revenge himself by this means on her; not
thinking it would cost him his own life."[6]

Mark Smeaton's Confession

Those of us who believe that Anne Boleyn was 100% innocent
of all the charges laid against her struggle to understand why Mark
Smeaton confessed to sleeping with the Queen.

- Was his confession tortured out of him?

- Did he confess in an attempt to save himself? Was he
  promised a pardon if he confessed?

- Was Mark promised a swifter and more merciful death if he
  complied and confessed?

- Was he living in some kind of fantasy world? Did he actually
  believe that Anne loved him and that they had a relationship?

- Was it revenge for Anne rejecting him and humiliating him?

- Did he see sin where there was none and see himself as guilty
  of adultery for fantasizing about Anne?

- Was Smeaton tortured?

Unfortunately, we just don't know whether Mark Smeaton was tortured. He was taken to Cromwell's house in Stepney for interrogation and although I cannot see Cromwell having a racking room there, Smeaton could have been tortured psychologically. He was certainly the only one of the accused to be kept in irons in the Tower.

The Spanish Chronicle has Smeaton being tortured with a rope and cudgel:

> "Then he [Cromwell] called two stout young
> fellows of his, and asked for a rope and a cudgel,
> and ordered them to put the rope, which was full
> of knots, round Mark's head, and twisted it with
> the cudgel until Mark cried out, "Sir Secretary,
> no more, I will tell the truth, " and then he said,
> "The Queen gave me the money. " "Ah, Mark, "
> said Cromwell, "I know the Queen gave you a
> hundred nobles, but what you have bought has
> cost over a thousand, and that is a great gift even
> for a Queen to a servant of low degree such as
> you. If you do not tell me all the truth I swear
> by the life of the King I will torture you till you
> do." Mark replied, "Sir, I tell you truly that she
> gave it to me." Then Cromwell ordered him a
> few more twists of the cord, and poor Mark,
> overcome by the torment, cried out, "No more,
> Sir, I will tell you everything that has happened."
> And then he confessed all, and told everything
> as we have related it, and how it came to pass."[7]

Although this is what is recorded in The Spanish Chronicle, we have no other primary source evidence to back this up. George Constantine, one of Henry Norris's servants, said that "the sayeing was that he was fyrst grevously racked, which I cowlde never know of a trewth"[8] but Lancelot de Carles wrote that Mark confessed without being tortured.[9] There is no mention of Smeaton having any physical injury at his trial or execution; if he had been severely racked then he would have had to have been helped or carried to the scaffold. Whatever the truth regarding his alleged torture, Mark Smeaton was interrogated for around twenty-four hours, which suggests that he didn't willingly confess and that some pressure was put on him. This pressure could have been physical or psychological, or he could have been offered some kind of deal.

Mark Smeaton was a lowly court musician and may have been seen as expendable. Perhaps Cromwell and his men could get away with torturing him, something that they could not risk doing with the likes of Sir Henry Norris, a nobleman and groom of the stool. Lancelot de Carles writes that when Henry VIII rode back from the May Day joust with Sir Henry Norris, the former accused the latter of committing adultery with Anne and then offered to spare Norris if he would confess. Did Cromwell try to strike some similar deal with Mark Smeaton and then break that deal after Mark confessed? Perhaps so.

I doubt that we will ever know what caused Mark Smeaton to confess to sleeping with the Queen and why he didn't later retract his confession, but this young musician's life was cut short on the 17th May 1536 when he was beheaded on Tower Hill. My own personal belief is that Smeaton was offered a deal – a more merciful death by axe, rather than the usual horrific and slow traitor's death, if he confessed and stuck to his confession.

Historian Eric Ives writes of how Henry's anger may have subsided long enough for him to continue with the May Day jousts the next day. However, it was ominous that the King postponed the court's move to Rochester and his plans to go from there on to Calais. Was he aware that Thomas Cromwell was interrogating Mark Smeaton? We just don't know.

Mark Smeaton

Mark Smeaton (Smeton) was a misfit in that he had not been part of the Boleyn faction or Anne's circle of friends for very long. Unlike the other men, it is thought that he was from a humble background, being the son of a carpenter.[1] It is thought that his family were Flemish.

Mark was a talented musician and it was through this talent that he got a position at Henry VIII's court. His gifts included dancing, singing and playing instruments such as the portable organ, lute and virginals. His beautiful voice was noticed by Cardinal Wolsey, who recruited him for his choir. At Wolsey's fall, Mark managed to move to the Henry VIII's Chapel Royal and get promoted to the position of Groom of the Privy Chamber in 1529. Everyone called him "Mark", rather than Smeaton; this familiar address shows that although Mark was a member of the Privy Chamber he was still rather "lowly". It also shows that he was probably younger than the others.

The Privy Purse Expenses of November 1529 to December 1532 show frequent mentions of "marke". In the introduction, the editor explains that it is clear that Smeaton was "wholly supported and clothed" by Henry VIII. There are many mentions of payments for "shert"s and "hosen". His rise in favour is evident from the increase in his rewards during the period, from "xx s"[2] (20 shillings) in December 1530 to "iii li. vi s. viii d."[3] (£3 6 shillings and 8 pence) in October 1532. The increase in payments for clothing would also indicate this rise in favour.

Mark and the Boleyn Faction

An inscription in a manuscript of Jean Lefèvres translation of Mathieu of Boulogne's 13th century satirical poem "Liber lamentationum Matheoluli" ("The Lamentations of Matheolus") is evidence that Smeaton was friends with George Boleyn and a part of the Boleyn circle of friends. The manuscript, which can now be found in the British Library, is inscribed, "Thys boke ys myn, George Boleyn. 1526", and then, near the end of the volume, "Amoy m marc S", showing that it had also belonged to Smeaton. The fact that the poem is an attack on women and the institution of marriage has been used as evidence of a sexual relationship between Smeaton and George Boleyn.[4] However, there are also scribblings on the fly leaf by Thomas Wyatt; and this was a text that was widely circulated amongst scholars in Europe at that time. It was simply a circle of friends sharing fashionable literature.

Smeaton was a talented young man and it is likely that his gifts would have been well appreciated by this group of intellectuals and lovers of the arts and entertainment. However, due to his humble backgrounds, he may have been on the fringes of this circle and looked upon as a source of entertainment rather than as an equal.

1st May 1536 - The May Day Joust

The May Day joust of 1st May 1536 should have been like every other May Day joust. It should have been a day of celebration, of fun and joy. Instead, it was to be the first outward sign that something was wrong in Tudor Paradise.

Anne Boleyn sat watching the May Day jousting at Greenwich with her husband, King Henry VIII, who was sitting it out for the first time due to his accident in the January. Anne was blissfully unaware of the interrogation of Mark Smeaton the day before, although she may have had an inkling that something was going on. She may well have been pre-occupied about the conversation she had had with Sir Henry Norris, her husband's Groom of the Stool; a conversation which could be misconstrued and used against her by her enemies. Anne may also have been concerned about her husband's interest in a certain Jane Seymour, one of her ladies, but she had no clue about the events which were shortly to unfold.

In his poem "De la royne d'Angleterre"[1], Lancelot de Carles, secretary to the French ambassador, wrote of how there was no sign of anything being wrong between the King and Norris during the joust. He describes how Norris was armed and ready to joust, but his horse refused to run. The King stepped in and offered Norris his own horse – an act of kindness and chivalry. The Queen's brother, George Boleyn, was also involved in the joust. He led the challengers and Norris led the defenders.[2]

Everything changed at the end of the joust when the King suddenly got up, abandoning his wife, and riding instead to Westminster with Norris. According to George Constantine, one of Norris's servants, the King interrogated Norris the whole way and offered him a pardon "in case he wolde utter the trewth".[3] Gilbert Burnet, Bishop of Salisbury, corroborated this offer of a pardon, writing that Norris said "that in his conscience he thought her innocent of these things laid to her charge; but whether she was or not, he would not accuse her of anything; and he would die a thousand times, rather than ruin an innocent person."[4] A courageous answer.

The Spanish Chronicle explains that Norris's interrogation was due to Smeaton's confession:

> "The Secretary at once [after Smeaton had confessed] wrote to the King, and sent Mark's confession to him by a nephew of his called Richard Cromwell, the letter being conceived as follows: "Your Majesty will understand that jealous of your honour, and seeing certain things passing in your palace, I determined to investigate and discover the truth. Your Majesty will recollect that Mark has hardly been in your service four months and only has £100 salary, and yet all the Court notices his splendour, and that he has spent a large sum for these jousts, all of which has aroused suspicions in the minds of certain gentleman, and I have examined Mark, who has made the confession which I enclose to your Majesty in this letter."[5]

The Spanish Chronicle then has the King leaving by boat for Westminster, whereas Constantine has them riding. Norris would not confess to anything and protested his innocence, but he was taken to the Tower of London the next morning.

2nd May 1536 – Arrests

At dawn on 2nd May 1536, Sir Henry Norris, Henry VIII's Groom of the Stool and great friend, was taken to the Tower of London. Mark Smeaton had also been taken there, and the imperial ambassador, Eustace Chapuys, wrote to Charles V on 2nd May telling him that George Boleyn, Lord Rochford, was also in the Tower:

> "The Concubine's brother, named Rochefort,
> has also been lodged in the Tower, but
> more than six hours after the others,
> and three or four before his sister."[1]

The Tudor chronicler, Charles Wriothesley,[2] was in agreement, writing that Norris and Rochford were both taken to the Tower on 2nd May. However, nowhere is there any mention of George Boleyn being interrogated prior to his arrest. He was also apprehended so discreetly that his sister, Anne Boleyn, knew nothing about it. Historian Eric Ives believes that the fact that George was arrested at Whitehall, rather than Greenwich (like his sister), suggests that he may have been on his way to see the King to find out what was going on.[3]

In "Las nuevas de Ynglaterra de la presion de la Manceba del Rey", recorded in Letters and Paper on 2nd May, it reports Rochford's arrest as being to do with him covering up his sister's crimes and being an accessory, rather than his being one of her lovers:

> "The Emperor has letters from England of 2
> May, stating that the mistress of the king of
> England, who is called queen, had been put
> in the Tower for adultery with an organist
> of her chamber, and the King's most private
> "sommelier de corps." Her brother is imprisoned

for not giving information of her crime. It is
said that, even if it had not been discovered,
the King had determined to leave her, as he
had been informed that she had consummated
a marriage with the earl of Nortemberlano
(Northumberland) nine years ago."[4]

This leaves us wondering whether George Boleyn was arrested
first and then the charge of incest made up later, a shocking and
horrific allegation intended to turn everyone against him and his
sister.

It appears that Anne Boleyn was watching a game of real tennis
on 2nd May when a messenger arrived telling her that the King
had ordered her to present herself to his privy council. Although
Anne was unaware that her brother had been arrested, this
message, along with her husband's abrupt departure from the May
Day jousts the day before, must have frightened her. Anne was an
intelligent woman who realised the potential repercussions of her
reckless words to Sir Henry Norris; she must have been worried
about what was going to happen next. So worried had Anne been
that she had appealed to the King with Elizabeth in her arms. On
Wednesday 26th April, as mentioned earlier, she had also asked
her chaplain, Matthew Parker, to take care of Elizabeth if anything
happened to her.[5] The fact that she approached Parker days before
she quarrelled with Norris suggests that Anne was already worried
about her precarious position.

Anne Boleyn left the tennis match and presented herself in
the council chamber in front of a royal commission consisting
of the Duke of Norfolk (her uncle), Sir William Fitzwilliam and
Sir William Paulet. There she was informed that she was being
accused of committing adultery with three different men: Mark
Smeaton, Sir Henry Norris and a third, unnamed at this stage.
She was also told that Smeaton and Norris had confessed. Anne
remonstrated with her accusers, but her words had no effect and
the royal commission ordered her arrest. Anne was then taken

to her apartments until the tide of the Thames turned and then, at two o'clock in the afternoon, she was escorted by barge to the Tower of London.

Upon arrival at the Tower, it is likely that Anne's barge would have entered through the Court Gate[6] (Tower Gate[7]) of the Byward Tower, rather than through Traitors' Gate. She was met by Sir Edmund Walsingham, the Lieutenant of the Tower, and taken to the Royal Palace where she encountered the Constable of the Tower, Sir William Kingston. Kingston wrote letters to Thomas Cromwell to keep him informed of Anne's behaviour and the things she said during her imprisonment. In a letter dated 3rd May, he wrote of Anne's arrival at the Tower:

> "On my lord of Norfolk and the King's Council
> departing from the Tower, I went before the
> Queen into her lodging. She said unto me,
> "Mr. Kingston, shall I go into a dungeon?"
> I said, "No, Madam. You shall go into the
> lodging you lay in at your coronation." "It is
> too good for me, she said; Jesu have mercy
> on me;" and kneeled down, weeping a good
> pace, and in the same sorrow fell into a great
> laughing, as she has done many times since."

> "She desired me to move the King's highness
> that she might have the sacrament in the closet
> by her chamber, that she might pray for mercy,
> for I am as clear from the company of man
> as for sin as I am clear from you, and am the
> King's true wedded wife. And then she said,
> Mr. Kingston, do you know where for I am
> here? and I said, Nay. And then she asked me,
> When saw you the King? and I said I saw him
> not since I saw [him in] the Tiltyard. And then,
> Mr. K., I pray you to tell me where my Lord my

father is? And I told her I saw him afore dinner
in the Court. O where is my sweet brother? I
said I left him at York Place; and so I did."

"I hear say, said she, that I should be accused
with three men; and I can say no more but nay,
without I should open my body. And there with
opened her gown. O, Norris, hast thou accused
me? Thou are in the Tower with me, and thou
and I shall die together; and, Mark, thou art here
to. O, my mother, thou wilt die with sorrow;
and much lamented my lady of Worcester, for
by cause that her child did not stir in her body.
And my wife said, what should be the cause? And
she said, for the sorrow she took for me. And
then she said, Mr. Kyngston, shall I die without
justice? And I said, the poorest subject the Kyng
hath, hath justice. And there with she laughed"[8]

It is hard to imagine how Anne felt as she entered the Tower of
London. How ironic for her to be imprisoned in the very lodgings
in which she spent the night before her coronation – the sumptuous
Queen's apartments in the Royal Palace. No wonder she collapsed
weeping and moved from tears to laughter. Her hysteria was caused
by her realising the full extent of what was happening. After all, she
knew her husband well and she had seen what had happened to the
likes of Sir Thomas More. She knew that real justice was unlikely.

We can see from her speech to Kingston that she was stricken
with anxiety, but more about others than herself. In April 1536,
Elizabeth Boleyn had been reported as being ill;[9] Anne was
obviously worried that news of her arrest would affect her mother's
health for the worse. Anne was also worried that the news would
affect her friend Elizabeth Browne's pregnancy. George was preying
on Anne's mind, too. She obviously realised that he may have been
in danger as well. Kingston lied to her. He knew full well that her

brother was also in the Tower, but it is likely that he was trying to be kind to an already hysterical woman.

Kingston would report Anne's ramblings to Cromwell over the next few days and these words, spoken by a desperate and frightened woman, would lead to the arrest of Sir Francis Weston. They would also be used as evidence against her and the men concerned. We can wonder what would have happened if Anne had stayed silent in the Tower. Perhaps Weston would have been saved. However, there was no hope for Anne, George, Norris, Brereton and Smeaton. They were facing a certain death.

On the very afternoon that Anne Boleyn was arrested and taken to the Tower of London, the King's illegitimate son, Henry Fitzroy, Duke of Richmond, visited his father. According to Chapuys, the King broke down in tears, telling Richmond "that both he and his sister, meaning the Princess, ought to thank God for having escaped from the hands of that woman[Anne Boleyn], who had planned their death by poison, from which I conclude that the King knew something of her wicked intentions."[10]There had been rumours that Anne Boleyn had poisoned Catherine of Aragon, causing her death four months earlier, so did Henry really believe that his wife was capable of murder? Did he truly believe what he was saying or was he trying to justify what was going on? We will never know.

George Boleyn, Lord Rochford

George Boleyn was born around 1504, making him the youngest of the three famous Boleyn children. His father was courtier and diplomat, Thomas Boleyn, and his mother was Elizabeth Howard, daughter of Thomas Howard, Earl of Surrey.

George's later fluency in French, along with his aptitude for poetry and translating, points to an excellent education. His "connaissance parfaite" of French, his interest in French literature and the "New Religion", and his close relationship with his sister in the 1520s and 1530s suggest that he spent part of his youth in France, possibly accompanying his father in diplomatic missions. George also spent time at court, quickly becoming a favourite with a king who enjoyed surrounding himself with intelligent, fun-loving and quick-witted young men. George Boleyn was the perfect Tudor courtier; he had charisma and brains, he was a sportsman and he was a talented musician and poet. His contemporaries listed him as a court poet along with Thomas Wyatt and Henry Howard, Earl of Surrey.

George married Jane Parker, daughter of Lord Morley, in late 1524/early 1525. Although the marriage has been viewed as loveless, with George being portrayed as homosexual and his wife as a spiteful and jealous shrew, we just don't know what their relationship was like and it is unlikely that a zealous evangelical would have put his life and his mortal soul in peril by committing 'buggery'.

In 1525 George was appointed a member of the King's privy chamber and in 1529 he was appointed as ambassador to France at such a young age that it drew comment from Jean du Bellay, a French diplomat. Like his father, George became a trusted diplomat, carrying out many important embassies.

George Boleyn was a man on the rise in the 1520s and 30s, and he enjoyed a high profile career at Henry VIII's court. He was rewarded with grants such as the keepership of the Palace of

Beaulieu in 1528, a knighthood in 1529, and, in the same year, the governorship of Bethlehem Hospital. So intimate was he with the King that Henry even trusted him to be the bearer of the love letters he wrote to George's sister, Anne.

George was active in pushing for Henry VIII's annulment. His signature can be found on the deposition signed by the Spiritual and Temporal Lords of England, which was sent to the Pope asking for his consent to the annulment and pointing out the evils which would arise from delay. As ambassador to France, he was also active in seeking French support for the annulment.

He carried on being a busy diplomat when Anne became Queen, even missing her coronation because he was in France. He was also involved in the League of Schmalkalden in 1535 and was a regular attendee of Parliament.

George was a zealous reformer and presented Anne with two beautiful manuscripts of works by French reformer Jacques Lefèvre d'Étaples which he had translated himself. Chapuys, the imperial ambassador, spoke of how, when he met with George Boleyn in April 1536, the former avoided "all occasions of entering into Lutheran discussions, from which he [George] could not refrain". George obviously liked to share his religious beliefs and opinions!

3rd May 1536
– I Had Never Better
Opinion of Woman

On 3rd May 1536, Archbishop Thomas Cranmer wrote a letter to King Henry VIII showing his shock and amazement at the arrest of his patron Anne Boleyn:

"Have come to Lambeth, according to Mr. Secretary's letters, to know your Grace's pleasure. Dare not, contrary to the said letters, presume to come to your presence, but of my bounden duty I beg you "somewhat to suppress the deep sorrows of your Grace's heart," and take adversity patiently. Cannot deny that you have great causes of heaviness, and that your honor is highly touched. God never sent you a like trial; but if He find you no less patient and thankful than when all things succeeded to your wish, I suppose you never did thing more acceptable to Him. You will give Him occasion to increase His benefits, as He did to Job.

If the reports of the Queen be true, they are only to her dishonor, not yours. I am clean amazed, for I had never better opinion of woman; but I think your Highness would not have gone so far if she had not been culpable. I was most bound to her of all creatures living, and therefore beg that I may, with your Grace's favor, wish and pray that she may declare herself innocent. Yet if she be found guilty, I repute him not a faithful subject who would not wish her punished without mercy. "And as I loved her not a little for the love which I judged her to bear towards God and His Gospel, so if she be proved culpable there is not one that loveth God and His Gospel that ever will favor her, but must hate her above all other; and the more they favor the Gospel the more they will hate her, for then there was never creature in our time that so much slandered the Gospel; and God hath sent her this punishment for that she feignedly hath professed his Gospel in her mouth and not in heart and deed." And though she have so offended, yet God has shown His goodness towards your Grace and never offended you. "But your Grace, I am sure, knowledgeth that you have offended Him." I trust, therefore, you will bear no less zeal to the Gospel than you did before, as your favor to the Gospel was not led by affection to her. Lambeth, 3 May.

Since writing, my lords Chancellor, Oxford, Sussex, and my Lord Chamberlain of your Grace's house, sent for me to come to the Star Chamber, and there declared to me such things as you wished to make me privy to. For this I am much bounden to your Grace. They will report our conference. I am sorry such faults can be proved against the Queen as they report."[1]

From this letter we can see Cramner's shock at the events unravelling around him. However, he is still careful in his support of Anne. Whilst he supports her by saying that he "had never better opinion of woman", that he was "most bound to her of all creatures living" and that he was praying that she would show herself to be innocent, he also tempers this support of her by showing his allegiance to the King above all else. Cranmer's zeal for reform, and probably fear for his life, stop him from giving his full unswerving support to Anne Boleyn, the woman who helped to make him Archbishop of Canterbury. It must have been a very difficult letter to write. Diarmaid MacCulloch writes of how this letter and Cranmer's handling of the situation show his wisdom and courage, rather than his cowardice as some have said.[2] Cranmer knew how to handle the King and when not to question the King's actions. Angering the King would not have helped Anne.

While Archbishop Cranmer was writing to the King, Sir William Kingston, Constable of the Tower of London, was writing to Thomas Cromwell. He had been charged with reporting everything that the Queen said to her ladies, who were acting as spies. In his letter of 3rd May 1536, Kingston reports Anne Boleyn's ramblings in the Tower as she tried to figure out why Norris had been arrested and what could have led to her own arrest. The letter was damaged by a fire in 1731, hence the missing parts:

> "and this morning did talk with Mistress Coffin.
> And she said, Mr Norris did say on Sunday last
> unto the Queen's almoner that he would swear
> to the Queen that she was a good woman. And
> then said Mrs Coffin, "Why should there be
> any such matters spoken of", "Marry", said she,
> "I bade him do so: for I asked him why he did
> not go through with his marriage and he made
> answer that he would tarry a time. Then I said,
> You look for dead men's shoes, for if aught
> came to the King but good, you would look
> to have me. And he said if he should have any
> such thought he would his head were off.""[3]

Later in the same letter Kingston reported how the Queen said that "she more feared Weston".[4] She explained how she had reprimanded him for loving her relative, Mistress Shelton, and not his wife, and he "made answer to her again that he loved on in her house better than them both". When Anne asked who, he replied

"It is yourself". The Queen then "defied him".[5]

Sir Henry Norris was already imprisoned in the Tower, but these words spoken by Anne may have been responsible for the arrest of Sir Francis Weston the following day.

Anne Boleyn and Archbishop Thomas Cranmer

In 1529, Thomas Cranmer was called on to advise the King on his quest for the annulment of his marriage to Catherine of Aragon. It was at this time that Cranmer began lodging with Thomas Boleyn, father of Anne, at Durham Place, and he may well have acted as the family chaplain. His appointment to the office of Archbishop of Canterbury in 1533 was not only a reward for his work on the King's Great Matter, it was also a result of his close relationship with Anne Boleyn and her family.

It is easy for us to look at the words written by Archbishop Cranmer in defence of Anne Boleyn in May 1536, and at his subsequent actions, and see him as a spineless man who sat by and let an innocent woman and five innocent men go to their deaths. His subsequent actions certainly did not support Anne:

- He helped the King find legal reasons for the marriage to be annulled, while acting as Anne's confessor.

- He visited her on 16th May to obtain from her an admission that there had been an impediment to her marriage to the King and convinced her to give her consent to the annulment of the marriage, thus making her daughter, Elizabeth, illegitimate.

- He may have misled Anne, offering her mercy in exchange for her compliance.

At dinner on 16th May, Anne Boleyn told Sir William Kingston that she was going to a nunnery and that she was "in hope of life". This suggests that Cranmer may well have offered her this chance of escape if she agreed to the annulment of her marriage. Perhaps Cranmer had been misled by Cromwell or by the King; we'll never know.

It is hard to judge Cranmer. He was a man running scared. He owed his position to Anne Boleyn, he had been friends with Anne and her family, he had close ties to the Boleyn faction and he must have had many sleepless nights wondering if he would be brought down too. He had to obey the King or risk losing his head, and we can only imagine the emotional pain he felt witnessing and being involved in the goings-on of May 1536. It is sad that it was Anne's friend who had a hand in annulling her marriage and bastardising Elizabeth, but he had little choice in the matter.

Sir Edward Baynton to William Fitzwilliam

Also around 3rd May 1536, Sir Edward Baynton, Anne Boleyn's vice-chamberlain, wrote to William Fitzwilliam, treasurer of the household:-

> "This shalbe to advertyse yow that here is
> myche communycacion that noman will
> confesse any thynge agaynst her, but allonly
> Marke of any actuell thynge. Wherfore (in my
> folishe conceyte) it shulde myche toche the
> kings honor if it shulde no farther appeere.
>
> And I cannot beleve but that the other two bee
> as f[ully] culpapull as ever was hee. And I thynke
> assur[edly] the on kepith the others conncell.
> As many .... conjectures in my mynde causeth
> me to thynk . . . specially of the communycacion
> that was last bet[wene] the qnene and Master
> Norres. Mr. Aumener [tolde] me as I wolde
> I myght speke with Mr. S[ecretorie] and yow
> together more playnely expresse my . . . yf case be
> that they have confessyd like wret... all thyngs as
> they shulde do than my n... ...at apoynte. I have
> mewsed myche at... ...of mastres Margery whiche
> hath used her .... strangely toward me of late,

being her fry[nde] as I have ben. But no dowte
it cann[ot be] but that she must be of councell
therewith, [there] hath ben great fryndeship
betwene the q[ene and] her of late. I here farther
that the que[ne] standith styfly in her opjmyon
that she wo... ...whiche I thynke is in the trust that
she... ...ther two. But if yor busynes be suche...
...not com, I wolde gladly com and wayte... ...ke it
requysyte. From Grenewy[che]... ...mornyng."[6]

The letter is mutilated, but we can see that he mentions Margery
Lyster (née Horsman), one of Anne Boleyn's ladies-in-waiting, as
being Anne's confidante. She would, therefore, have been someone
who'd know what was going if Anne was having any affairs. Eric
Ives[7] points out that Margery was not arrested and, instead, moved
into the service of Jane Seymour after Anne's execution, something
that just would not have happened if the King had thought that
Margery helped cover up his wife's affairs. The fact that none of
Anne's ladies were arrested suggests that Anne was innocent.

Sir Francis Weston

It is thought that Sir Francis Weston was born around 1511 to Sir Richard Weston, a former Under-Treasurer of the Exchequer, and to his wife, Anne Sandys who had been one of Catherine of Aragon's ladies.[1] In 1521, Henry VIII gave Sir Richard the beautiful house and estate of Sutton Place, near Guildford in Surrey, and this became the Weston family home. In May 1530, Sir Francis Weston married Anne Pickering, the daughter of Sir Christopher Pickering of Killington, Cumberland. The couple went on to have a son, Henry, in 1535.

In 1532 Weston was made a gentleman of the Privy Chamber; in 1533 he became, with his father, joint governor of Guernsey. Records show that he was a favourite of both the King and Anne Boleyn, a friend of Lord Rochford (George Boleyn), a member of the rising Boleyn faction and a popular man of the King's court. He was also a talented lute player, a first class athlete and often played tennis, bowls and cards with the King. In 1530, the King paid him sixteen angels after Weston beat him at Tennis four times.[2]

At Anne Boleyn's coronation in 1533, Weston was made a Knight of the Bath, showing that he was a royal favourite and on the rise.

Quotes about Sir Francis Weston

George Cavendish, Cardinal Wolsey's gentleman usher and biographer, said of Weston:

"in active things, who might with thee compare?"

Thomas Wyatt, Weston's contemporary and a man who was also imprisoned, albeit briefly, in the coup against Anne Boleyn, said that Weston was "pleasant" and "well-esteemed".

Both Cavendish and Paul Friedmann,[3] Anne Boleyn's biographer, wrote of how Weston received a number of grants and pensions from the King, showing what a favourite he was. Cavendish commented that Weston was "daintily nourished under the King's wing".

As well as praising Weston's athletic abilities, Cavendish also wrote about Weston's not so wonderful traits, describing him as

"Weston the wanton...that wantonly lived without fear or dread,...following his fantasy and his wanton lust" and said "hot lust kindled the fire of filthy concupiscence".[4]

Sir Francis Weston's Sexuality

If we are to believe historian Retha Warnicke, then Sir Francis Weston and the other four men arrested, tried and executed in the coup against Anne Boleyn were all known libertines; and libertines apparently progressed "from adultery and fornication to 'buggery' and bestiality".[5] In Philippa Gregory's historical novel, "The Other Boleyn Girl", Sir Francis Weston and George Boleyn, Lord Rochford, were lovers. However, as far as I can tell from my research, there is no historical evidence to back up the idea that Weston was Rochford's lover or that he committed the illegal act of buggery. We cannot even prove that he was a ladies' man, although it is thought that he may have had an affair, or at least a flirtation, with Anne Boleyn's cousin, Margaret Shelton.

4th May 1536 – Further Arrests

On 4th May 1536, a further two members of the King's privy chamber were arrested and taken to the Tower of London: Sir Francis Weston and Sir William Brereton. Weston's arrest was predictable, coming after the Queen's ramblings about him telling her he loved her, but Anne had not mentioned Brereton and he was not close to her.

Sir William Brereton was a rather colourful character with power in Chester and North Wales. He was also close to Henry Fitzroy, the Duke of Richmond, and the Duke of Norfolk. Maybe his arrest was more to do with Thomas Cromwell's plans for reform in the administration of North Wales.

George Constantine, Sir Henry Norris's servant, had this to say of Sir William Brereton:

> "By my troeth, yf any of them was innocent,
> it was he... And he tolde me that there was no
> way but one with any matter. For I did aske
> hym and was bold apon hym because were
> were borne within foure myles together, And
> also we wente to grammar scole together. And
> the same daye afore two of the clock was he in
> the towre as ferre as the best. What was layed
> against hym I know not nor never hearde."[1]

There were now five men in the Tower of London: Mark Smeaton, Sir Henry Norris, George Boleyn, Sir Francis Weston and Sir William Brereton.

Sir William Brereton

The William Brereton of "The Tudors" is a Jesuit priest hired by the Pope to assassinate Queen Anne Boleyn, and a man who gives a false confession, saying that he slept with the Queen, in order to bring her down. The real Sir William Brereton was nothing like this character. He was, in fact, a groom of the privy chamber and a man who protested his innocence in the coup against Anne Boleyn in May 1536.

Sir William Brereton (or Bryerton) was the sixth son of a leading, landowning Cheshire family. He was born between 1487 and 1490; his father was Sir Randolph Brereton of Malpas, chamberlain of the county palatine of Cheshire.[1] Randolph became a knight of the body in 1513. William's mother was Eleanor Dutton, daughter of Piers Dutton of Halton. Brereton, like three of his brothers, entered royal service and by 1524 (perhaps even 1521)[2] he had become a groom of the privy chamber.

Eric Ives[3] writes of how Brereton was "the dominant royal servant in Cheshire and north Wales" due to his wealth, his royal grants and his father's power in Cheshire. In the mid to late 1520s, he was able to secure the reversion of the stewardship of Longdendale, the position of sergeant of the peace in Bromfield and Yale, the lordship of Chirk, the escheator of the county palatine and ranger of Delamere Forest, keepership of Merseley Park, the post of sheriff of Merioneth and Flint, constable of Chester Castle and steward and controller of Halton – quite a list of offices, and those are just some of them! On his father's death, he was appointed Chamberlain of Chester. When Henry finally separated from Catherine of Aragon, Brereton was made receiver-general in Cheshire and Flint to Catherine, in her new position as Dowager Princess of Wales.[4] Ives estimates that Brereton's gross income in the early 1530s was around £1300 a year, a large amount in those days.

In 1529/1530, Brereton married Lady Elizabeth Savage,

widow of Sir John Savage of Clifton, Cheshire, and daughter of
Charles Somerset, 1st Earl of Worcester, the King's second cousin.
Her brother was Henry Somerset who had become the 2nd Earl
of Worcester in 1526 on the death of his father. This marriage
brought Brereton closer to the King, who trusted Brereton enough
in 1531 to give him the job of delivering jewels to Anne Boleyn.
He may also have been chosen to be present at the King's secret
marriage, to Anne, in January 1533. Brereton's name was also on
the list of those who attended Anne's coronation celebrations
when Henry VIII dubbed around 50 knights bachelor.

Eric Ives also writes of how Brereton was in charge, helped
by Thomas Wriothesley, of riding around the country in 1530 to
collect signatures from the "elite of England" on a petition begging
the Pope for Henry's divorce. Brereton's friendship with the
King is shown also by the fact that he accompanied the King and
Anne on many hunting expeditions and the fact that he enjoyed a
multitude of royal grants and Crown offices. He was definitely a
royal favourite! It was also Brereton who was responsible for giving
Anne her famous and treasured greyhound, Urian, who was named
after Brereton's brother, another of the King's grooms.

Brereton the Bad Boy

Sir William Brereton actually had a rather colourful reputation.
It seems that he used his power and influence for his own gain,
just as his father had. George Cavendish, Wolsey's faithful servant
and biographer, describes him as someone who persecuted the
innocent and who let personal animosity get in the way when he
was doing his job. Cavendish gives the example of John ap Griffith
Eyton, Brereton's former deputy, who was hanged in 1534. Eyton
had accused Brereton of being involved in various offences: the
robbery of cattle, the murder of a servant, the release of a monk
guilty of treason, the murder of Eyton's uncle (Constable of
Chirk) and another relative, and the murder of William Hamner
at Bromfield. Brereton denied any involvement in the offences
and blamed Eyton for the murder of Hamner. Even though Eyton

was acquitted by a London court after complaining to the Star Chamber about Brereton, it is alleged that he was rearrested and imprisoned at Holt Castle in July 1534 and subsequently hanged.

Brereton was not a member of Anne Boleyn's inner circle and it appears that his arrest and execution were more to do with his activities in Wales and his opposition to Cromwell's reforms there. Cromwell was planning further administrative reforms for Wales and did not want any obstacles in his path. He was the perfect fall guy for Cromwell, having already garnered a reputation for corruption. He may have been a corrupt character, but, as Norris's servant, George Constantine said, "yf any of them was innocent, it was he". He was the odd one out.

With Brereton gone, his monopoly in Cheshire and North Wales was also gone. His offices were distributed between a few men – his brother Urian, Sir Piers Dutton, Sir Rees Mauncell and Hugh Starkey[5]– so that the power was shared. Cromwell could now have his way in Cheshire and North Wales.

4th May 1536 –
Lady Rochford's Letter

Around 4th May 1536, George Boleyn's wife, Jane, Lady Rochford, sent a message of comfort to her husband via Sir William Kingston. The full content of the message is unknown, but Kingston wrote of how Lady Rochford had promised to "humbly [make] suit unto the king's highness" for George. This meant that she was going to petition the King or his council on behalf of her husband. George was understandably comforted by her words and replied that he wanted to "give her thanks".[1]

There is no record of Jane petitioning the King on behalf of George, but that doesn't mean that she didn't. It is hard to imagine how she was feeling. Her husband, her friend and mistress, and men she knew well had been arrested; and Anne's ladies were being examined. Jane had been at court many years, she had seen people go into the Tower and never come out. She must have been terrified.

Jane Boleyn –
History's Scapegoat

In "The Lady in the Tower: The Fall of Anne Boleyn", Alison Weir writes of how "most sources" concur that the evidence for Anne and George committing incest rested upon the testimony of George's wife, Jane.[1] The source she cites for this is the 17th century biographer Edward, Lord Herbert of Cherbury, who described Jane as the 'particular instrument' in the downfalls of Anne and George, and who based his account on eye-witness Anthony Anthony's lost journal. Other sources cited are Eustace Chapuys, the imperial ambassador; an anonymous Portuguese account; the writings of Lancelot de Carles, secretary to the French ambassador, and Jane's execution confession. According to Weir, these all back up the fact that Jane was the woman who gave evidence against the Boleyn siblings out of jealousy and resentment.

This picture of Jane also appears in the novels of Philippa Gregory and in the popular Showtime series, "The Tudors", so it is little wonder that many people hold her responsible for the deaths of George and Anne.

But did Jane betray Anne and George Boleyn?

No, I don't believe so; and I'm not the only one. Historian Julia Fox argues against this fallacy in her book on Jane, "Jane Boleyn: The Infamous Lady Rochford", calling Jane "a scapegoat". In a review of Alison Weir's "The Lady in the Tower, Fox's husband, historian John Guy,[2] points out the following:

- That Chapuys never named Jane Boleyn as the witness against George and Anne.

- That the Portuguese source also did not name Jane, writing of only "that person".

- That Lord Herbert of Cherbury was not quoting from Anthony Anthony's lost chronicle but from his own book.

- That Jane's execution confession was a forgery and the work of Gregorio Leti, a man know for making up stories and inventing sources.
- That Lancelot de Carles was talking about Lady Worcester, not Jane Boleyn.

But what about George Boleyn's own words at his trial? Yes, according to Lancelot de Carles, at his trial, George said:

> "On the evidence of only one woman
> you are willing to believe this great evil
> of me, and on the basis of her allegations
> you are deciding my judgement."[3]

But he doesn't say "On the evidence of my own wife you are willing...", he says "one woman". Since the Crown's main piece of evidence was the Countess of Worcester's conversation with her brother, regarding the Queen's inappropriate relationship George, I believe that George is referring here to the Countess and not to Jane. When George was imprisoned in the Tower of London, Jane wrote to him offering words of comfort.[4] Would she have done that if she was a star witness for the prosecution?

We have no concrete evidence that Jane did betray George and Anne or that she was the sort of woman who spied through keyholes and lied, like the Jane of "The Tudors", so I, for one, am not jumping to conclusions and using Jane as a scapegoat.

4th May 1536 Cruelly Handled –
Anne Boleyn in the Tower

As I have previously said, Sir William Kingston, the Constable of the Tower of London, was ordered to make regular reports to Thomas Cromwell regarding Anne Boleyn's imprisonment in the Tower. Obviously, Anne could say things that her enemies could use against her. For that reason her ladies in the Tower[1] were appointed by Cromwell and ordered not to speak to Anne unless Lady Kingston was present to remember or record what was said.

The ladies chosen to serve Anne in the Tower were:

- Mrs Mary Orchard – Anne's former nurse and the only one who would have been sympathetic to Anne's plight and shown her love.

- Mrs Stonor (Margaret or Anne Foliot) – Wife of Sir Walter Stonor, the King's sergeant-at-arms.

- Elizabeth Wood, Lady Boleyn – Wife of Thomas Boleyn's younger brother, Sir James Boleyn of Blickling Hall, and therefore Anne's aunt. Although Sir James Boleyn had served Anne as her chancellor, he was a supporter of the Lady Mary.

- Lady Anne Shelton – Thomas Boleyn's sister and the mother of Madge Shelton. In her book on Anne Boleyn's fall, Alison Weir puts forward the argument that Lady Shelton may have turned against Anne after her daughter was used by Anne to keep the King happy (as his mistress). Anne had also forced Lady Shelton to treat the Lady Mary cruelly.

- Mrs Margaret Coffin (Margaret Dymoke, also referred to as Mrs Cosyns) – Wife of William Coffin, the Queen's Master of the Horse, and a Gentleman of the Privy Chamber. The Coffins were related by marriage to the Boleyns, but Mrs Coffin had been appointed to spy on Anne in the Tower. She was the lady chosen, along with Lady Boleyn, to sleep "on the Quenes palet".[2]

- Mary Scrope, Lady Kingston – Sir William Kingston's wife. She had served Catherine of Aragon and was friends with the Lady Mary.

Anne Boleyn may have had a Queen's household and sumptuous lodgings, but she was still a prisoner and was surrounded by women who had little sympathy for her. No wonder Anne complained to Sir William Kingston, saying:

> "I think [much unkindness in the] King to
> put such about me as I never loved."[3]

Anne also complained of the treatment she had experienced at Greenwich, when she was arrested:

> "Then she began to talk, and said I was
> cruelly handled a . . . . a Greenwich with
> the King's council, with my lord of
> Norfolk, that he said Tut, [tut, tut!], and
> shaking her head two or three times."[4]

In her ramblings, Anne also wondered if Henry was testing her:

> "But s]he to be a Queen, and cruelly
> handled as was never seen; but I th[ink
> the King d]oes it to prove me;"[5]

and hoped that her bishops would speak up for her and the country pray for her:

> "then she said I would to God I had my
> bishops, for they would all go to the King
> for me, for I think the most part of England
> prays for me and if I died you shall see the
> greatest punishment for me within these
> seven years that ever came to England."[6]

After pondering this, she then talked of her death, the good deeds she had done in her life and the cruelty of the King who had surrounded her with enemies in the Tower:

> "And the[n, she said, shall I be in Heaven, for]
> I have done many good deeds in my days, but I
> think]much unkindness in the] King to put such
> about me as I never loved... I would have had of
> my own privy chamber which I favour most."[7]

In another letter, Kingston reported that Anne wanted him to bear a letter from her to Cromwell which stated that it would not rain until she was delivered out of the Tower.[8] John Strype commented that Anne was "thinking probably that God (who takes care of innocency) would vindicate her by giving or withholding the clouds of heaven."[9] Anne's ramblings show her fear, her panic and hysteria, but they also show her trying to hold on to some hope and faith. She was hoping that the King was simply testing her, and she was trying to reassure herself that at least she had a place in Heaven if things continued to go wrong. Poor Anne.

5th May 1536 –
Sir Thomas Wyatt, Sir Richard Page
and Sir Francis Bryan

By 5th May 1536, two further arrests had taken place: courtier
and poet Sir Thomas Wyatt, and Sir Richard Page, a Gentleman of
the Privy Chamber and a former favourite of Thomas Cromwell.
There were now seven men in the Tower of London.

The Spanish Chronicle records Wyatt being apprehended at
the May Day joust, although no other source backs up this date:

> "It seems that the King sent Cromwell to tell him
> to have Wyatt fetched in order to examine him.
> When they arrived in London Cromwell took
> Master Wyatt apart, and said to him, "Master
> Wyatt, you well know the great love I have always
> borne you, and I must tell you that it would cut
> me to the heart if you were guilty in the matter of
> which I wish to speak." Then he told him all that
> had passed; and Master Wyatt was astounded,
> and replied with great spirit, "Sir Secretary, by
> the faith I owe to God and my King and lord, I
> have no reason to distrust, for I have not wronged
> him even in thought. The King well knows what I
> told him before he was married." Then Cromwell
> told him he would have to go to the Tower, but
> he would promise to stand by his friend, to which
> Wyatt answered, "I will go willingly, for as I am
> stainless I have nothing to fear." He went out
> with Richard Cromwell, and nobody suspected
> that he was a prisoner, and when he arrived at the
> Tower Richard said to the captain of the Tower,
> "Sir Captain, Secretary Cromwell send to beg

you to do all honour to Master Wyatt." So the
captain put him into a chamber over the door..."[1]

In Letters and Papers, there is a letter from Wyatt's father, Sir
Henry Wyatt, to Cromwell in which he writes that he:

> "Received his letter on the 10th, and thanks him
> for the comfortable articles therein touching
> his son Thomas and himself. Asks Cromwell
> when it shall be the King's pleasure to deliver
> him, to show him "that this punishment
> that he hath for this matter is more for
> the displeasure that he hath done to God
> otherwise," and to admonish him to fly vice
> and serve God better. Alington, 11 May."[2]

This shows that Cromwell had written to Sir Henry regarding
his son and had offered him some comfort. Sir Henry is obviously
grateful for that but is worried that his son's moral conduct would
be his undoing. This was not to be the case. Sir Thomas Wyatt was
not mentioned in the Middlesex or Kent indictments and was not
tried with Weston, Norris, Brereton and Smeaton on 12th May. In
a letter written on the 12th May to Lord Lisle, Hussey writes:

> "Mr. Payge and Mr. W[y]at are in the Tower,
> but it is thought without danger of life."[3]

Hussey changes his mind in his next letter to Lord Lisle on
13th May, where he says that

> "This day, some say, young Weston shall scape,
> and some that none shall die but the Queen
> and her brother; others, that Wyat and Mr.
> Payge are as like to suffer as the others."[4]

Thomas Cromwell wrote to Sir Henry Wyatt on 11th June
reassuring him that his son was going to be released and there is a
reply in Letters and Papers from Sir Henry Wyatt, on 14th June,

saying that:

> "On the receipt of Cromwell's letters declaring
> the King's pleasure, and his favorable warnings
> to his son to address himself better than his wit
> can consider, sent for him and commanded his
> obedience in all points to the King's pleasure,
> and the leaving of such slanderous fashion as
> hath engendered unto him the displeasure of
> God and of his master. Found it not now to
> do in him, but already done. Has charged him
> to follow Cromwell's commandments, and
> repute him as his father. Assured him that if
> he had not this sure printed in his heart, he
> would refuse him for his son. Begs Cromwell
> to continue the same to him, and he will not
> find it evil employed. Alington, 14 June."[5]

It seems that Cromwell had advised Sir Henry to speak to his son and warn him to mend his ways and here Sir Henry Wyatt confirms that he has followed Cromwell's orders. His son had escaped death by the skin of his teeth and Sir Henry was not going to let him forget it!

Sir Thomas Wyatt would have been the perfect scapegoat or fall guy in this coup, yet he escaped to live another day (or another six years!). It would have been easy for Cromwell or the King to frame him for adultery or to claim that Anne had not been a virgin when she married the King because she had already slept with Wyatt. So, why was Wyatt not a major part of the coup? How did he escape?

It is likely that his escape was mostly down to Cromwell, who had close ties with the Wyatt family. However, he would not have been able to secure Wyatt's release without the King's blessing. It appears that the King saw Wyatt as innocent, as someone who had not had much to do with Anne since he (Wyatt) had given up on her and let the King have her. Wyatt had distanced himself from Anne Boleyn and it looks like this saved him.

Sir Francis Bryan Questioned

Also around the 5th May 1536, the courtier and diplomat Sir Francis Bryan, 'christened' the "Vicar of Hell"[6] by Thomas Cromwell, was ordered to London for questioning. This was an interesting move because Bryan, although related to Queen Anne Boleyn and having benefited from her patronage in the past, was no friend of the Queen and was very good friends with Sir Nicholas Carew, the man said to be coaching the Lady Jane Seymour. Bryan was questioned, but not arrested.

Sir Thomas Wyatt

Sir Thomas Wyatt was born in 1503 at Allington Castle, Kent. His father, Henry Wyatt, was a Lancastrian who had been imprisoned during Richard III's reign. He was released on the accession of Henry VII, who rewarded him with many grants and titles. Wyatt's mother was Anne Skinner, daughter of John Skinner of Reigate, a woman famed for her hospitality. Henry Wyatt became a Privy Councillor under Henry VII and acted as an executor for the King's will on his death in 1509. He went on to serve the new king, Henry VIII and was made a Knight of the Bath at his coronation in June 1509.

Little is known of Thomas Wyatt's childhood, apart from the story of the lion. It is said that Wyatt, or his father, was raising a lion cub as a pet when it turned on Sir Henry as he entered Allington and knocked him to the ground. Thomas Wyatt had the presence of mind to grab his rapier and run it through the lion's heart. When Henry VIII heard of this story, he commented "Oh, he will tame lions".[1]

In 1516, Wyatt, along with his friend Thomas Poynings, served as a sewer extraordinary at Princess Mary's christening. Later that year he was sent to St John's College, Cambridge, which was known for Humanism. In 1520, Wyatt married Elizabeth Brooke, the daughter of Lord Cobham, and the couple had a son, Thomas Wyatt the Younger, in 1521. The Duke of Norfolk stood as a godfather at the baby's christening.

In 1524, Wyatt followed his father's example and started a career at court as Clerk of the King's jewels. In 1525 he was made Esquire of the Body and he went on to become an ambassador, undertaking many foreign missions for his master, King Henry VIII. These included one to France in 1526 and one to the Papal Court in Rome in 1527, this last an embassy to try to convince Pope Clement VII to annul the King's marriage to Catherine of Aragon. In 1528 Wyatt was made High Marshal of Calais and in 1532 he

was made Commissioner of the Peace in Essex. Wyatt was also
one of the men chosen to accompany the King and Anne Boleyn
on their visit to Calais in late 1532 and he served Anne at her
coronation in the summer of 1533. He was knighted in 1535.

Thomas Wyatt and Anne Boleyn

It is thought that Wyatt fell in love with Anne Boleyn when
she first arrived at the English court in 1522. He was unhappily
married and it seems to have been love at first sight for Thomas.
In his biography "The Life of Anne Boleigne", Thomas Wyatt's
grandson, George Wyatt, wrote that when Wyatt saw Anne, "this
new beauty", he was "surprised somewhat with the sight thereof"
and that he "could gladly yield to be tied for ever with the knot
of her love".[2] At this time, though, Anne and Henry Percy were
in love.

In 1524, Wyatt became clerk of the King's jewels and would
have seen Anne at court because she was a member of Queen
Catherine of Aragon's household. There is no real evidence that
there was any relationship between Anne and Wyatt at this time,
and in any case, by Shrovetide 1526 Anne had a new admirer; the
King. At the Shrovetide joust, Henry VIII rode out "resplendent
in cloth of gold and silver, richly embroidered with a man's heart
gripped in a press and engulfed in flames. The motto read declare ie
nose – "declare I dare not"." The King had a new love.

Some people believe that Wyatt's poetry is evidence of a
relationship between Anne Boleyn and Thomas Wyatt. For
example, his riddle poem "What wourde is that that chaungeth
not" has the answer "Anna", and in "The Lover Confesseth Him
in Love with Phyllis", he writes of "That Brunet" which is taken
to refer to Anne. Further evidence (if you believe The Spanish
Chronicle!) is the story of Wyatt visiting Anne at Hever, finding
her in bed, declaring his love for her, kissing her and touching her
breasts and then being disturbed by stamping from upstairs from
another of Anne's lovers![3]

Another story is told by George Wyatt. Thomas was

entertaining Anne one day as she did needlework and playfully grabbed a jewel hanging by a lace from her pocket. He decided to keep it as a trophy, wearing it around his neck. When the King and Wyatt were playing bowls one day, they argued over a shot. Wyatt declared that it was his, but the King declared "Wiatt, I tell thee it is mine" as he pointed to the wood with the finger on which he wore Anne's ring. Wyatt saw the ring and replied "And if it may like your majesty to give me leave to measure it, I hope it will be mine" and he took the jewel from around his neck and began to measure the cast with the ribbon. This angered the King, who broke up the game and then demanded an explanation from Anne, who told him how Wyatt had stolen her jewel.[4]

Whatever the truth of George Wyatt's story, Anne and Thomas Wyatt's relationship seems nothing more than a case of unrequited love. Wyatt's poem "Whoso list to hunt" tells of a man (Wyatt) hunting a hind with little chance of success, and then withdrawing from the hunt because of another hunter. If we see Anne as the hind, then Wyatt is talking of withdrawing his suit of Anne because she is now the property of the King: "Noli me tangere; for Caesar's I am".

Sir Richard Page

Nothing is known about Sir Richard Page's background and early life, all we know is that he started his career working for Cardinal Wolsey as the latter's chamberlain. In the Royal Household records of December 1516,[1] Page is listed as "Sir Ric.Page", a gentleman of the privy chamber, so he was serving Henry VIII then and had also been knighted by this point.

Page served as a Justice of the Peace for Surrey between 1522 and 26, and again in 1528, and for Middlesex in 1524. In January 1522 he was appointed as comptroller of the customs in the port of London "during good behaviour, in consideration of his services to the King and cardinal Wolsey"[2]. In 1525, he was chosen to help administer the household of Henry Fitzroy, Duke of Richmond, the illegitimate son of Henry VIII, and served on the Council of the North. It is thought that he also served as recorder of Hull and chief steward of Beverley around this time.[3]

His biographer, Catharine Davies, writes of how he accompanied Cardinal Wolsey to Calais in 1527 wearing a great chain which weighed 200 pounds, and in 1528 Page and Sir John Wallop were chosen "To be surveyors and receivers, &c. of the subsidy of cloths called karseys, in the ports of London and Southampton, with an annuity of 100l. T"[4]

On 3rd December 1530, after the fall of his master, Cardinal Wolsey, Page was awarded "Grant of the site of the late priory of St. Leonard, Thoby, Essex, and the manors of Thoby and Bluntzwall, Essex; with messuages, lands, &c. in Thoby, Gingemountney alias Mountnesing, Bluntzwall, Cupsolde, Wyndall, Parva Warley, Marses, Nosells alias Norlsells, Rome, Maylond, Mowlond, Wyndhull, Runwell, Bobyngworth, Springfeld, Hereford, Stoke Paching, Shenfeld, Ingraf, Raureth, Colchester, Borhame, Stondon, Wryttell, Shelowe, Gingemargaret, Cubsant, and Shenfeld, Essex; which belonged to Thos. cardinal archbishop of York, attainted."[5] Page surely must have had mixed feelings about that reward!

By 1532, he was working alongside the likes of Sir Nicholas Carew and Sir John Russell in the privy chamber in a climate of rivalry. Carew was one of the Seymour faction, so this may explain Page's arrest. Page was a close friend of the Queen's. He had carried out "sundry little services" for Anne and she had rewarded him with gifts,[6] so there was a connection. Paul Friedmann writes of how his links to the Fitzwilliams and Russells may explain his eventual release[7] in July 1536.

Sir Francis Bryan

Sir Francis Bryan is thought to have been born around 1490 and was the first surviving son of Sir Thomas Bryan. His mother was Lady Margaret Bryan (née Bourchier), lady-in-waiting to Queen Catherine of Aragon and the future governess of Princess Mary, Princess Elizabeth and Prince Edward. Bryan was a second cousin to both Anne Boleyn and Jane Seymour.

In 1516, he became the King's cupbearer and then, in 1518, master of the toils. He also became a gentleman of the privy chamber in 1518, but lost this position in Wolsey's purge. He regained the position in 1528, probably due to the influence of Anne Boleyn. He was knighted in 1522 for his courage during the capture of Morlaix in Brittany, serving under the Earl of Surrey, and by 1526 he held the position of chief cupbearer and master of the henchmen. During the King's Great Matter, Bryan was Henry VIII's trusted messenger to the Pope and Francis I. He even went as far as sleeping with a courtesan at the Papal court to get inside information.

Thomas Cromwell referred to Bryan as "the vicar of Hell" in a letter to Gardiner and Wallop on the 14th May 1536,[1] and, according to Catholic recusant Nicholas Sander, the King also referred to him by this nickname. Sander writes "This man was once asked by the king to tell him what sort of a sin it was to ruin the mother and then the child. Bryan replied that it was a sin like that of eating a hen first and its chicken afterwards. The king burst forth into loud laughter, and said to Bryan, "Well, you certainly are my vicar of hell". The man had been long ago called the vicar of hell on account of his notorious impiety, henceforth he was called also the king's vicar of hell."[2]

Bryan was a staunch Catholic and his motto was *Je tens grace* ('I look for salvation'). Historian Susan Brigden[3] writes of how he owned a copy of the 1537 Matthew Bible and that he acted as a patron of scholars who could translate the Bible from the original

Greek. Like his good friend, Thomas Wyatt, Bryan was also a poet.

It seems that he felt no guilt in conspiring with Cromwell to bring down the Boleyn faction. Cromwell ordering Bryan back to London for interrogation was probably for show, a tactical move.

Robert, Abbot of Woburn, made a declaration in 1538 regarding Sir Francis Bryan's involvement in the fall of Anne Boleyn, which he likened to the fall of Lucifer. Of Bryan, he said:

> "At the fall of queen Anne Mr. Bryan was sent
> for by the lord Privy Seal in all haste "upon
> his allegiance." At his next repair to Ampthill
> the abbot went to visit him, being in the
> Court with lord Grey of Wilton and others.
> Sir Francis espied the abbot at the gate, and of
> his gentleness came to meet him. Said, "Now
> welcome home and never so welcome." He,
> astonished, asked, Why so? Said he would explain
> at leisure. Afterwards, in the great chamber with
> the others, drew a parallel between the fall of
> Lucifer and that of queen Anne, congratulating
> Sir Francis that he was not implicated. He
> replied it was true that when he was suddenly
> sent for he marvelled; but knowing his truth to
> his prince he never hesitated but went straight
> to my lord Privy Seal, and then to the King,
> and there was "nothing found" in him."[4]

Sir Francis Bryan was probably never in any danger; after all, he had allied himself with the Seymours and the anti-Boleyn faction. He was probably hoping to profit from Jane Seymour's rise, just as he had with his other cousin, Anne Boleyn. The fact that just three hours after Anne Boleyn's condemnation Bryan was sent to tell Jane Seymour the news is proof indeed that he was never in any real danger. After Anne Boleyn's fall, he replaced the late Sir Henry Norris as Chief Gentleman of the King's Privy Chamber and got his share of the spoils. In 1539, Bryan was removed from this post as Cromwell turned against him and others of that faction, but he gained favour again after Cromwell's fall and became vice-admiral of the fleet. During the reign of Edward VI, Bryan was made Lord Chief Justice of Ireland. He died in Ireland in 1550.

6th May 1536 –
From the Lady in the Tower

On 6th May 1536, it is said that Anne Boleyn wrote the following letter to her husband, King Henry VIII, from the Tower of London:

"To the King from the Lady in the Tower" [Heading said to have been added by Thomas Cromwell]

"Sir, your Grace's displeasure, and my Imprisonment are Things so strange unto me, as what to Write, or what to Excuse, I am altogether ignorant; whereas you sent unto me (willing me to confess a Truth, and so obtain your Favour) by such a one, whom you know to be my ancient and professed Enemy; I no sooner received the Message by him, than I rightly conceived your Meaning; and if, as you say, confessing Truth indeed may procure my safety, I shall with all Willingness and Duty perform your Command.

But let not your Grace ever imagine that your poor Wife will ever be brought to acknowledge a Fault, where not so much as Thought thereof proceeded. And to speak a truth, never Prince had Wife more Loyal in all Duty, and in all true Affection, than you have found in Anne Boleyn, with which Name and Place could willingly have contented my self, as if God, and your Grace's Pleasure had been so pleased. Neither did I at any time so far forge my self in

my Exaltation, or received Queenship, but that
I always looked for such an Alteration as now I
find; for the ground of my preferment being on
no surer Foundation than your Grace's Fancy,
the least Alteration, I knew, was fit and sufficient
to draw that Fancy to some other subject.

You have chosen me, from a low Estate, to
be your Queen and Companion, far beyond
my Desert or Desire. If then you found me
worthy of such Honour, Good your Grace, let
not any light Fancy, or bad Counsel of mine
Enemies, withdraw your Princely Favour from
me; neither let that Stain, that unworthy Stain
of a Disloyal Heart towards your good Grace,
ever cast so foul a Blot on your most Dutiful
Wife, and the Infant Princess your Daughter.

Try me, good King, but let me have a Lawful
Trial, and let not my sworn Enemies sit as my
Accusers and Judges; yes, let me receive an open
Trial, for my Truth shall fear no open shame;
then shall you see, either mine Innocency cleared,
your Suspicion and Conscience satisfied, the
Ignominy and Slander of the World stopped, or
my Guilt openly declared. So that whatsoever
God or you may determine of me, your Grace
may be freed from an open Censure; and mine
Offence being so lawfully proved, your Grace
is at liberty, both before God and Man, not
only to execute worthy Punishment on me as
an unlawful Wife, but to follow your Affection
already settled on that party, for whose sake
I am now as I am, whose Name I could some
good while since have pointed unto: Your Grace

being not ignorant of my Suspicion therein.

But if you have already determined of me,
and that not only my Death, but an Infamous
Slander must bring you the enjoying of your
desired Happiness; then I desire of God, that
he will pardon your great Sin therein, and
likewise mine Enemies, the Instruments thereof;
that he will not call you to a strict Account
for your unprincely and cruel usage of me,
at his General Judgement-Seat, where both
you and my self must shortly appear, and in
whose Judgement, I doubt not, (whatsover the
World may think of me) mine Innocence shall
be openly known, and sufficiently cleared.

My last and only Request shall be, That my
self may only bear the Burthen of your Grace's
Displeasure, and that it may not touch the
Innocent Souls of those poor Gentlemen, who (as
I understand) are likewise in strait Imprisonment
for my sake. If ever I have found favour in your
Sight; if ever the Name of Anne Boleyn hath
been pleasing to your Ears, then let me obtain
this Request; and I will so leave to trouble your
Grace any further, with mine earnest Prayers
to the Trinity to have your Grace in his good
keeping, and to direct you in all your Actions.

Your most Loyal and ever Faithful
Wife, Anne Bullen

From my doleful Prison the
Tower, this 6th of May."[1]

The Words of Anne Boleyn or a Forgery?

The letter first appeared in Lord Edward Herbert's 1649 book "The Life and Raigne of King Henry the Eighth".[2] Herbert was sceptical, believing that the letter may have been a fake penned in the reign of Elizabeth I, but Gilbert Burnet, Bishop of Salibury,[3] writing in 1679, believed it to be genuine. It was claimed that the letter was found with Sir William Kingston's letters in Cromwell's papers and, like Kingston's letters to Cromwell, it had been damaged during a fire in 1731.

This letter has often been considered a forgery, mainly due to the handwriting which differs from other authenticated letters by Anne. However, at the time of publication, the claim was made that the letter found was a copy made by Cromwell. This would explain why it was not in Anne's handwriting. Although Burnet and Victorian historian J.A. Froude[4] believed that the letter was authentic, historians such as Agnes Strickland and James Gairdner thought it to be a forgery, with Gairdner[5] believing it to be written in an Elizabethan hand. Other historians, like Paul Friedmann and P W Sergeant, also thought it to be a forgery. Modern day historian Alison Weir[6] makes a further point when she draws our attention to Henry Savage's view. Savage states that the difference in handwriting could be due to this letter being written a decade later than Anne's other authenticated letters, which date from the 1520s, and also the fact that she was imprisoned and living in fear of her life. Weir also cites Jasper Ridley, editor of "The Love Letters of Henry VIII"[7], as pointing out that the letter "bears all the marks of Anne's character, of her spirit, her impudence and her recklessness".

There are, however, anomalies which suggest that the letter is a forgery:

- The signature "Anne Bullen" rather than the usual "Anne Boleyn", "Anne de Boulaine" or "Anne the Queen".
- The fact that Cromwell kept it rather than destroying it.
- The heading at the top: "To the King from the Lady in the

Tower" – wouldn't Cromwell have referred to her as the Queen or as Anne Boleyn? "The Lady in the Tower" is rather poetic and romantic.

- The style, which is not consistent with Anne's other letters.
- The reproving tone and provocative content – The writer is claiming that the King instigated the plot so that he could marry Jane Seymour. Would Anne risk angering and insulting Henry in this way?

BUT these anomalies can be thrown out of the window:

- If the letter was a copy then this could have been Cromwell referring to Anne.
- It wasn't discovered until the 17th century so it was obviously kept hidden and not made public.
- Perhaps Cromwell no longer saw her as Queen and nicknamed her "The Lady in the Tower".
- Anne was not writing a normal letter, she had the shadow of the axe (or rather, sword) hanging over her.
- Anne could be provocative when she wanted to be. It may have been a huge risk to take but perhaps she wanted this one opportunity to tell the King what she thought of him and his plot.

The handwriting issue and the use of "Bullen" can also be explained away. The letter could have been a copy made by Cromwell. It could be, as argued by Jasper Ridley,[8] a late 16th century copy of the earlier original, or Anne may have been so distraught that she dictated it to one of her ladies. Ultimately, there is no way we can be certain one way or the other, but I hope that Anne did write it or something like it. Anne's execution speech stuck to the usual rules, in that she accepted her sentence and praised the King, but I'd like to think that Anne had some opportunity to let the King know what she really thought.

7th May 1536 –
A Chaplain is Searched

On Sunday 7th May 1536, Queen Anne Boleyn's chaplain, William Latymer, was searched on his arrival at Sandwich in Kent. He was returning from a business visit to Flanders, a visit he had undertaken on behalf of the Queen.

A letter from the Mayor and Jurates of Sandwich to Henry VIII recorded the search:

> "On Sunday, 7 May, Sir Wm. Latymer, one of the Queen's chaplains, arrived at Sandwich, where he was told that the Queen and others were prisoners in the Tower. He said that he had come from Flanders on her business, and showed the contents of his budget and purse to the mayor and jurates, as Thos. Boys, one of the King's servants then present, can testify. Enclose a list written by him of the books he had with him, and of others in his mail, which had not yet arrived, but which were to be conveyed to London to one Mrs. Wilkinson. Boys will convey Latymer himself to the King. Sandwich, 8 May."[1]

It does not appear that they found in his possession any books of an heretical nature, which was fortunate for Latymer considering what was going on in May 1536. Latymer was a keen reformer and did bring religious texts back from the Continent for Anne, so he was lucky this time. After the search, Latymer was escorted to London.

William Latymer

It is thought that William Latymer was introduced to Anne Boleyn by one of her other chaplains, Matthew Parker, who knew Latymer from their Cambridge days. As I have said, Anne used Latymer to procure evangelical texts for her and Anne's patronage was often sought through Latymer. In 1536, Tristram Revell tried to present her with his version of Lambertus' "Farrago Rerum Theologicarum" through William Latymer - Anne refused it, probably because it denied transubstantiation, salvation through good deeds and the power of prayers for the dead. Radical views. We don't know for sure what Anne believed about these issues, but in 1536 she was in a rather precarious position, having miscarried a son, so she just could not put her name to such a radical text.[2]

William Latymer survived the fall of the Boleyns in 1536 and went on to become master of the College of St Laurence Pountney in London in 1538. He also served as rector of Witnesham in Suffolk between 1538 and 1554, and then a number of benefices in Kent, London, Nottingham and Suffolk

In 1547, Latymer voted in favour of clerical marriage at convocation and married a widow, Ellen English. In 1549, he was a key prosecution witness, with the future Marian martyr John Hooper, in the case against Bishop Edmund Bonner who subsequently lost his bishopric.[3]

When the Catholic Mary I came to the throne in 1553, Latymer was deprived of his living, due to his marriage. He separated from Ellen in order to serve a parish in Ipswich, Suffolk, but the couple never actually separated in reality; Ellen conceived a son, Edward, by Latymer during their separation!

When Anne Boleyn's daughter, Elizabeth I, became Queen, Latymer was appointed as one of her chaplains. In 1559, he was appointed dean of Peterborough. In addition, Elizabeth made him a prebendary of Westminster Abbey, where he also served as archdeacon and treasurer. It was during Elizabeth's reign that Latymer wrote his biography or treatise of Anne Boleyn,

the "Chronickille of Anne Bulleyne". On the Queen's visit to
Cambridge in August 1564, Latymer was made Clerk of the Closet
and Doctor of Divinity.

Latymer died in 1583, in his early 80s, and was laid to rest in
Peterborough Cathedral on 28th August 1583. He was outlived by
his wife Ellen and two sons - Edward and Joshua.

Anne Boleyn's Desire for Spiritual Comfort

Also around 7th May, in a letter to Thomas Cromwell, Sir
William Kingston wrote of Anne's requests to the King that "she
[might] have the sacrament in the closet by her chamber" and that
her almoner, John Skip, should also be permitted to visit her. Anne
had asked for the sacrament when Kingston had first taken her to
her lodgings in the Tower, but she had obviously reminded him
of this. The problem was that Anne was charged with a sexual sin,
a sin that she had not confessed to or done penance for. It would,
therefore, "have been highly inappropriate for an adulteress to
have the Host displayed in her rooms".[4] Poor Anne - she was in the
Tower of London surrounded by women who were unsympathetic
to her plight and who were acting as spies, and she was being
denied spiritual comfort. All she could do was pray to her Father
in Heaven.

Kingston also reported Anne's hope that her bishops would
appeal to the King on her behalf, but her steadfast faith in the face
of death, if the appeals did not work: "And then, she said, shall I be
in Heaven, for I have done many good deeds in my days".[5]

8th May 1536 – The Vultures Circle

While Anne Boleyn, Mark Smeaton, Sir Henry Norris, Sir Francis Weston, Sir William Brereton, George Boleyn, Sir Richard Page and Sir Thomas Wyatt were in prison awaiting their trials, courtiers were already clamouring over the spoils that might result from the fall of grace of the former personages. These people were like vultures circling a corpse, like the Roman soldiers casting lots over Christ's clothes. Three of these 'vultures' were Sir Henry Fitzroy (the Duke of Richmond and the illegitimate son of the King), landowner and lawyer Richard Staverton and Lord Lisle.

Here are three letters which show the true character of these men:

Vulture One – Arthur Plantagenet, Lord Lisle

Letter from Lord Lisle to Thomas Cromwell, 8th May 1536

> "And seeing there are many things now in
> his gracious disposition and hands by reason
> of the most mischievous, heinous, and most
> abominable treasons against his most gracious
> and royal Crown and person committed, I
> wholly trust that his Grace, being good lord
> unto me, will vouchsafe to employ some
> part of those same upon me, which I do well
> know may so much the rather be obtained by
> your good mediation and furtherance."[1]

Vulture Two – Richard Staverton of Warfield, Berkshire

Richard Staverton was a lawyer and landowner who may have been related by marriage to Sir Francis Weston. He wrote to Cromwell on 2nd May, just two days after Sir Henry Norris had been detained for questioning:

> "It pleased you to write to me of your good
> will to my preferment. Various offenders have
> been committed to the Tower, among others
> Master Henry Norris, who has various rooms
> in the parts about me near Windsor, for which
> I hope you will have me in remembrance. He
> has the Little Park, the Park of Holy John (Foly
> John), Perlam (Perlaunt) Park, and the room
> of the Black Rod, in Windsor Castle, which I
> shall be glad to have, as I have 14 children."[2]

Vulture Three – Henry Fitzroy, Duke of Richmond

The following is a letter from the Duke of Richmond to John
Longland, Bishop of Lincoln, 8th May 1536:

> "As the stewardship of Banbury is like shortly
> to be vacant in consequence of Mr. Norres'
> trouble (many men thinking that there is no
> way but one with him,) asks the Bishop for a
> grant thereof under the chapter seal, that he may
> exercise the office by his deputy Gyles Forster,
> master of his horse, the bearer. London, 8 May"[3]

Unfortunately for Richmond, the post had already been given
to Thomas Cromwell. Here is an extract from a letter from the
Bishop of Lincoln to Cromwell, dated 5th May:

> "If it is true that Norrys has not used himself
> according to his duty to his sovereign lord, offers
> Cromwell the stewardship of the University
> of Oxford, if he will accept so small a fee as 5l.
> When the duke of Suffolk exchanged his lands
> in Oxfordshire with the King, he gave up the
> stewardship of Banbury to the behoof of Norris,

on condition that in the new grant to Norris
he might be joined with him for the longest
liver. Advises Cromwell to ask the Duke to
give up his interest in it. The fee is only 6l. 13s.
4d. Will then give Cromwell a new patent."[4]

This clamouring over the spoils makes you wonder if there
was any chance of justice for Anne Boleyn and these men. These
'vultures' seemed to think that it was a done deal.

9th May 1536 – Meetings

On Tuesday 9th May 1536, King Henry VIII wrote to Thomas Cromwell summoning him to meet with the King "for the treaty of such great and weighty matters as whereupon doth consist the surety of our person, the preservation of our honour, and the tranquillity and quietness of you and all other our loving and faithful subjects, like as at your arrival here ye shall more plainly perceive and understand.".[1] On the same day, the King summoned a group of noblemen and gentleman to a Council meeting at Hampton Court Palace. Among their number were the Duke of Norfolk and Suffolk, the Marquis of Exeter and the Earls of Oxford, Arundel, Westmoreland, Essex, Derby, Worcester, Sussex and Huntingdon.[2] We don't know what was discussed, but it is plausible that they discussed Cromwell's investigation into the alleged offences of Anne Boleyn and the men imprisoned in the Tower.

It was just one week since Anne Boleyn's arrest, but Thomas Cromwell felt that he had gathered enough evidence to move forward and start the judicial process. According to the Baga de Secretis (now held in the National Archives), 9th May was also the day that the justices of the King's Bench at Westminster ordered the sheriffs of London assemble a grand jury the following day to rule on the offences alleged to have taken place at Whitehall and Hampton Court Palace. The sheriffs were able to make a list of 48 men to go before the Chief Justice of the Common Pleas, John Baldwin (Sir Henry Norris's brother-in-law), on 10th May at Westminster.[3]

10th May 1536 –
The Middlesex Indictment

On 10th May 1536, Giles Heron, foreman of the Grand Jury of Middlesex and son-in-law of the late Sir Thomas More, announced that the jury had decided that there was sufficient evidence to suggest that Anne Boleyn, George Boleyn, Mark Smeaton, Sir Henry Norris, Sir Francis Weston and Sir William Brereton were guilty of the alleged crimes carried out at Hampton Court Palace and Whitehall, and that they should be indicted and sent to trial before a jury.

Here is the full Middlesex indictment drawn up by the Grand Jury of Middlesex:

"Indictment found at Westminster on Wednesday next after three weeks of Easter, 28 Hen. VIII. before Sir John Baldwin, &c., by the oaths of Giles Heron, Roger More, Ric. Awnsham, Thos. Byllyngton, Gregory Lovell, Jo. Worsop, Will. Goddard, Will. Blakwall, Jo. Wylford, Will. Berd, Hen. Hubbylthorn, Will. Hunyng, Rob. Walys, John England, Hen. Lodysman, and John Averey; who present that whereas queen Anne has been the wife of Henry VIII. for three years and more, she, despising her marriage, and entertaining malice against the King, and following daily her frail and carnal lust, did falsely and traitorously procure by base conversations and kisses, touchings, gifts, and other infamous incitations, divers of the King's daily and familiar servants to be her adulterers and concubines, so that several of the King's servants yielded to her vile provocations; viz., on 6th Oct. 25 Hen. VIII.,

at Westminster, and divers days before and after,
she procured, by sweet words, kisses, touches,
and otherwise, Hen. Noreys, of Westminster,
gentle man of the privy chamber, to violate her,
by reason whereof he did so at Westminster
on the 12th Oct. 25 Hen. VIII.; and they had
illicit intercourse at various other times, both
before and after, sometimes by his procurement,
and sometimes by that of the Queen.

Also the Queen, 2 Nov. 27 Hen. VIII. and
several times before and after, at Westminster,
procured and incited her own natural brother,
Geo. Boleyn, lord Rocheford, gentleman of the
privy chamber, to violate her, alluring him with
her tongue in the said George's mouth, and
the said George's tongue in hers, and also with
kisses, presents, and jewels; whereby he, despising
the commands of God, and all human laws, 5
Nov. 27 Hen. VIII., violated and carnally knew
the said Queen, his own sister, at Westminster;
which he also did on divers other days before and
after at the same place, sometimes by his own
procurement and sometimes by the Queen's.

Also the Queen, 3 Dec. 25 Hen. VIII., and
divers days before and after, at Westminster,
procured one Will. Bryerton, late of
Westminster, gentleman of the privy chamber,
to violate her, whereby he did so on 8 Dec.
25 Hen. VIII., at Hampton Court, in the
parish of Lytel Hampton, and on several other
days before and after, sometimes by his own
procurement and sometimes by the Queen's.

Also the Queen, 8 May 26 Hen. VIII., and
at other times before and since, procured Sir
Fras. Weston, of Westminster, gentleman of
the privy chamber, &c., whereby he did so on
the 20 May, &c. Also the Queen, 12 April 26
Hen. VIII., and divers days before and since, at
Westminster, procured Mark Smeton, groom
of the privy chamber, to violate her, whereby he
did so at Westminster, 26 April 27 Hen. VIII.

Moreover, the said lord Rocheford, Norreys,
Bryerton, Weston, and Smeton, being thus
inflamed with carnal love of the Queen, and
having become very jealous of each other, gave
her secret gifts and pledges while carrying on
this illicit intercourse; and the Queen, on her
part, could not endure any of them to converse
with any other woman, without showing great
displeasure; and on the 27 Nov. 27 Hen. VIII.,
and other days before and after, at Westminster,
she gave them great gifts to encourage them in
their crimes. And further the said Queen and
these other traitors, 31 Oct. 27 Hen. VIII., at
Westminster, conspired the death and destruction
of the King, the Queen often saying she would
marry one of them as soon as the King died, and
affirming that she would never love the King in
her heart. And the King having a short time since
become aware of the said abominable crimes
and treasons against himself, took such inward
displeasure and heaviness, especially from his
said Queen's malice and adultery, that certain
harms and perils have befallen his royal body.

And thus the said Queen and the other traitors

aforesaid have committed their treasons in
contempt of the Crown, and of the issue
and heirs of the said King and Queen".[1]

The language used in the indictment and the details of the
alleged offences aim to shock those reading or listening. Anne
Boleyn is described as "seduced by evil" and having malice in her
heart and "frail and carnal appetites", and then we have the details
of her seducing her brother by "alluring him with her tongue". Anne
was being painted as the Devil incarnate, a woman so possessed
with evil and lust that she would even seduce her brother, and who
appetites were so insatiable that rather than just taking one lover,
she took five! Her lust and appetite knew no end. Shock was the
aim and shock was what was achieved.

The Queen was accused of:-

- "Entertaining malice against the King" and following her
  lustful desires.

- Procuring her servants to be her lovers.

- Seducing and committing adultery with Sir Henry Norris,
  Sir William Brereton, Sir Francis Weston and Mark Smeaton.

- Committing incest with her brother, George Boleyn, Lord
  Rochford.

- Encouraging the men with gifts.

- Plotting with the men to kill the King.

- Agreeing to marry one of them after the King's death.

- Never having loved the King.

- Causing harm to the King.

- Committing treason by her actions.

The five named men were also obviously accused of these crimes,
but there was no mention of Sir Richard Page or Sir Thomas Wyatt
who were also among those imprisoned in the Tower of London at
that time.

The Middlesex Indictment had covered all the bases – Anne

Boleyn and the men were guilty of adultery and high treason (by plotting the King's death), and Anne was an evil seductress who had caused the King great harm. Any problem with the dates chosen for the alleged offences was covered by "divers days before and since" and "several times before and after", wonderful catch-all phrases which made it impossible to refute these dates. The Crown must have been pleased with itself – the jury would be shocked by Anne's behaviour and also by the harm done to their lord, the King, and they would surely want to please the King by doing his will. Anne Boleyn never stood a chance.

Arrangements for Trial

Also on 10th May 1536, Sir William Kingston, the Constable of the Tower of London, was ordered "to bring up the bodies of Sir Francis Weston, knt. Henry Noreys, esq.William Bryerton, esq. and Mark Smeton,gent. at Westminster, on Friday next after three weeks of Easter"[2], i.e. 12th May. Both Alison Weir[3] and Eric Ives[4] point out that this order was sent before the meeting of the Grand Jury in Kent and may even have been sent before the Middlesex meeting. Sir John Dudley wrote to Lady Lisle on the 10th May:

"Is sure there is no need to write the news,
for all the world knows them by this time.
Today Mr. Norres, Mr. Weston, William a
Brearton, Markes, and lord Rocheforde were
indicted, and on Friday they will be arraigned
at Westminster. The Queen herself will be
condemned by Parliament. Wednesday, 10 May."[5]

Obviously Dudley did not realise that Rochford, like the Queen, would be tried on the 15th May, but he correctly predicted that she would be condemned.

11th May 1536 –
The Kent Indictment

Just as the Grand Jury of Middlesex met at Westminster on 10th May 1536, the Grand Jury of Kent met on 11th May in front of Chief Justice John Baldwin and six of his colleagues at Deptford. They met to rule on the alleged crimes committed at Greenwich Palace, East Greenwich, and Eltham Palace by Queen Anne Boleyn, Sir Henry Norris, Sir William Brereton, Sir Francis Weston, George Boleyn (Lord Rochford) and Mark Smeaton. Unsurprisingly, this was a repeat of the previous day's meeting and it was ruled that the Queen and the five men would stand trial.

Here is a transcript of the Kent Indictment:

> "Record of indictment and process before
> Baldewyn, Luke, and others, in co. Kent.
>
> The indictment found at Deptford, on Thursday,
> 11 May 28 Hen. VIII., is precisely similar in
> character to the Middlesex indictment, except
> as regards times and places; viz., that the
> Queen at Estgrenewyche [East Greenwich],
> 12 Nov. 25 Hen. VIII., and divers days before
> and since, allured one Hen. Noreys, late of Est
> Grenewyche, to violate her, whereby he did
> so on the 19 Nov., &c.; that on 22 Dec. 27
> Hen. VIII., and divers other days, at Eltham,
> she allured Geo. Boleyn, lord Rocheford, &c.,
> whereby he did so, 29 Dec., &c.; that on the
> 16 Nov. 25 Hen. VIII., and divers, &c., at Est
> Grenewyche, she allured one Will. Bryerton,
> late of Est Grenewyche, &c., whereby he did
> so, 27 Nov., &c.; that on the 6 June 26 Hen.

VIII., &c., at Est Grenewyche, she allured Sir
Fras. Weston, &c., whereby he did so, 20 June,
&c.; that on the 13 May 26 Hen. VIII. &c., at
Est Grenewyche, she allured Mark Smeton,
&c., whereby he did so, 19 May 26 Hen. VIII.

And further that the said Boleyn, &c. grew
jealous of each other; and the Queen, to
encourage them, at Eltham, 31 Dec. 27 Hen.
VIII., and divers times before and since, made
them presents, &c.; that the Queen and the
others, 8 Jan. 27 Hen. VIII., conspired the King's
death, &c., and that she promised to marry one
of the traitors whenever the King was dead,
affirming she would never love him, &c."[1]

The alleged offences were the same as the Middlesex indictment
– seduction, adultery, incest, jealousy, plotting to kill the king etc.
– just at different venues, so it is no wonder that the jury decided to
send it to trial after the previous day's decision. The indictment also
included the same catch-all phrase as the Middlesex Indictment,
regarding various days before and after these dates.

The Dates of the Alleged Offences

If we combine the Kent and Middlesex Indictments, we get a
clearer picture of the dates of the alleged offences:

- 6th and 12th October 1533 – Anne and Sir Henry Norris at
  Westminster.

- 16th and 27th November 1533 – Anne and Sir William
  Brereton at Greenwich.

- 3rd and 8th December 1533 – Anne and Sir William
  Brereton at Hampton Court.

- 12th April 1534 – Anne and Mark Smeaton at Westminster
  (date for Anne procuring Smeaton).

- 8th and 20th May 1534 – Anne and Sir Francis Weston at Westminster.
- 6th and 20th June 1534 – Anne and Sir Francis Weston at Greenwich.
- 26th April 1535 – Anne and Mark Smeaton at Westminster.
- 13th and 19th May 1535 – Anne and Mark Smeaton at Greenwich.
- 31st October 1535 – Anne and some of the men plotted the King's death at Westminster.
- 2nd and 5th November 1535 – Anne and her brother George Boleyn,Lord Rochford at Westminster.
- 27th November 1535 – Anne gave gifts to the men at Westminster.
- 22nd and 29th December 1535 – Anne and her brother George Boleyn, Lord Rochford, at Eltham Palace.
- 8th January 1536 – Anne plotted the King's death with Rochford, Norris, Weston and Brereton at Greenwich.

These dates actually do not make sense. Historian Eric Ives[2] comments that three quarters of the alleged offences can be disproven because Anne Boleyn or the man involved were actually somewhere else, as shown below.

The Case for the Defence

On 6th and 12th October 1533, Anne Boleyn would still have been unchurched after giving birth to her daughter, Elizabeth, the previous month. Furthermore, at the time she was at Greenwich, not Westminster.

3rd and 8th December 1533 – Records[3] show that the royal court was at Greenwich on 8th December, so Anne could not have been committing adultery with Sir William Brereton at Hampton Court Palace.

April, May and June 1534 - A letter from George Taylor to

Lady Lisle dated 27th April 1534 says that "The Queen hath a goodly belly, praying our Lord to send us a prince"[4] and in July, Anne's brother, Lord Rochford, was sent on a diplomatic mission to France to ask for the postponement of a meeting between Henry VIII and Francis I because of Anne's condition: "being so far gone with child she could not cross the sea with the King".[5] So, there is evidence that Anne was visibly pregnant at this time, a time when she was allegedly seducing and sleeping with Mark Smeaton and Sir Francis Weston. Sexual intercourse was not commonly practised when the woman was pregnant.

Anne could also not have slept with Weston on 20th June at Greenwich when the court was at Hampton Court from 3rd to 26th June.

13th and 19th May 1535 – It would have been difficult for Anne to be sleeping with Mark Smeaton at Greenwich on the 19th when she was in Richmond at the time.[6]

27th November 1535 - Seeing as Anne Boleyn miscarried a baby of 15 weeks' gestation on the 29th January 1536, she would have been pregnant at this time, although in the early stages. If she had had an inkling that she was pregnant, what benefit would it be for her to give gifts to the men to get them on side? Also, Anne was not at Westminster on this date, she was at Windsor.

22nd and 29th December 1535 - Would a woman in the early stages of pregnancy really have the reason or the inclination to seduce her brother?

8th January 1536 – Would Anne really be plotting the King's death while also celebrating Catherine of Aragon's death with Henry?

The dates listed in the indictments are pure nonsense, but the catch-all phrases "and on divers other days and places" and "on several days before and after" meant that if the dates were challenged then the indictment was still valid. Interestingly, the date that Anne Boleyn argued with Sir Henry Norris and accused him of looking "for dead men's shoes", the 30th April, is not in the indictments, yet Anne admitted to talking to Norris on that day and mentioning the King's death. Odd!

Looking at the dates of Anne's alleged adultery I find it difficult to believe that a woman, never-mind a queen, could hop from bed to bed like that over a period of just over 2 years and not be caught sooner. How could she possibly have had five lovers and not have been gossiped about? It beggars belief.

The Prisoners Interrogated

Sometime shortly before their trials, Anne Boleyn, George Boleyn, Sir Henry Norris, Sir Francis Weston, Sir William Brereton and Mark Smeaton were visited in the Tower of London by members of the King's council. The Spanish Chronicle records that Thomas Cromwell, the Duke of Norfolk, Chancellor Thomas Audley and Archbishop Cranmer were the ones chosen for this mission and were ordered by the King "to treat her with no respect or consideration".[1] Cranmer was chosen as the spokesperson and he addressed the Queen:

> "Madam, there is no one in the realm, after my
> lord the King, who is so distressed at your bad
> conduct as I am, for all these gentlemen well
> know I owe my dignity to your good-will;"

Anne interrupted him, saying, "My lord Bishop, I know what is your errand; waste no more time; I have never wronged the King, but I know well that he is tired of me, as he was before of the good lady Katharine."

Archbishop Cranmer, responded, "Say no such thing, Madam, for your evil courses have been clearly seen ; and if you desire to read the confession which Mark has made, it will be shown to you."

Anne then replied to him "in a great rage", crying "Go to ! It has all been done as I say, because the King has fallen in love, as I know, with Jane Seymour, and does not know how to get rid of me. Well, let him do as he likes, he will get nothing more out of me; and any confession that has been made is false."

According to the Chronicle, the men then decided to leave because they knew that they would get nothing further from Anne, but Norfolk couldn't resist having another go at the Queen, saying, "Madam, if it be true that the Duke your brother has shared your guilt, a great punishment indeed should be yours and his as well." To which Anne replied, "Duke, say no such thing; my brother is blameless; and if he has been in my chamber to speak with me, surely he might do so without suspicion, being my brother, and they cannot accuse him for that. I know that the King has had him arrested, so that there should be none left to take my part. You need not trouble to stop talking with me, for you will find out no more."

When they reported Anne's words back to the King, he allegedly commented that she had a "stout heart" but that she would "pay for it".

A French poem[2] in Letters and Papers corroborates the Spanish report, in so far as saying that the Queen and the five men were interrogated. It records that when they spoke to George Boleyn, Lord Rochford, he raised his eyes to heaven and denied the accusations. Norris, Weston and Brereton also continued denying the charges laid against them.

12th May 1536 – The Trial of Norris, Weston, Brereton and Smeaton

On 12th May 1536, Mark Smeaton, Sir Henry Norris, Sir Francis Weston and Sir William Brereton were tried at a special commission of oyer and terminer, just a day after the Grand Jury of Kent had assembled and only eight days after Weston and Brereton had been arrested. The legal machinery had worked incredibly quickly.

The four men were tried separately from Anne Boleyn and George Boleyn, Lord Rochford, who, as members of the aristocracy, were entitled to be tried in the court of the Lord High Steward of England by a jury of their peers. Sir William Kingston, Constable of the Tower of London, escorted the four men by barge along the Thames and brought them to the bar of the special commission of oyer and terminer at Westminster Hall, where all four were arraigned for high treason.

The Jury

The men's hearts must have sunk into their shoes when they saw the jury. Any hopes they had held of being acquitted and released must have been dashed as soon as they saw the men sitting in judgement on them. Although the jury included Thomas Boleyn, Earl of Wiltshire, a man who would certainly not benefit from these men being found guilty when it would prejudice the trial of his son and daughter, it also included men who owed Cromwell or the King a favour and those who would love to see the Boleyn faction spectacularly brought down. There were no two ways about it; the jury was a hostile one.

Those who could be described as hostile included:-
- Sir William Fitzwilliam – The man who had interrogated Smeaton and Norris and persuaded them to confess, if indeed Norris had ever confessed.

- Edward Willoughby, foreman – This man owed Sir William Brereton money so it was definitely in his interests to get rid of him.

- Sir Giles Alington – Husband of Sir Thomas More's stepdaughter. More had been executed for treason for refusing to swear the oath of succession.

- William Askew – A religious conservative and supporter of the Lady Mary. Interestingly, he was also the father of the Protestant martyr Anne Askew.

- Walter Hungerford – Eric Ives describes this man as "a scapegrace dependant of Cromwell's and a homosexual"[1] and Paul Friedmann describes him as "the son-in-law of Lord Hussey, Anne's bitter enemy".[2]

- Sir John Hampden – A man whose daughter was sister-in-law to the comptroller of the royal household, William Paulet.

- William Musgrave – A man keen to do the right thing and win favour with Cromwell and the King after failing to make stick the treason charges against Lord Dacre. He had also signed a bond for 2,000 marks to Cromwell and others of the King's officers: Friedmann makes the point that this could be demanded at any time.

- Robert Dormer – A religious conservative who had opposed the Break with Rome.

- Thomas Palmer – A client of William Fitzwilliam and also one of the King's gambling buddies.

- Richard Tempest – A relation and ally of Lord Darcy (a conservative) and a man close to Cromwell. According to Friedmann, he was also related to Lady Boleyn, Anne Boleyn's aunt, but no friend of Anne.

- William Sidney – A friend of Charles Brandon, the Duke of Suffolk, who was known to be hostile to the Boleyns.

- Anthony Hungerford – A relation of the King's new love, Jane Seymour.

We also have to take into account the Tudor legal machinery. Defendants did not have counsel, they were not aware of what evidence was being presented against them, they could not prepare their defence case and all they could do was react to what was said in court.[3] Talk about being at a disadvantage! When you combine this disadvantage with the hostile jury and the fact that the onus was on the accused to prove their innocence, rather than the Crown proving their guilt,[4] then there was little chance of justice for these men. They were dead men even before the trial began.

The Trial

Unfortunately, records of this special commission of oyer and terminer no longer exist. They may have been destroyed in the same fire that damaged Sir William Kingston's letters to Cromwell in 1731, or perhaps they were purposely destroyed. However, we do have some accounts of what happened at Westminster Hall on the 12th May 1536. From Letters and Papers, we know that:

> "Noreys, Bryerton, Weston, and Smeton were brought up in the custody of the constable of the Tower, when Smeton pleaded guilty of violation and carnal knowledge of the Queen, and put himself in the King's mercy. Noreys, Bryerton, and Weston pleaded Not guilty. The jury return a verdict of Guilty, and that they have no lands, goods, or chattels.
>
> Judgment against all four as in cases of treason; execution to be at Tyburn."[5]

On the 19th May 1536, Eustace Chapuys, the Imperial Ambassador, wrote to Charles V to keep him up to date with events, saying:

"On the 11th were condemned as traitors Master
Noris, the King's chief butler, (sommelier de
corps) Master Ubaston (Weston), who used to
lie with the King, Master Bruton (Brereton),
gentleman of the Chamber, and the groom
(varlet de chambre), of whom I wrote to
your Majesty by my man. Only the groom
confessed that he had been three times with the
said putain and Concubine. The others were
condemned upon presumption and certain
indications, without valid proof or confession."[6]

He gets the date wrong, but both Chapuys and the records in
Letters and Papers agree that Mark Smeaton confessed and pleaded
"guilty" to sleeping with the Queen, whereas Norris, Brereton and
Weston pleaded "not guilty" to all charges. According to George
Constantine, Sir Henry Norris's manservant, when Norris was
presented with his confession he declared "that he was deceived"
into making it by Sir William Fitzwilliam, the Earl of Southampton,
and thus retracted it.[7] Mark Smeaton did not retract his confession.

All four men were found guilty on all charges, declared traitors
and sentenced to the usual traitor's death, to be hanged, drawn and
quartered at Tyburn.[8] A date was not set due to the forthcoming
trial of Anne Boleyn and Lord Rochford, but the axe was turned
towards them and their fates were sealed.

Another Event

Also on 12th May 1536, the Duke of Norfolk, uncle of Anne
and George Boleyn, was appointed Lord High Steward of England
in readiness for ruling, as Lord President, over the trials of his niece
and nephew.[9]

13th May 1536 –
Henry Percy and the Pre-contract

On 13th May 1536, Henry Percy, Earl of Northumberland wrote to Thomas Cromwell. The subject of his letter was the alleged pre-contract which was said to have existed between himself and Anne Boleyn before she married Henry VIII. From his home in Newington Green, Henry Percy wrote:

> "I perceive by Raynold Carnaby that there is
> supposed a pre-contract between the Queen
> and me; whereupon I was not only heretofore
> examined upon my oath before the archbishops
> of Canterbury and York, but also received the
> blessed sacrament upon the same before the
> duke of Norfolk and other the King's highness'
> council learned in the spiritual law, assuring
> you, Mr. Secretary, by the said oath and blessed
> body, which afore I received and hereafter
> intend to receive, that the same may be to my
> damnation if ever there were any contract or
> promise of marriage between her and me."[1]

Percy had already denied the existence of such a pre-contract when interrogated by the Duke of Norfolk and two archbishops in 1532. His wife, Mary Talbot, had sought an annulment from their very unhappy marriage by claiming that he had previously been contracted to marry Anne Boleyn who was, at that time, being courted by the King. Percy had denied this by swearing an oath on the Blessed Sacrament, in front of Norfolk, the archbishops and the King's canon lawyers.

Thomas Cromwell decided to resurrect the issue in May 1536, in an effort to get Anne's marriage to the King annulled. He sent Sir Reynold Carnaby to exert some pressure on Henry Percy and to try and make him confess that he and Anne had been pre-contracted to marry. Carnaby was a King's officer in the north of England, and someone Percy knew well, but Percy refused to be bullied into confessing. His letter to Cromwell shows Percy affirming that in no uncertain terms.

Cranmer's Light Bulb Moment

As Percy wouldn't play ball, Cromwell had to give up on the idea of getting the marriage between Anne Boleyn and Henry VIII annulled on the grounds of a pre-contract. There was just no evidence to prove that a precontract had existed. Cromwell was not ready to give up yet though, so he asked Thomas Cranmer, the Archbishop of Canterbury, to find another way round it. Cranmer must have been torn. After all he knew the Boleyns well and his rise had been due to Anne's patronage and support. He knew, however, that he had to do his job and give Cromwell what he wanted and needed. It was not enough for Cromwell and the King to merely get rid of Anne by execution. They needed her marriage to the King to be erased; to be annulled and declared invalid. Complete annihilation was what was required. Fortunately for Cranmer, he had a brainwave, and used the King's past relationship with Mary Boleyn, Anne's sister, as an impediment of consanguinity to the marriage. The marriage could be seen as incestuous because Henry had already slept with Mary. Clever!

13th May 1536 – The Queen's Household is Broken Up

On 13th May 1536, two days before Queen Anne Boleyn was tried and found guilty, her household was broken up. The chronicler Charles Wriothesley wrote:

> "And the morrowe after, beinge Satterdaie, and the thirtenth daie of Maie, Maister Fittes-Williams [Sir William Fitzwilliam], Treasorer of the Kinges howse, and Mr. Controoler [Sir Edward Poynings], deposed and brooke upp the Queenes househoulde at Greenewich, and so discharged all of her servantes of their offices clearlye."[1]

Fitzwilliam and Poynings would only have broken up Anne's household on the King's orders, so the King was obviously confident that Anne was going to be condemned. Of course, some of the Queen's staff would be back at court within just a few weeks to serve the new queen, Jane Seymour. William Coffin, Anne's master of the horse and the husband of one of her attendants in the Tower, went on to serve Jane Seymour, as did her vice chamberlain, Sir Edward Baynton, and her surveyor, John Smith. Ladies who moved on to serve Queen Jane, included Anne's sister in law, Jane Boleyn, Lady Rochford; Anne Gainsford, Lady Zouche; Bess Holland and Margery Horsman.

14th May 1536 – Jane Seymour

On 14th May 1536, Henry VIII sent Sir Nicholas Carew to fetch Jane Seymour and to install her in a house in Chelsea, within a mile of the King's own lodgings. Eustace Chapuys, the imperial ambassador, wrote to his master Charles V, that Jane was "most richly dressed" and "splendidly served by the King's cook and other officers".[1] Her sumptuous dress, her proximity to the King and the way she was being served by the King's own servants, suggest that Jane was being treated like the Queen of England and thus that Henry VIII knew that this position would need filling soon.

The gossip around court in early May had been that the King was trying to rid himself of Queen Anne Boleyn so that he could replace her with Lady Jane Seymour, but until this point the King had been careful to distance himself from Jane, going so far as to even spend time with other women. Chapuys reported that Henry VIII had "been going about banqueting with ladies, sometimes remaining after midnight, and returning by the river" and that he had also "supped lately with several ladies in the house of the bishop of Carlisle, and showed an extravagant joy".[2] The King also spoke about Anne Boleyn's arrest with the bishop, telling that "he had before composed a tragedy, which he carried with him". Chapuys wondered if this was a book of "certain ballads that the King has composed, at which the putain and her brother laughed as foolish things, which was objected to them as a great crime". Making fun of the King obviously did not help their cause.

Chapuys had also reported that earlier in May the King had ordered Sir Nicholas Carew to move Jane out of London, to Carew's country home, in order to prevent gossip:

> "To cover the affection he has for the said Semel
> he has lodged her seven miles hence in the house
> of the grand esquire, and says publicly that he

has no desire in the world to get married again
unless he is constrained by his subjects to do so."[3]

By 14th May, however, the King was confident enough to bring
his relationship with Jane out into the open and to have her close
to him.

We have no way of knowing how Jane felt about the situation.
She must have known that she was being groomed to take Anne
Boleyn's place as queen and that Anne was in the Tower, but she
may not have known all of the details. Did she feel guilty about
Anne's predicament? Did she believe that Anne was guilty? Did
she think that Anne deserved it for taking Catherine of Aragon's
crown from her? Did she worry about her own future? We just
don't know what Jane was thinking at this time, but how awful to
be planning a marriage while your predecessor is waiting to die.

No Great Beauty

Chapuys seems to have been bemused by the King's behaviour
and his attraction to Jane. Chapuys was no friend of Anne Boleyn,
referring to her frequently as "the Concubine" or "the putain"
(whore), but he was also highly critical of the King's new flame too.
In a letter to Antoine Perrenot, Chapuys wrote:

> "I have no news to add to what I write to His
> Majesty, except to tell you something of the
> quality of the King's new lady, which the Emperor
> and Granvelle would perhaps like to hear. She
> is sister of one Edward Semel[Seymour], "qua
> este a sa mate," of middle stature and no great
> beauty, so fair that one would call her rather
> pale than otherwise. She is over 25 years old. I
> leave you to judge whether, being English and
> having long frequented the Court, "si elle ne
> tiendroit pas a conscience de navoir pourveu
> et prevenu de savoir que cest de faire nopces."
> Perhaps this King will only be too glad to be

so far relieved from trouble. Also, according to the account given of him by the Concubine, he has neither vigour nor virtue; and besides he may make a condition in the marriage that she be a virgin, and when he has a mind to divorce her he will find enough of witnesses. The said Semel [Seymour] is not a woman of great wit, but she may have good understanding (un bel enigm, qu. engin?). It is said she inclines to be proud and haughty. She bears great love and reverence to the Princess. I know not if honors will make her change hereafter."[4]

No great beauty, possibly not a virgin, proud and haughty; but at least she cares about the Princess Mary! That was Chapuys' summation of Jane Seymour.

Henry VIII's
Letter to Jane Seymour

In the few days between Jane arriving at Chelsea on 14th May and Anne Boleyn's execution on 19th May, Henry VIII sent a message to Jane which was accompanied by a gift, a token of the King's "true affection":

"My dear friend and mistress,

The bearer of these few lines from thy entirely devoted servant will deliver into thy fair hands a token of my true affection for thee, hoping you will keep it for ever in your sincere love for me. Advertising you that there is a ballad made lately of great derision against us, which if it go much abroad and is seen by you, I pray you to pay no manner of regard to it. I am not at present informed who is the setter forth of this malignant writing, but if he is found out he shall be straitly punished for it. For the things ye lacked I have minded my lord to supply them to you as soon as he can buy them. Thus hoping shortly to receive you in these arms, I end for the present your own loving servant and sovereign,

H. R."[1]

We can see from the King's words that pamphlets were being published and circulated which derided Henry and Jane's relationship. Anne Boleyn may have been unpopular in some quarters but her imprisonment and the King's behaviour with Jane Seymour were causing gossip and disapproval. In this letter, the King is promising Jane that he'll get to the bottom of it, and asking her not to worry.

This is the only surviving letter which Henry wrote Jane and it is hard not to compare it to the gushing letters Henry wrote to Anne during their courtship, letters in which he wrote of being "stricken with the dart of love" and which he ended with words like

"Written by the hand of that secretary,
who in heart, body, and will, is, Your
loyal and most assured Servant,

H. aultre A.B. ne cherse R" or "H.
no other (AB) seeks. R"[2]

with the "A.B." written in a heart.

Maybe there were other letters to Jane, and maybe this was a purely functional, quick message to alert her to what was going on, but it definitely lacks passion and romance.

14th May 1536 -
The Queen's Incontinent Living

Also on 14th May 1536, Master Secretary Cromwell wrote to Stephen Gardiner and John Wallop, the King's ambassadors in France. In this letter, which was written to inform Gardiner and Wallop of recent events in England, the man who was once happy to be the Queen's right hand man and friend showed his true colours and his fickle nature:

> "The King has deferred answering their
> letters sent by Salisbury till the arrival of
> the bailly of Troyes. Has to inform them,
> however, of a most detestable scheme, happily
> discovered and notoriously known to all men.
> They may have heard the rumour of it. Will
> express to them, however, some part of the
> coming out, and of the King's proceeding.

> The Queen's incontinent living was so rank and
> common that the ladies of her privy chamber
> could not conceal it. It came to the ears of some
> of the Council, who told his Majesty, although
> with great fear, as the case enforced. Certain
> persons of the privy chamber and others of her
> side were examined, and the matter appeared
> so evident that, besides that crime, "there brake
> out a certain conspiracy of the King's death,
> which extended so far that all we that had the
> examination of it quaked at the danger his Grace
> was in, and on our knees gave him (God ?) laud
> and praise that he had preserved him so long from
> it." Certain men were committed to the Tower,

viz., Marks and Norris and the Queen's brother;
then she herself was apprehended and committed
to the same place; after her Sir Fras. Weston and
Wm. Brereton. Norris, Weston, Brereton, and
Marks are already condemned to death, having
been arraigned at Westminster on Friday last.
The Queen and her brother are to be arraigned
tomorrow, and will undoubtedly go the same way.

"I write no particularities; the things be so
abominable that I think the like was never
heard. Gardiner will receive 200l. of the
300l. "that were out amongst these men,
notwithstanding great suit hath been made for
the whole; which though the King's highness
might give in this case, yet his Majesty doth
not forget your service; and the third 100l. is
bestowed of the vicar of Hell [Sir Fras. Brian],
upon [whom] though it be some charge unto
you, his Highness trusteth ye will think it well
bestowed." From the Rolls in haste, 14 May.

P.S.—Wallop will not be forgotten, though
Cromwell cannot tell at present how
much he is to have. The King is highly
pleased with the services of both."[1]

Cromwell was not holding back, was he?

"Incontinent", in this case, means lacking self-control, so
Cromwell was painting Anne Boleyn as a queen of debauchery
instead of a queen of virtue. So scandalous was her behaviour,
according to Cromwell, that her ladies could no longer keep it
secret.

The letter read just like the Middlesex and Kent indictments,
using language that was intended to shock. Cromwell's words

regarding the upcoming trial of the Queen and Lord Rochford, that they "will undoubtedly go the same way" were obviously not due to Cromwell being psychic but rather, down to him knowing that their trials had been prejudiced by the trials of Norris, Weston, Brereton and Smeaton. The Queen was unlikely to be found innocent of adultery and treason when those four men had already been found guilty of sleeping with her and plotting with her! Cromwell would, of course, have been pretty confident that the jury would do his bidding.

Cromwell finished his letter by promising that both Gardiner and Wallop would benefit from the fall of Queen Anne Boleyn, as would Sir Francis Bryan.

Notice that Cromwell is not taking any credit for the Queen's downfall. He quite clearly states that the investigation was "the King's proceeding". His biographer John Schofield uses this as evidence that Cromwell was commissioned by Henry VIII to do what was needed to remove Anne Boleyn and to replace her with his new love, Jane Seymour. However, it could be that Cromwell did not want Gardiner and Wallop to know of his precise involvement in the plot, or that it was a plot rather than an investigation.

15th May 1536 –
The King to Take a New Wife

On 15th May 1536, before Anne Boleyn had even been tried, Charles V, the Holy Roman Emperor, wrote to his ambassador, Eustace Chapuys, regarding what he had heard about Queen Anne Boleyn, the allegations against her and the King's plans to remove her and remarry. What is interesting about this letter is that it shows quite clearly the assumption that Anne would die and that Henry would need a new Queen – Charles obviously had not yet received the news about Jane Seymour.

Here is the part of the letter relating to Anne Boleyn:

> "Hannaert has written to Granvelle on the 9th
> that he had just heard that the king of England's
> concubine had been surprised in bed with the
> King's organist. If this be so, as it is very probable
> that God has permitted it after her damnable
> life, we think the King will be more inclined to
> treat, especially as regards our cousin; but you
> must use great dexterity lest the King intend a
> marriage in France, and that he should rather
> choose one of his own subjects, either the one
> with whom he is in love or some other. We trust
> that if there be anything in it you will let us know
> with diligence. We send letters of credence for
> you for the dukes of Richmond, Norfolk, and
> Suffolk, and also for Cromwell, such as you will
> see by the copies. Pontremulo, 15 May 1536.
>
> P.S.—Since the above was written your man
> George has arrived, who confirms the news
> touching the King's concubine, and, as we

suppose that the King will put her and her
accomplices to death and take another wife, as
he is of amorous complexion and always desires
to have a male child, and as on the side of France
they will not fail to offer him a match, you will
suggest, when you can, to him or Cromwell, a
marriage with the Infanta of Portugal, daughter of
our sister the queen of France, who has 400,000
ducats dowry by testament. Another marriage
might be arranged for the Infant Don Loys of
Portugal, our brother-in-law, with the princess
of England. You must point out to them that
these matches would be very expedient, both to
remove past scruples and to promote strict amity
between us, him, and Portugal, and would be very
advantageous to England in case the King should
have a male child by this marriage, as he may
reasonably hope from the youth and bringing up
of the Infanta. If you see the King not inclined to
these marriages you might propose one between
the King and our niece, the duchess dowager
of Milan, a beautiful young lady, well brought
up and with a good dowry; treating at the same
time of the other marriage between Don Loys
and our cousin. But we should greatly prefer the
former match with the Infanta, for the good of
both, and in order to be able to dispose of our
niece of Milan otherwise. Bersel, 15 May 1536."[1]

I find it rather chilling that Charles V just accepted the situation
and even thought it was good news. From his perspective, it meant
that he could secure a good marriage alliance for his niece and
stop Henry VIII aligning himself with France. As far as Anne was
concerned, Charles seemed to think that she deserved it for her
"damnable life". I know that he was Catherine of Aragon's nephew

but even so, such cold, harsh talk gives me goosebumps!

15th May 1536 –
The Trial of Anne Boleyn

On the morning of 15th May 1536, while Anne Boleyn prepared herself for her trial, Jane Seymour received a message from the King telling her that "he would send her news at 3 o'clock of the condemnation of the putain."[1] Obviously there was no need for a trial, really, when the King already knew that Anne would be condemned!

Queen Anne Boleyn was tried in the King's Hall of the Tower of London in front of an estimated 2,000 spectators. A great platform[2] had been erected in the hall so that everybody could see. The Lord High Steward, the Duke of Norfolk, who was representing the King, sat on a special throne underneath the canopy of estate. In his hand was the white staff of office and at his feet sat his son, the Earl of Surrey, holding, on his father's behalf, the golden staff of the Earl Marshal of England.[3] Sir Thomas Audley, the Lord Chancellor, and Charles Brandon, the Duke of Suffolk, were on either side of the Duke.

As Queen, Anne Boleyn was given the privilege, if it can be called that, of being tried by a jury of her peers, rather than by the commission of oyer and terminer who sat in judgement on Norris, Weston, Smeaton and Brereton. In reality, this was no privilege. Her trial had already been prejudiced by the guilty verdicts of the four men, and her jury was made up of her enemies. Here are just a few of them[4]:

- Charles Brandon, Duke of Suffolk – Henry VIII's brother-in-law and good friend. A man who disliked the Queen and who would, of course, support the King and do the King's will.

- Henry Courtenay, Marquis of Exeter, and his cousin Henry Pole, Baron Montague – Both men were supporters of the Lady Mary, daughter of Henry VIII and Catherine of Aragon.

Chapuys had also linked them to Sir Nicholas Carew and the plotting to replace Anne with Jane Seymour.

- John de Vere, 15th Earl of Oxford – Oxford bore the crown at Queen Anne's coronation in 1533, but he was a good friend of the King's.

- Henry Percy, Earl of Northumberland – The Earl had once been in love with Anne Boleyn, but that love seemed to have turned into bitterness and hatred.

- Ralph Neville, the Earl of Westmoreland – A loyal servant to the King in the North.

- Henry Somerset, Earl of Worcester – It was rumoured that his wife, Elizabeth Browne, the Countess of Worcester, gave evidence against the Queen to Cromwell and was the prosecution's key witness.

- Thomas Manners, the Earl of Rutland, George Hastings, Earl of Huntingdon – Both men were related to the King and were royal favourites.

- Robert Radcliffe, Earl of Sussex – One of the King's best friends.

- Henry Parker, Lord Morley – Father of Jane Boleyn (George Boleyn's wife), one time servant to Lady Margaret Beaufort (Henry VIII's grandmother), staunch conservative and a supporter of the Lady Mary.

- Thomas Fiennes, Lord Dacre – A man with a rather colourful past who needed to please the King.

- George Brooke, Lord Cobham – Brother-in-law of Thomas Wyatt, close friend of Henry VIII and husband of Anne Braye (Nan Cobham), one of the Queen's ladies who is thought to have given evidence against the Queen.

- Edward Grey, Baron Grey of Powys, and Thomas Stanley, Lord Monteagle – Both were son-in-laws of the Duke of Suffolk, so their allegiance lay with him and, of course, with the King.

- Edward Clinton (Fiennes), Lord Clinton – Husband of Elizabeth (Bessie) Blount and stepfather of the King's illegitimate son, the Duke of Richmond.

- William, Lord Sandys – A great friend of the King and also Lord Chamberlain. Sandys was one of the men who escorted the Queen to the Tower of London on the 2nd May.

- Andrew, Lord Windsor – Another friend of the King.

- Thomas, Lord Wentworth – A cousin of Lady Jane Seymour, the King's new flame.

Lancelot de Carles, secretary to the French ambassador, described Queen Anne Boleyn as she entered the hall, commenting on her grace, her beauty, her lack of fear and how she entered the court "with the bearing of one coming to great honour",[5] "comme venant a l'honneur d'un grant bien".[6] Other witnesses described that she was wearing a black velvet gown, a scarlet damask petticoat and a cap decorated with a black and white feather.[7] She looked every inch a queen and the proceedings did not seem to faze her. She defended her honour "soberly" and although she said little, her face showed that she was not guilty of the crimes she was accused of.[8] Anne pleaded "not guilty", after which the Attorney General, Sir Christopher Hales, put forward the case against her. He accused the Queen of incest, adultery, plotting the King's death, promising to marry Sir Henry Norris after the King's death, and of making fun of the King and his dress. Chapuys also reported that Anne and George had laughed at "certain ballads that the King has composed".[9] No witnesses gave evidence against her.

The chronicler Charles Wriothesley, recorded that after her indictment was read out, Anne "made so wise and discreet aunsweres to all thinges layde against her, excusing herselfe with her wordes so clearlie, as thoughe she had never bene faultie to the same".[10]

The Queen defended herself admirably, denying all of these preposterous charges and admitting only to giving money to Sir Francis Weston, just as she gave money to many young gentlemen at court.Notwithstanding, the jury were unanimous in their verdict: "guilty". The Queen was then stripped of her crown and her titles, all except that of "Queen". With tears running down his cheeks, Anne's uncle, the Duke of Norfolk, pronounced the sentence:

> "Because thou hast offended against our sovereign
> the King's Grace in committing treason against
> his person, and here attainted of the same, the law
> of the realm is this, that thou hast deserved death,
> and thy judgment is tis: that thou shalt be burned
> here within the Tower of London on the Green,
> else to have thy head smitten off, as the King's
> pleasure shall be further known of the same."[11,12]

The shock was too much for the Earl of Northumberland, who collapsed and had to be taken out of the hall, and also for Mrs Orchard, a lady who had cared for the Queen when she was a child, who "shrieked out dreadfully".[13] The Queen kept her composure. Although she did not argue against the sentence, she said that she "believed there was some other reason for which she was condemned than the cause alleged".[14] Lancelot de Carles recorded that Anne then addressed the court, saying:

> "I do not say that I have been as humble
> towards the King as he deserved, considering
> the humanity and kindness he showed me,
> and the great honour he has always paid
> me; I know that my fantasies have led me
> to be jealous... but God knows that I have
> never done him any other wrong."[15]

Victorian historian Agnes Strickland records another speech by Anne Boleyn at court that day, recorded by Crispin, Lord of Milherve:-

"My lords, I will not say your sentence is unjust,
nor presume that my reasons can prevail against
your convictions. I am willing to believe that you
have sufficient reasons for what you have done,
but then they must be other than those which
have been produced in court, for I am clear of all
the offences which you then laid to my charge.
I have ever been a faithful wife to the king,
though I do not say I have always shown him
that humility which his goodness to me and the
honour to which he raised me merited. I confess
I have had jealous fancies and suspicions of him
which I had not discretion and wisdom enough
to conceal at all times. But God knows, and is
my witness, that I never sinned against him in
any other way. Think not I say this in the hope
to prolong my life, God hath taught me how to
die, and he will strengthen my faith. Think not
that I am so bewildered in my mind as not to
lay the honour of my chastity to heart now in
mine extremity, when I have maintained it all
my life long, much as ever queen did. I know
these my last words will avail me nothing but
for the justification of my chastity and honour.
As for my brother and those others who are
unjustly condemned, I would willingly suffer
many deaths to deliver them; but since I see it
so pleases the king, I shall willingly accompany
them in death, with this assurance, that I shall
lead an endless life with them in peace."

Similarities can be seen between this speech and the words
recorded by Lancelot de Carles and this is because, as historian John
Guy has pointed out, Crispin de Milherve is actually a 'phantom'
and his poem was written by Lancelot de Carles.[16]

Anne Boleyn was then escorted out of the court by her gaoler, Sir William Kingston, with the axe turned against her to show that she had been sentenced to death. It was now her brother's turn to face the hostile panel.

The Trial of George Boleyn

While Anne Boleyn was taken back to her lodgings in the Tower of London, her brother, George Boleyn, Lord Rochford, was taken to the King's Hall to stand before the same jury. George's trial is mentioned briefly in Letters and Papers:

> "The same day, lord Rocheford is brought
> before the High Steward in the custody of Sir
> Will. Kingston, and pleads not guilty. The peers
> are charged, with the exception of the earl of
> Northumberland, who was suddenly taken ill,
> and each of them severally saith that he is guilty.
>
> Judgment: - To be taken to prison in the
> Tower, and then drawn through the city
> of London, to the gallows at Tyburn,
> &c., as usual in high treason."[17]

All witnesses agree that George put up a good fight in the court room that day. In his Chronicle, Charles Wriothesley recorded that after George pleaded not guilty, "he made answer so prudently and wisely to all articles laid against him, that marvel it was to hear, but never would confess anything, but made himself as clear as though he had never offended"[18] and Lancelot de Carles commented on George's good defence and his eloquence, which de Carles likened to that of Sir Thomas More.[19]

But George wasn't just prudent, he was also rather spirited, as my friend Clare Cherry says in her research into George Boleyn's life:

> "Ironically, during life it was Anne who was
> the more tempestuous and reckless of the

two siblings. Yet she faced her accusers with
the quiet and restrained dignity of a true
Queen. It was her brother who approached
the trial with all guns blazing."[20]

When the only evidence for George committing incest with
Anne was that "he had been once found a long time with her",
George "replied so well that several of those present wagered 10
to 1 that he would be acquitted, especially as no witnesses were
produced against either him or her".[21] And when he was handed
a note regarding the King's impotence, George recklessly read
it aloud even though he had been commanded not to. Chapuys
recorded this incident in a letter to Charles V:

> "I must not omit, that among other things
> charged against him as a crime was, that his
> sister had told his wife that the King "nestoit
> habile en cas de soy copuler avec femme, et
> quil navoit ne vertu ne puissance." This he was
> not openly charged with, but it was shown
> him in writing, with a warning not to repeat
> it. But he immediately declared the matter, in
> great contempt of Cromwell and some others,
> saying he would not in this point arouse any
> suspicion which might prejudice the King's
> issue. He was also charged with having spread
> reports which called in question whether his
> sister's daughter was the King's child."[22]

Not only had George joked or gossiped about the King's sexual
problems, his lack of sexual prowess, he had also joked about
Elizabeth not being the King's daughter. This meant that he had
unwittingly committed treason because this kind of talk impugned
the King's issue. What was worse was that George had disobeyed
instructions and read out this note in court, embarrassing the King
and not endearing himself to the jury.

George Wyatt, Thomas Wyatt's grandson, wrote a few years later that "the young nobleman the Lord Rochford, by the common opinion of men of best understanding in those days, was counted and then openly spoken, condemned only upon some point of a statute of words then in force".[23] Even "the judges at first were of different opinions".[24] However, they were able to give an unanimous decision in the end. No witnesses and an eloquent defence, but George was still found guilty by a jury of his peers. His uncle, the Duke of Norfolk, then sentenced George to a traitor's death:

> "that he should goe agayne to prison in the
> Tower from whence he came, and to be drawne
> from the saide Tower of London thorowe the
> Cittie of London to the place of execution
> called Tyburne, and there to be hanged, beinge
> alyve cutt downe, and then his members cutt
> of and his bowells taken owt of his bodie and
> brent[burnt] before him, and then his head
> cutt of and his bodie to be divided into quarter
> peeces, and his head and bodie to be sett at
> suche places as the King should assigne."[25]

Chapuys records George's reaction to his sentence:

> "Her brother, after his condemnation, said
> that since he must die, he would no longer
> maintain his innocence, but confessed that
> he had deserved death. He only begged the
> King that his debts, which he recounted,
> might be paid out of his goods."[26]

Some might read Chapuys' words and conclude that George Boleyn thought it was not worth maintaining the pretence any more and so confessed to committing incest with his sister, but I do not agree. I think that George was simply admitting to being a sinner, a sinner who deserved judgement from God. People who were convicted of a crime, even if they were innocent, "did not doubt that they deserved to die"[27] and that it was a punishment from God for their sinful life. There was a strong belief in original sin.

George Boleyn was then taken back to his prison in the Tower to prepare himself for death.

16th May 1536 –
Archbishop Cranmer Visits
Anne Boleyn

In a letter to Thomas Cromwell, on 16th May, Sir William Kingston wrote of how he had seen the King that day regarding "the petitions of my Lord of Rochford", which must have been about the debts that George Boleyn was worrying about during his imprisonment, things that were "touching his conscience." Kingston wrote that the King had told him that the men were going to be executed the next day but that Kingston needed to know from Cromwell "the preparation for the scaffolds and other necessaries concerning".[1]

Kingston also reported that the King had finally agreed to Anne Boleyn's request to have a confessor. In addition, he states that Archbishop Thomas Cranmer, the man who had once Anne Boleyn's family chaplain and a man she had helped rise to prominence at the English court, had visited her that day. Cranmer may have been chosen as the Queen's confessor, but that was not the real reason for his visit.

Archbishop Cranmer was actually visiting Anne Boleyn to get her to confess to an impediment to her marriage. He wanted obtain her consent to dissolve the marriage and to disinherit and bastardise her daughter Elizabeth. In the same letter to Cromwell, Kingston reported that "Yet this day at dinner the Queen said she would go to "anonre" [a nunnery], and is in hope of life",[2] which suggests that Anne was offered a deal by Cranmer – say yes to an annulment and you can go to a nunnery. Of course, even though she did comply she was not sent to a nunnery. Perhaps the more merciful death by a sword, rather than by axe, was her reward. What we don't know is whether Cranmer was, himself, being misled by Cromwell and the King, or whether he was lying to Anne.

While Cranmer was visiting Anne in the Tower, Henry VIII's new flame, Jane Seymour, was receiving guests at her lodgings in Chelsea – courtiers who were there to curry favour with the woman who was sure to be their new queen. As for the King, he was signing death warrants, one of them his wife's.

George Boleyn, Sir Francis Weston, Sir Henry Norris, Sir William Brereton and Mark Smeaton prepared for their deaths by confessing their sins to Dr Allryge (or Alridge), the chaplain sent to them.[3] Sir Francis Weston wrote out a list of his debts, which can be found in Letters and Papers,[4] and then wrote a farewell letter to his parents, which was to be included with the list of creditors:

> "Father and mother and wife, I shall humbly
> desire you, for the salvation of my soul, to
> discharge me of this bill, and for to forgive
> me of all the offences that I have done to you,
> and in especial to my wife, which I desire for
> the love of God to forgive me, and to pray
> for me: for I believe prayer will do me good.
> God's blessing have my children and mine.
>
> By me, a great offender to God."

As Alison Weir points out,[5] Weston is not confessing to his alleged crimes; he is simply asking his family's forgiveness for the sins he had committed during his lifetime. As I said earlier, Tudor people believed very strongly in the concept of original sin and their sinful natures.

I suspect that after their confessions, the men would have spent time praying to their Father in Heaven, the maker they would be meeting very soon.

17th May 1536 –
The Executions of
5 Men and a Marriage Destroyed

On 17th May 1536, Sir Henry Norris, Sir Francis Weston, Mark Smeaton, Sir William Brereton and George Boleyn, Lord Rochford, were led out of the Tower of London to a scaffold which had been erected on Tower Hill. I cannot imagine how they felt as they surveyed the scene and realised that death was closing in on them. Their only comfort was that their sentences had been commuted to beheading, a much more merciful death than being hanged, drawn and quartered.

Thomas Wyatt, the poet who at that point was himself imprisoned in the Tower of London, wrote a poem about their executions, entitled "In Mourning wise since daily I increase". I have included excerpts of this poem throughout the accounts of the men's executions.

George Boleyn, Lord Rochford

George had fretted the whole time he'd been in the Tower. He wasn't afraid of dying, but he was afraid that his debtors would not be paid and that those who owed him money would end up getting into trouble if they had to pay the King instead. So worked up was George that Sir William Kingston wrote to Cromwell twice, firstly saying "The said Lord desires to speak with you on a matter which touches his conscience"[1] and then reiterating it in a second letter: "You must help my lord of Rochford's conscience".[2] One person George was concerned about was a monk who, with Cromwell's help, George had got promoted. The monk had paid George £100 and owed a further £100, but the Abbey had now been "suppressed". The monk had no way of paying George back and George was worried that the Crown would demand the payment. Kingston begged Cromwell to step in and help George. We do not know if Cromwell ever visited George, but his worries would soon be over.

As the highest in rank, Anne Boleyn's brother, George Boleyn, Lord Rochford, was the first to be executed. This at least spared him the ordeal of watching as his friends and colleagues were killed one by one. Before he knelt at the block, he made a speech, but it is hard to know exactly what he said; there are a few different versions of his final speech.

According to a Spanish record in Letters and Papers:

> "The count (viscount) Rochefort, brother of the queen (unjustly so called) Anne Boleyn, was beheaded with an axe upon a scaffold before the Tower of London. He made a very catholic address to the people, saying he had not come thither to preach, but to serve as a mirror and example, acknowledging his sins against God and the King, and declaring he need not recite the causes why he was condemned, as it could give no pleasure to hear them. He first desired mercy and pardon of God, and afterwards of the King and all others whom he might have offended, and hoped that men would not follow the vanities of the world and the flatteries of the Court, which had brought him to that shameful end. He said if he had followed the teachings of the Gospel, which he had often read, he would not have fallen into this danger, for a good doer was far better than a good reader. In the end, he pardoned those who had condemned him to death, and asked the people to pray for his soul."[3]

The Chronicle of King Henry VIII (The Spanish Chronicle) says:

"Then the Duke turned to the people and said
in the hearing of many "I beg you to pray to God
for me; for by the trial I have to pass through
I am blameless, and never even knew that my
sister was bad. Guiltless as I am, I pray God to
have mercy upon my soul." Then he lay upon the
ground with his head on the block, the headsman
gave three strokes, and so died this poor duke."[4]

The Chronicle of Calais records George Boleyn's execution speech as:

"Christen men, I am borne undar the lawe, and
judged undar the lawe, and dye undar the lawe,
and the lawe hathe condemned me. Mastars all, I
am not come hether for to preche, but for to dye,
for I have deserved for to dye yf I had xx. lyves,
more shamefully than can be devysed, for I am a
wreched synnar, and I have synned shamefully,
I have knowne no man so evell, and to reherse
my synnes openly it were no pleaswre to you to
here them, nor yet for me to reherse them, for
God knowethe all; therefore, mastars all, I pray
yow take hede by me, and especially my lords
and gentlemen of the cowrte, the whiche I have
bene amonge, take hede by me, and beware of
suche a fall, and I pray to God the Fathar, the
Sonne, and the Holy Ghoste, thre persons and
one God, that my deathe may be an example
unto yow all, and beware, trust not in the vanitie
of the worlde, and especially in the flateringe of
the cowrte. And I cry God mercy, and aske all
the worlde forgevenes, as willingly as I wowld
have forgevenes of God ; and yf I have offendyd
any man that is not here now, eythar in thowght,
worde, or dede, and yf ye here any suche, I pray

yow hertely in my behalfe, pray them to forgyve
me for God's sake. And yet, my mastars all, I have
one thinge for to say to yow, men do comon and
saye that I have bene a settar forthe of the worde
of God, and one that have favored the Ghospell
of Christ ; and bycawse I would not that God's
word shuld be slaundered by me, I say unto yow
all, that yf I had followecl God's worde in dede
as I dyd rede it and set it forthe to my power,
I had not come to this. I dyd red the Ghospell
of Christe, but I dyd not follow it; yf I had, I
had bene a lyves man amonge yow : therefore
I pray yow, mastars all, for God's sake sticke to
the trwthe and folowe it, for one good followere
is worthe thre redars, as God knowethe."[5]

The editor of The Chronicle of Calais points out that this
speech is very similar to the one given in the Excerpta Historica,
1831, in a contemporary account by a Portuguese man. In that
sense, therefore, these words are corroborated.

George followed convention by acknowledging that he had
been condemned by the law and confessing that he was a sinner
who deserved death. However, although he the started by saying
that he was not going to preach a sermon, he "spoke the language
of Zion",[6] urging those witnessing his death to "stick to the truth
and follow it", and not make the mistakes that he had. Powerful
words indeed, especially when spoken by a man who believed that
he was justified by faith, even though he may not have had the most
perfect of lives.

George then knelt at the block and was beheaded. I do hope
that the Spanish Chronicle is wrong when it says that three strokes
were required.

"As for them all I do not thus lament,
But as of right my reason doth me bind;
But as the most doth all their deaths repent,

Even so do I by force of mourning mind.
Some say, 'Rochford, haddest thou been not
so proud,
For thy great wit each man would thee bemoan,
Since as it is so, many cry aloud
It is great loss that thou art dead and gone."

Thomas Wyatt

Sir Henry Norris

As the next in rank, Sir Henry Norris followed George Boleyn onto the scaffold. George Constantine, Norris's manservant and a witness of these bloody events, recorded that the others confessed, "all but Mr. Norice, who sayed allmost nothinge at all".[7] I do not think that Constantine means that the men confessed to sleeping with the queen, rather that they had confessed to being sinners, as was usual at executions.

The Spanish Chronicle[8] reported that Sir Henry Norris "made a great long prayer" and declared that he deserved death because he had been ungrateful to the King. He then knelt at the block and was beheaded.

"Ah! Norris, Norris, my tears begin to run
To think what hap did thee so lead or guide
Whereby thou hast both thee and thine undone
That is bewailed in court of every side;
In place also where thou hast never been
Both man and child doth piteously thee moan.
They say, 'Alas, thou art far overseen
By thine offences to be thus deat and gone.'"

Thomas Wyatt

Sir Francis Weston

Sir Francis Weston's family had fought hard for his release. However, even offers of money and the intercession of the French ambassadors, Jean, Sieur de Dinteville (one of the men portrayed in Holbein's The Ambassadors painting), and Antoine de Castelnau, Bishop of Tarbes, could not save him.[9]

Sir Francis Weston was the third of the men to be executed. Before he knelt at the bloody block he warned people to learn by his example, saying:

> "I had thought to have lyved in abhominacion
> yet this twenty or thrittie yeres and
> then to have made amendes. I thought
> little it wold have come to this."[10]

Weston mentions living in "abomination", rather than being just a plain common and garden sinner, and this word has been used by some historians as evidence of homosexuality and illicit sexual acts. It is more likely that Weston is just referring to the fact that he, like everyone, was a sinner and that he had hoped to have had an opportunity to have put things right and to live a better life.

Weston then knelt at the bloodsoaked block and his life was taken.

> "Ah! Weston, Weston, that pleasant was
> and young,
> In active things who might with thee compare?
> All words accept that thou diddest speak with
> tongue,
> So well esteemed with each where thou
> diddest fare.
> And we that now in court doth lead our life
> Most part in mind doth thee lament and moan;
> But that thy faults we daily hear so rife,
> All we should weep that thou are dead and gone."

Thomas Wyatt

Sir William Brereton

Sir William Brereton was the fourth man to climb the scaffold. According to The Spanish Chronicle, he simply said, "I have offended God and the King; pray for me", but other reports have him repeating the phrase:

> "I have deserved to dye if it were a thousande deethes. But the cause wherfore I dye, judge not. But yf ye judge, judge the best."[11]

Was Brereton simply exaggerating in his fear or do his words about deserving a thousand deaths suggest that he had led a criminal life and perhaps been involved in sodomy and illicit sexual acts? I cannot see any evidence for Retha Warnicke's view that all five men were libertines who committed sodomy on a regular basis, but it does appear that Brereton was a bit of a Tudor 'bad boy'. In his "Metrical Visions", George Cavendish, Wolsey's faithful servant and biographer, has Brereton lamenting the malicious streak which led to him causing the execution of John ap Griffith Eyton "by colour of justice".[12]

Norris's servant George Constantine wrote of how Brereton repeated "But if ye judge, judge the best" three or four times. Constantine felt that "If he were gyltie, I say therefore that he dyed worst of them all",[13] meaning that if Brereton had been guilty then he would surely have confessed his guilt and asked God's forgiveness, rather than risking eternal damnation by dying with sins still unconfessed. Eric Ives[14] points out that Brereton's wife, Elizabeth, certainly believed her husband to be innocent. The proof of this is that, at her death in 1545, she bequeathed a bracelet of "gold and Jasyndte stone"[15] to her youngest son, Thomas, describing it as "the last token his father sent me".

> "Brereton farewell, as one that least I knew.
> Great was thy love with divers as I hear,

But common voice doth not so sore thee rue
As other twain that doth before appear;
But yet no doubt but they friends thee lament
And other hear their piteous cry and moan.
So doth each heart for thee likewise relent
That thou givest cause thus to be dead and gone."

Thomas Wyatt

Mark Smeaton

Mark Smeaton was the final man to be executed. How awful it must have been to stand by as the four men died such violent deaths in front of him, knowing that he himself had only minutes to live. He was lucky, however. As a man of lower class he could have ended his life in a much more brutal way by being hanged, drawn and quartered. The axe was preferable.

According to George Constantine, Smeaton addressed the crowd, saying:

"Masters I pray you all praye for me,
for I have deserved the deeth"[16]

and then he was beheaded. He did not take the opportunity to retract his confession and when Anne Boleyn heard of this she said, "Did he not exonerate me... before he died, of the public infamy he laid on me? Alas! I fear his soul will suffer for it."[17]

"Ah! Mark, what moan should I for thee
make more,
Since that thy death thou hast deserved best,
Save only that mine eye is forced sore
With piteous plaint to moan thee with the rest?
A time thou haddest above thy poor degree,
The fall whereof thy friends may well bemoan:
A rotten twig upon so high a tree
Hath slipped thy hold, and thou art dead

and gone.
And thus farewell each one in hearty wise!"

Thomas Wyatt

Burials

Because they were commoners, Sir Henry Norris, Mark Smeaton, Sir William Brereton and Sir Francis Weston were buried in the churchyard of the Chapel of St Peter ad Vincula. George Boleyn's head and body were taken inside the Chapel, however, and interred in the chancel area before the high altar. Just two days later, his sister's head and body would be joining him.

"And thus farewell each one in hearty wise!
The axe is home, your heads be in the street;
The trickling tears doth fall so from my eyes
I scarce may write, my paper is so wet.
But what can hope when death hath played
his part,
Though nature's course will thus lament
and moan?
Leave sobs therefore, and every Christian heart
Pray for the souls of those be dead and gone."

Thomas Wyatt

Was Anne Boleyn a Witness?

The men were executed on Tower Hill, outside the confines of the Tower of London, so it would have been impossible for Anne to witness their harrowing deaths from her lodgings in the royal palace. However, Gareth Russell[18] points out that Anne may have asked Sir William Kingston to move her to either the Byward Tower or Bell Tower so that she could witness her brother's last moments. In his report to the Emperor, Chapuys, the imperial ambassador, recorded Anne witnessing the executions: "the Concubine saw them executed from the Tower, to aggravate her grief".[19]

A Marriage Destroyed

Also on 17th May 1536, at Lambeth, Archbishop Thomas Cranmer, in the presence of Sir Thomas Audley, the Duke of Suffolk, the Earl of Oxford and others, declared that the marriage between Henry VIII and Anne Boleyn was null and void.[20] This sentence of "nullity" meant that it was as if the marriage had never happened and automatically rendered the couple's daughter, Elizabeth, illegitimate. The King could now forget the woman waiting for her death in the Tower and move on with his life and marry again.

We do not know the grounds for the annulment. The Archbishop simply said that it was "in consequence of certain just and lawful impediments which, it was said, were unknown at the time of the union, but had lately been confessed to the Archbishop by the lady herself."[21] Charles Wriothesley[22] took this to mean that the Queen confessed to a pre-contract with Henry Percy, Earl of Northumberland. However, the Imperial ambassador, Eustace Chapuys, believed that "the said Archbishop had pronounced the marriage of the King and Concubine invalid on account of the King having had connection with her sister, and that, as both parties knew of this, the good faith of the parents cannot make the said bastard legitimate."[23] Thus, the impediment referred to here was that of consanguinity. In other words, the marriage was deemed incestuous because the King had had a previous sexual relationship with Anne Boleyn's sister, Mary Boleyn.

18th May 1536 – Anne Prepares

On the night of 17th May 1536, while the carpenters built her scaffold within the grounds of the Tower of London, Anne Boleyn prepared herself for her execution, which was scheduled for 9am on the 18th. At 2am, her almoner, John Skip (some say her confessor Father Thirwell[1]), arrived to pray with her. She was still in prayer when Archbishop Cranmer arrived just after dawn to hear her final confession and to celebrate the Mass.

Anne Boleyn thought she would be dying in just a few hours, so she wanted the Sacrament. She asked for Sir William Kingston, the Constable of the Tower, to be present and he agreed. As Anne took the sacrament she swore on it twice, before and after receiving the body of Christ. She solemnly swore that she had not been unfaithful to the King, as Chapuys reported in a letter to Charles V:

> "The lady who had charge of her has sent to tell
> me in great secresy that the Concubine, before
> and after receiving the sacrament, affirmed
> to her, on the damnation of her soul, that she
> had never been unfaithful to the King."[2]

Anne obviously wanted Kingston to pass this information on to Thomas Cromwell and he did:

> "for this mornynge she sent for me that I myght
> be with hyr at [such time] as she reysayved the
> gud Lord, to the intent I shuld here hy[r] s[peak
> as] towchyng hyr innosensy alway to be clere."[3]

It changed nothing. Anne could have sworn her innocence until she was blue in the face but the swordsman of Calais was on his way, the scaffold was being erected and her marriage had been annulled. Anne had been abandoned by Henry VIII and she was to suffer death.

Anne then made arrangements for the customary distribution

of alms using the £20 given to her by the King for this purpose, and then she waited for 9am, the moment she thought she would take her final walk. She went back to her prayers.

When nothing happened at 9am, Anne sent for Kingston. She had heard that her execution had been postponed until noon:

> "Mr. Kyngston, I h[ear say I shall] not dy affore
> none, and I am very sory therfore, for I thowt[h
> to] be dede [by this time], and past my payne."

Kingston knew full well that Anne was not being executed that day as he had received orders from Cromwell to clear the Tower of foreigners first, perhaps so that foreign diplomats could not send home sympathetic reports of Anne execution. Kingston kept Anne in the dark for a while longer and tried to comfort her by explaining that her execution would not be painful and that the blow was "so subtle". To this, Anne replied with characteristic black humour, "I heard say the executioner was very good, and I have a little neck", after which she put her hands around her throat and laughed heartily.[4] Kingston was impressed with Anne Boleyn's composure, commenting to Cromwell that "thys lady hasse mech joy and plesure in dethe"[5] and writing of how her almoner was with her continually.

Anne's black humour in those dark hours showed through as she joked with her ladies that the people would be able to give her the nickname "la Royne Anne Sans Tete"[6] or Queen Anne Lackhead, and then she laughed. Regardless, those hours of waiting and not knowing what was going on must have been pure hell for Anne, who had prepared herself to die that day.

She was finally put out of her misery when noon passed and Kingston informed her that her execution had been postponed until the next day, the 19th. According to Chapuys, "when the command came to put off the execution till today [19th], Anne appeared very sorry, praying the Captain of the Tower that for the honor of God he would beg the King that, since she was in good state and disposed for death, she might be dispatched immediately".[7] Lanceleot de Carles has her adding that it was "not that she desired death, but thought herself prepared to die and feared that delay would weaken her". De Carles writes of how she then "consoled her ladies several times, telling them that was not a thing to be regretted by Christians, and she hoped to be quit of all unhappiness, with various other good counsels."[8]

There was nothing that Sir William Kingston could do to ease Anne's suffering; all Anne could do was return to prayer and wait.

Catherine's Tomb

Elsewhere on 18th May 1536, it was reported to Cromwell by a Frenchman that the wax tapers set around Catherine of Aragon's tomb in Peterborough Abbey "had been lighted of their own accord".[9] Spooky!

19th May 1536 –
The Execution of
Queen Anne Boleyn

At dawn on 19th May 1536, Queen Anne Boleyn celebrated the Mass for the last time, receiving the Sacrament from her almoner, John Skip. She then ate breakfast and waited to hear Sir William Kingston's footsteps outside her door. At 8am, the Constable appeared, informing Anne that the hour of her death was near and that she should get herself ready. But Anne was already prepared. She had taken special care with her outfit – the ermine trim symbolised royalty and crimson, the colour of her kirtle, was associated with martyrdom. Her hood was the traditional English gable hood, rather than her usual stylish French hood.

Anne left the sumptuous royal palace for the last time, walking past the Great Hall, through Cole Harbour Gate and along the western side of the White Tower. There, ahead of her, was the newly erected black-draped scaffold.[1] Kingston helped his prisoner up the scaffold steps and Anne stepped forward to address the crowd. The crowd fell silent as they gazed at their queen, a woman "with an untroubled countenance".[2] Anne then delivered her final speech:

> "Good Christian people, I have not come here
> to preach a sermon; I have come here to die.
> For according to the law and by the law I am
> judged to die, and therefore I will speak nothing
> against it. I am come hither to accuse no man,
> nor to speak of that whereof I am accused and
> condemned to die, but I pray God save the
> King and send him long to reign over you, for
> a gentler nor a more merciful prince was there
> never, and to me he was ever a good, a gentle, and

sovereign lord. And if any person will meddle of
my cause, I require them to judge the best. And
thus I take my leave of the world and of you all,
and I heartily desire you all to pray for me."

(The speech is corroborated by Edward Hall, George Wyatt,
John Foxe and Lord Herbert of Cherbury)

Unlike her brother, Anne did not protest her innocence and
preach to the crowd; she simply did what was expected of her.
Executions were carefully choreographed, with a set format for
execution speeches which Anne followed to to the letter. There
was no way that she would risk her daughter's safety by defying
the King and proclaiming her innocence. Elizabeth's safety and her
future relationship with her father, the King, were paramount in
Anne's mind as she prepared to meet her Maker.

Anne paid the "distressed"[3] executioner who asked Anne's
forgiveness. Her ladies then removed Anne's mantle and Anne
lifted off her gable hood. "A young lady presented her with a linen
cap, with which she covered her hair, and she knelt down, fastening
her clothes about her feet, and one of the said ladies bandaged her
eyes."[4] The crowd, who would have been well used to executions by
this time, were moved by the Queen's plight, many of them crying.[5]
As Anne sank to her knees in readiness, the crowd too sank to its
knees, following the example of Sir John Aleyn, the Lord Mayor.
Only Charles Brandon, Duke of Suffolk, and Henry Fitzroy, Duke
of Richmond, remained on their feet.[6]

As Anne waited for the executioner to strike, she started
praying, "O Lord have mercy on me, to God I commend my soul.
To Jesus Christ I commend my soul; Lord Jesu receive my soul."
Eric Ives[7] writes that her only show of fear was the way that she kept
looking behind her to check that the executioner was not going to
strike the fatal blow too soon. As Anne prayed, the executioner
called out to his assistant to pass him his sword. As Anne moved
her head to follow what the assistant was doing, the executioner
came up unnoticed behind her and beheaded her with one stroke

of his sword. It was over.

As the shocked crowd dispersed, Anne's ladies, who were described as "bereft of their souls, such was their weakness",[8] wrapped her head and body in white cloth and took them to the Chapel of St Peter ad Vincula for burial. No casket had been provided, so a yeoman warder fetched an old elm chest which had once contained bow staves from the Tower armoury.[9] Anne Boleyn, Queen of England and mother of Elizabeth I, was then buried as a traitor in an unmarked grave. The Tower cannons fired to tell London that its Queen was dead.

Sir William Kingston was paid £100 by the Crown for Anne Boleyn's "jewels and apparel"[10] and that was that. One queen was dead and another was about to take her place. Sir Francis Bryan took the news of Anne's death to her replacement, Jane Seymour; who knows what she thought of the bloody events of the past few days?

Scottish theologian Alexander Alesius had woken up in the early hours of 19th May from a nightmare about the Queen's severed neck in which he "could count the nerves, the veins, and the arteries". He went to visit his friend Archbishop Cranmer in his garden at Lambeth. Alesius was unaware of Anne's imminent execution, having remained at home since the day of Anne's imprisonment, but as he told the Archbishop of his dream, Cranmer "raised his eyes to heaven and said, 'She who has been the Queen of England upon earth will to-day become a Queen in heaven.' So great was his grief that he could say nothing more, and then he burst into tears."[11] The Archbishop who owed his rise to the patronage of the Queen and her family was a broken man, and perhaps he felt some guilt for his part in recent events. It is hard to imagine how he would have felt on hearing the cannons ring out over London, announcing the Queen's death.

Queen Anne Boleyn was gone, gone to a better place.

Anne Boleyn's Resting Place

Anne Boleyn's remains lay in peace in the Chapel of St Peter ad Vincula until 1876 when much-needed restoration work was carried out on the chapel. During the work, it was found that the pavement of the chancel area, where Anne Boleyn, Catherine Howard and Lady Jane Grey were buried, was sinking. It was decided that proper foundations were needed so the chancel area was dug up and the remains exhumed.

In the area where Anne Boleyn was recorded to have been buried, the bones of a female were found at a depth of about two feet. The remains were examined by Dr Mouat who confirmed that they belonged to "a female of between twenty-five and thirty years of age, of a delicate frame of body, and who had been of slender and perfect proportions". He went on to say that "the forehead and lower jaw were small and especially well formed. The vertebrae were particularly small, especially one joint (the atlas), which was that next to the skull, and they bore witness to the Queen's 'lyttel neck'."[1] Although the bones were mixed up, they had been heaped together in a small space and there were no further female remains at that spot. Dr Mouat's memorandum said of Anne Boleyn's remains:

"The bones found in the place where Queen Anne Boleyn is said to have been buried are certainly those of a female in the prime of life, all perfectly consolidated and symmetrical, and belong to the same person.

"The bones of the head indicate a well-formed round skull, with an intellectual forehead, straight orbital ridge, large eyes, oval face and rather square full chin. The remains of the vertebrae, and the bones of the lower limbs, indicate a well-formed woman of middle height, with a short and slender neck. The ribs show depth and roundness of chest. The hands and feet bones indicate delicate and well-shaped hands and feet, with tapering fingers and a narrow foot."[2]

He noted that she had been around 5' to 5'3 inches in height. Both hands were entirely normal and no extra finger was found.

After the work had been completed, the remains found in the chancel area were "soldered up in thick leaden coffers, and then fastened down with copper screws in boxes made of oak plank, one inch in thickness. Each box bore a leaden escutcheon, on which was engraved the name of the person whose supposed remains were thus enclosed, together with the dates of death, and of the year (1877) of the reinterment. They were then placed in the respective positions in the chancel in which the remains had been found, and the ground having been opened, they were all buried about four inches below the surface, the earth was then filled in, and concrete immediately spread over them".[3] Algernon Bertram Freeman-Mitford, Lord Redesdale,[4] recorded how a plan of the burials was deposited amongst the Tower of London records and a "solemn ceremony" was carried out, presided over by the chaplain, the Reverend E. Jordan Roberts. Beautiful memorial tiles were used to mark the resting places of those buried in the chancel and these can still be seen today, although a rope cordons off the chancel area and some tiles lie underneath the altar table. As you look at the altar, Anne Boleyn's tile is to the left of the table.

The royal palace where Anne Boleyn was imprisoned, and the Great Hall in which she was tried, no longer exist, having been demolished by the end of the 18th century. However, the Queen's lodgings stood between the Lanthorn Tower and the Wardrobe Tower, on the South Lawn behind the White Tower. The half-timbered Queen's House which overlooks Tower Green is not where Anne was imprisoned; these apartments were not built until after Anne's death. The men, however, were imprisoned in other parts of the Tower and there are two carvings in the stone which are thought to have been made by the prisoner in 1536 – one of a rose with what looks like a letter "H" and the name "Boullan" in the Martin Tower, and Anne's falcon badge in the Beauchamp Tower. Tellingly, the falcon is missing its crown and scepter; it is no royal bird.

I find it moving to make a 'pilgrimage' to Anne's resting place on 19th May. Every year, a basket of red roses is delivered to the Tower with instructions to lay it on Anne Boleyn's memorial tile. The card always has the same message: "Queen Anne Boleyn, 19th May 1536". According to a Sunday Telegraph article,[5] a former director-general of the Tower of London, Major General Chris Tyler, tracked down the roses to a florist local to the Tower who had been receiving an annual order for the roses since the 1850s with instructions to keep the sender's details private. In recent years, the order had been handled by the same florist company, but at a branch in Kent. Major Tyler was apparently able to track down Boleyn family descendants who admitted to sending the roses. It appears that the sending of the roses was part of a bequest and that there is enough money to send the roses for many more years. It is a beautiful tradition and one which the Yeoman Warders take very seriously.

For me, though, Anne isn't at the Tower; she's at Hever Castle, her family home. That is where I like to go to pay my respects to her and George, in the place where they grew up. Although Lord Astor renovated it in the early 20th century, adding a whole wing (the 'Tudor village'), creating the gardens and lake, the castle, or rather Tudor manor house, is still the structure Anne would have known. I feel close to her when I gaze at her Book of Hours and stand in the castle courtyard. This is the place Anne played with her siblings, where she spent time with her parents, where she retreated to get away from Henry's advances and where she fought off the deadly sweating sickness. This was her home.

20th May 1536 –
The Betrothal of
Henry VIII and Jane Seymour

On 20th May 1536, Eustace Chapuys, the Imperial Ambassador, wrote to Seigneur de Granvelle informing him of the latest developments in London:

> "Has just been informed, the bearer of this having already mounted, that Mrs. Semel [Seymour] came secretly by river this morning to the King's lodging, and that the promise and betrothal (desponsacion) was made at 9 o'clock. The King means it to be kept secret till Whitsuntide; but everybody begins already to murmur by suspicion, and several affirm that long before the death of the other there was some arrangement which sounds ill in the ears of the people; who will certainly be displeased at what has been told me, if it be true, viz., that yesterday the King, immediately on receiving news of the decapitation of the putain entered his barge and went to the said Semel, whom he has lodged a mile from him, in a house by the river."[1]

From this one letter we know that as soon as the King heard that Anne Boleyn was dead he was on his way to see his new love and that at 9am on 20th May, just one day after the execution of his previous wife, Henry VIII and Jane Seymour became officially betrothed. Talk about moving fast! Chapuys also makes the point that there was gossip about the King's relationship with Jane long before Anne's death, which, although Anne was not the most popular of people, caused ill feeling and sympathy for Anne's plight.

I suspect that Henry VIII saw nothing wrong with his actions as, after all, he was acting in the best interest of his country by providing England with a new Queen to give him a son and heir. What did it matter that he was planning a wedding while his current wife was in the Tower condemned to die? Henry had probably convinced himself that his marriage to Anne Boleyn was as cursed as his marriage to Catherine of Aragon had been, and that he was doing the world a favour by getting rid of Anne. Henry could move on to a new love and a new life, but Anne had been denied that chance. It is no wonder that Henry neglected his daughter Elizabeth for a time. How could he look into those dark eyes and not think of the woman he had fought so hard to possess but had ended up killing?

30th May 1536 –
Henry VIII Marries Jane Seymour

On Tuesday 30th May, just eleven days after the execution of his second wife, Anne Boleyn, Henry VIII married Jane Seymour in the Queen's Closet at York Place, the property renovated by himself and Anne.

The King and Jane Seymour had become betrothed on 20th May, a day after Anne's execution, but did not marry immediately because the speed of their relationship sounded "ill in the ears of his people".[1] As if an extra ten days made any difference!

David Starkey[2] writes that Jane was probably kept in seclusion at Chelsea between the betrothal and her wedding day, after which she took her place at the King's side as Queen. Sir John Russell wrote to Lord Lisle:

> "On Friday last [2nd June] the Queen sat
> abroad as Queen, and was served by her own
> servants, who were sworn that same day. The
> King came in his great boat to Greenwich
> that day with his privy chamber, and the
> Queen and the ladies in the great barge."[3]

The chronicler, Charles Wriothesley, writes that, on 4th June, Whitsunday, "the said Jane Seymor was proclaymed Queene at Greenewych, and went in procession, after the King, with a great traine of ladies followinge after her, and also ofred at masse as Queen, and began her howsehold that daie, dyning in her chamber of presence under the cloath of estate."[4]

Jane Seymour was now Queen of England. She had had an easier start than her predecessor, Anne Boleyn, who had waited seven years to be Queen. Jane's wait had been just a few weeks and her predecessor was dead, having first been labelled a traitor and whore.

"Whereas the crowned, the most happy falcon was no more, a Phoenix was rising."[5]

The Reaction

Although Cromwell's propaganda machine had been working flat out, spreading the salacious and shocking news that the King of England had been saved from a conspiracy instigated by his own wife and Queen, there were those who were cynical and could not quite believe the official line.

Etienne Dolet, the French scholar, printer, and Reformer, published an epigram, "Reginae Utopiae falso adulterii crimine damnatae, et capite mulctatae Epitaphium" ("Queen of Utopia condemned on a false charge of adultery, and deprived of an epitaph"). He knew of Anne through his friend, Nicholas Bourbon, a French Reformer, poet and scholar, who had been rescued by Anne in 1534 after he had got into trouble in France for his work, "Nugae". Bourbon's release from prison was down to Anne's influence over her husband, Henry VIII, and once Bourbon was in England she appointed him as tutor to her ward and nephew, Henry Carey. It is likely that it was Bourbon who told Dolet of the events of 1536 and that he knew Anne to be innocent of all of the charges.

The imperial ambassador, Eustace Chapuys, in reporting the trials to Charles V, wrote that the men "were condemned upon presumption and certain indications, without valid proof or confession", that George Boleyn was charged "by presumption" and that "those present wagered 10 to 1 that he would be acquitted, especially as no witnesses were produced against either him or her".[1] He also reported that "there are some who murmur at the mode of procedure against her and the others". Therefore, there were definitely those who thought that Anne and the men were framed due to the King's relationship with Jane Seymour.

Mary of Hungary, Emperor Charles V's sister, who knew Anne Boleyn from their time together at the court of Margaret of Austria, wrote that "As none but the organist confessed, nor herself either, people think he invented this device to get rid of her" and added, insightfully, that "when he is tired of this one he will find some occasion of getting rid of her."[2] So she too was cynical and thought that Anne's condemnation was more to do with the King wanting rid of her than any actual guilt.

George Constantine, Sir Henry Norris's servant, commented that "few men would believe that she was so abominable" and that he had "never suspected". He also said that "there was much muttering at the Queen's death".[3] George Wyatt, Sir Thomas Wyatt's grandson, writing in Elizabeth I's reign, commented on how those "abroad" found Anne "guiltless"[4] and that he, himself, believed the charges of incest and adultery to be "incredible" and "partly by the circumstances impossible", since Anne was always surrounded by her ladies.[5] Martyrologist, John Foxe, also writing in Elizabeth I's reign, blamed "crafty setters-on"[6] for poisoning the King's mind and turning him against his wife.

As for Henry VIII, he simply moved on with his life, marrying Jane Seymour. Whenever the latter dared to ask him for something he warned her to learn from the example of Anne Boleyn. This was reported by the diplomat Jean du Bellay:

> "At the beginning of the insurrection the Queen
> threw herself on her knees before the King and
> begged him to restore the abbeys, but he told
> her, prudently enough, to get up, and he had
> often told her not to meddle with his affairs,
> referring to the late Queen, which was enough
> to frighten a woman who is not very secure."[7]

So, according to Henry VIII, the Queen had come to a sticky end from 'meddling' rather than being guilty of treason! As Eric Ives[8] points out, Henry VIII also admitted years later that once a prisoner was in the Tower of London then false evidence could be used against him. Ralph Morice, secretary of Archbishop Cranmer, recorded the following warning issued by the King to Cranmer in 1546 when the conservatives targeted him and tried to bring him down:

"Oh Lorde God ! (quod the king) what fonde
symplicitie have you : so to permitt yourself
to be ymprisoned, that every enemy of yours
may take vantage againste you. Doo not you
thincke that yf thei have you ones in prison, iij
or iiij false knaves wilbe sone procured to witnes
againste you and to condempne you, whiche
els now being at your libertie dare not ones
open thair lipps or appere before your face."[9]

I find it rather telling that Henry VIII knew that it was 'the
done thing' to procure false witnesses to condemn a prisoner!

A Foregone Conclusion

I am convinced that the removal of Anne Boleyn from her position as Queen by execution was a foregone conclusion and that Anne never stood a chance of clearing her name and escaping death. There was shock at the allegations against Anne Boleyn and the five men, as shown in a letter from Rowland Lee, Bishop of Coventry and Lichfield, written on the 7th May 1536, acknowledging receipt of letters from the Privy Council:-

> "As the news in this letter is very doleful to
> this Council and all the liege people of this
> realm, God forbid it should be true."[1]

But records of another letter written on the same day by Sir Henry Wyatt to his son Thomas Wyatt, who was a prisoner in the Tower, show how Anne's guilt was generally accepted:

> "Considers himself most unfortunate that he
> cannot go nor ride without danger to his life,
> or do his duty to the King in this dangerous
> time that his Grace has suffered by false
> traitors. Desires his son to give the King due
> attendance night and day. "I pray to God
> give him grace long to be with him and about
> him that hath found out this matter, which
> hath been given him of God, and the false
> traitors to be punished according to justice to
> the example of others." Alington, 7 May."[2]

Henry Wyatt believed in his son's innocence but seemed convinced of the guilt of "the false traitors", namely Anne Boleyn, Sir Henry Norris, Sir Francis Weston, Sir William Brereton, Mark Smeaton and Anne's brother, George Boleyn. The fact that Sir Henry believed in his son and did not believe in the innocence of the others implies that their guilt was generally accepted by

people. If Cromwell's motives in arresting Sir Thomas Wyatt and
Sir Richard Page, and in questioning Sir Francis Bryan had been to
make people believe that he was investigating the case thoroughly,
then his plan had worked.

Shall I Die Without Justice

On entering the Tower of London on 2nd May 1536, Anne
Boleyn had asked Sir William Kingston, the Constable of the
Tower, "shall I die with]yowt justes?"[3] ("shall I die without justice?")
and although Sir William Kingston replied that "the porest sugett
the Ky[ng hath, hath justice"[4] (the poorest of the King's subjects
has justice), Anne's laugh at his statement shows that she did not
believe him. Just as I am convinced that Anne's conviction and
execution were foregone conclusions, I also think that she was
intelligent enough to realise this, even at that early stage.

Why do I think that it was all a foregone conclusion?

The Commissions of Oyer and Terminer

Two commissions of oyer and terminer were set up on 24th
April 1536 by Cromwell and Audley to cover criminal offences in
the counties of Kent and Middlesex, the two counties which were
the locations of the alleged criminal offences committed by Anne
Boleyn and the five men in the indictments. Coincidence? I think
not, particularly when you consider how rarely these commissions
were used.

Parliament

On 27th April 1536 writs were issued summoning Parliament
and a letter was sent to the Archbishop of Canterbury asking him
to attend Parliament. This was followed up on 7th May 1536 by
letters being sent out to every sheriff in England explaining that:
"since the dissolution of the late Parliament matters of high
importance have chanced, which render it necessary to discuss the
establishment of the succession in a Parliament assembled for that

purpose. Writs have been already sent, which the King doubts not he will execute. Desires him to declare to the people that the calling of a Parliament is so necessary, both for the treating of matters tending to their weal and the surety of our person, that they will have cause to think their charge and time, which will be very little and short, well spent. Desires him to take care that persons are elected who will serve, and for their worship and qualities be most meet for this purpose." Westm., 7 May. Signed with a stamp.[5] The fact that the succession is mentioned suggests that there was going to be some change in the succession.

The Dates on the Indictments

If you have read the sections on the Middlesex and Kent indictments, you will know that the dates just don't make sense. In the majority of cases Anne or the man named just were not present at that palace. Although historian G W Bernard[6] argues that the dates were probably just guesswork by the lawyers, because witnesses could not be expected to remember specific dates of events, I am of the opinion that the sloppiness of these indictments shows that the guilt of Anne Boleyn, Smeaton, Norris, Brereton, Weston and Rochford was a foregone conclusion. Dates did not matter. If the prosecution wanted to present a cast iron case against Anne in a fair and just court then they would have been more careful in picking the dates and at least avoided dates upon which Anne was recovering from childbirth or when she was with the King! Anne was deemed guilty before she ever set foot in that Tower or court room.

Henry VIII's behaviour

Chapuys wrote that "the King has shown himself more glad than ever since the arrest of the Concubine, for he has been going about banqueting with ladies, sometimes remaining after midnight, and returning by the river".[7] His merrymaking at such a time is rather tasteless and wouldn't the cuckolded husband be distraught at the love of his life betraying him? No, not if it wasn't true and if he had conspired against her. Being seen to be consorting with other women at this time, rather than being in the company of his mistress Jane Seymour, may well have been a tactic on Henry's part. He may have been distancing himself from Jane Seymour so that he didn't look like the baddie, the man who was getting rid of one wife for a new model. Jane Seymour was actually given lodgings within a mile of the King's residence so that they could see each other easily.

Chapuys' letter to Charles V

Chapuys wrote to Charles V on the 19th May: "I hear that, even before the arrest of the Concubine, the King, speaking with Mistress Jane Semel[Seymour] of their future marriage, the latter suggested that the Princess should be replaced in her former position".[8] So Henry had mentioned marriage to Jane Seymour before Anne was even arrested on 2nd May! Court gossip perhaps but it's interesting nonetheless.

Henry's Prediction

The fact that Henry VIII was able to tell Jane Seymour on the morning of Anne's trial that she would be condemned by three o'clock that afternoon.[9]

The Sword of Calais

Anne's executioner was a French swordsman from Calais[1011] and for him to get to London by 18th or 19th May he would have to have been ordered before Anne's trial had even taken place.

The Break-up of Anne's Household

Anne Boleyn's household was broken up on 13th May, before her trial. Why break up her household if she could still be found innocent?

The Speed of Events

Less than a month after the commissions of oyer and terminer were set up the Queen was dead. The King had a new wife just 11 days after Anne's death. Could thorough investigations really be carried out in such a short time? The Catherine Howard affair blew up in November 1541, yet Catherine was not executed until 13th February 1542. So how and why did events move so fast in Anne's case?

Even though Anne Boleyn was tried in front of a jury of her peers, she did not receive justice in any true sense of the word. While she was in court fighting for her life, the Sword of Calais was on his way to do his job and execute her, and Archbishop Cranmer was organising the annulment of her marriage to the King. Anne Boleyn's guilt and her death were foregone conclusions as far as Cromwell, the King and the jury were concerned.

Who was Responsible for
the Fall of Anne Boleyn?

I have been researching Anne Boleyn full-time for over three years now and this is still a question that gnaws at me, that keeps me awake at night and that quite literally drives me to distraction.

Through researching the primary sources I am confident that Anne Boleyn was innocent of the charges laid against her and that she died the victim of an awful miscarriage of justice, a victim of a brutal conspiracy. But who's to blame? Henry VIII? Thomas Cromwell? Jane Seymour? The Catholic conservatives? It just is not clear from the primary sources, and historians still argue over it today, all backing up their theories with solid evidence. It is frustrating and I don't believe it is something that we will ever have a definite answer to. All we can do is look at the primary sources, consider the arguments of the various Tudor experts and then come to our own conclusions.

On one side of the fence, we have historians such as Eric Ives and Alison Weir arguing that Thomas Cromwell was the instigator of the plot against Anne Boleyn and that he manipulated Henry VIII into believing that Anne was guilty. When I questioned, or rather grilled, Eric Ives on this subject last year, he commented that dominant men like Henry are often very malleable. So perhaps Cromwell simply preyed on the King's already paranoid and suspicious nature to make him believe that it was possible that Anne had betrayed him in some way. When Smeaton confessed, it appeared that Henry VIII's suspicions had been proved true. Once the legal wheels were in motion, it would have been very difficult for Henry to have stopped it without looking foolish. Everything happened so quickly. In her book "The Lady in the Tower", Alison Weir goes as far as to paint Henry VIII as a victim of the coup, alongside Anne, the men and the little Elizabeth.[1]

On the other side of the fence, we have historians like Derek

Wilson and John Schofield who see Henry VIII as the prime mover in the events of 1536. Wilson writes of the illegal and "extremely cumbersome" means used in Anne's fall, which included extending the treason law in a rather "unwarranted" manner.[2] Wilson concludes that Cromwell would only have gone ahead with such a complicated plot because it was the King's will. Schofield agrees, painting Cromwell as Henry's loyal servant who had a duty to obey his King and to do his wishes.

I respect all of the historians concerned, and Ives, Wilson and Schofield are incredibly good at backing up their arguments with primary sources. When I read Ives, it seems natural to believe that it was all down to Cromwell, and then Schofield has me thinking that it was all down to Henry! The problem is that sources can be interpreted in different ways and even the people there at the time didn't seem to have known who was responsible, so how can we today? It's a conundrum and I don't believe that we can say anyone is right or wrong in their views.

Suspect 1 – Thomas Cromwell

Those who believe that Thomas Cromwell was the one ultimately responsible for Anne Boleyn's fall cite the following reasons:

Cromwell and Anne Disagreeing over the Dissolution of the Monasteries

In his book "The Religious Orders in England: Volume 3", David Knowles writes that Cromwell had decided how to act against the monasteries because he had been advised that "This good law duly put in execution would bring back to the Crown lands worth 40,000l. a year."[3] This law, which Knowles explains was nothing new, was "not comprehensive enough" for Cromwell, His remembrances of February 1536 record "The abomination of religious persons throughout this realm, and a reformation to [be] devised therein".[4] He then went on to draft a bill which was presented before the Commons for debate on 11th March. He also released the Compendium Compertorum (Comperta), the reports of his commissioners, who had visited monasteries throughout the land in 1535 and early 1536 and found corruption, superstition and immorality. He hoped that these reports would enable him to get backing for his proposed reforms. Eric Ives[5] quotes Hugh Latimer's recollection of the response to the commissioners' report, from a sermon preached before King Edward VI in 1549. Latimer said that "when their enormities were first read in the Parliament-house, they were so great and abominable, that there was nothing but "down with them"."[6]

As historian R W Hoyle points out, the suppression statute which resulted from the debates in Parliament "touched the smaller monasteries only", portraying them as houses that were ill-managed and full of immorality.[7] These houses were to be dissolved, their members transferred to larger monasteries and their lands given to the King. Were the smaller monasteries the only ones that were corrupt? Of course not, so the Act of Suppression may have been more about funds than reform.

Anne Boleyn's almoner, John Skip, preached a sermon on Passion Sunday, 2nd April 1536, in which he claimed that "men" were rebuking the clergy "because they would have from the clergy their possessions." This was surely a reference to the reforms which Cromwell was pushing through Parliament. Skip went on to refer to the story of Esther, wife of King Ahasuerus. The King was deceived into ordering a massacre of his Jewish subjects by his adviser, Haman. Hower, "a good woman" whom the King loved and trusted, i.e. Esther, gave him different advice, stopped the massacre, and saved the Jews. Haman was hanged as a result. This sermon, which must have had Anne Boleyn's approval, was an attack on Cromwell and the advice he was giving the King. Anne was all for reforming the monasteries but only where needed. Moreover, she believed that the money should be used for educational and charitable causes. Skip referred to this, talking about "the great decay of the universities in this realm and how necessary the maintenance of them is for the continuance of Christ's faith and his religion."[8]

But Anne and Skip were not the only ones to disagree with Cromwell's plans for the monasteries. Reformers and humanists Robert Barnes and Thomas Starkey also wanted the money put to better use, yet Cromwell did not bring them down. John Skip also survived Anne's fall. Schofield[9] also points out that Cromwell was also working on a new act for poor relief, so he too was concerned with charity. It can also be said that Skip's attack may have been aimed at the King's council, not just Cromwell. When Skip was interrogated about his sermon the Esther-Haman reference was not mentioned.[10]

Anne Boleyn Had Threatened Cromwell

Eustace Chapuys, the imperial ambassador, recorded on the 5th June 1535 something Cromwell told him, "the Lady [Anne] telling him, among other things, that she would like to see his head off his shoulders."[11] Cromwell had seen Cardinal Wolsey fall, partly as a result of Anne Boleyn's influence over the King, so some historians argue that Cromwell needed to get rid of Anne before she could bring him down.

However, historians such as John Schofield, point out that Anne's threat was made back in 1535 and that Cromwell had shrugged it off, saying " I trust so much on my master, that I fancy she cannot do me any harm".[12] Chapuys was also sceptical, wondering if the threat was actually " an invention of Cromwell". We also know that Anne lashed out at people and said things in anger. For example, she said that she would "bring down the pride of this unbridled Spanish blood",[13] in reference to Mary, and that "she wished all the Spaniards in the world were in the sea".[14] These were empty threats borne out of frustration. Furthermore, Cromwell had no need to bring Anne down when he could just wait for the Conservatives and Henry VIII to do it for him. By spring 1536, Anne was losing her influence over the King anyway and wasn't so much of a threat as she had been in Wolsey's time.

Cromwell Took Responsibility for Anne's Fall

Cromwell boasted that he was responsible for the coup against the Boleyns. In a letter to the Emperor dated 6th June 1536, Chapuys related a conversation he had had with Cromwell in which Cromwell had said that "it was he who, in consequence of the disappointment and anger he had felt on hearing the King's answer to me on the third day of Easter, had planned and brought about the whole affair."[15] Chapuys credited Cromwell's claim about being responsible for the plot; he was an experienced ambassador who had had many dealings with Cromwell. He did not doubt that Cromwell was to blame.

However, John Schofield points out that in the part of the sentence before Cromwell said that "he had planned and brought about the whole affair, he also said that he had been "authorised and commissioned by the king to prosecute and bring to an end the mistress's trial".[16] Cromwell's plotting was due to orders from Henry and not of his own volition. Greg Walker puts forward the argument that Cromwell simply investigated the allegations made against Anne, rather than being the one to initiate them.[17] Cromwell reacted to events rather than causing them, but may have wished to come across as "a clever Machiavell" to Chapuys, rather than a minister who had not spotted the Queen's immoral behaviour.

Two Birds With One Stone

As well as Anne, who had become a thorn in his side regarding foreign policy, Cromwell wanted to remove powerful and influential men who were affecting his own standing with the King. Sir Henry Norris was one of the King's closest friends and, as Groom of the Stool, had considerable influence over the King, and Sir William Brereton was causing problems for Cromwell in Wales. Eric Ives points out that Brereton reigned supreme in North Wales and Cheshire, having "a virtual monopoly" of royal appointments made in the region,[18] and that he used his authority there to push his own agenda. Brereton had had run-ins with Bishop Rowland Lee, Cromwell's representative there, and he was obviously going to be a fly in the ointment for Cromwell's planned reforms in the Welsh borders. Brereton was also a corrupt character, having caused the hanging of John ap Griffith Eyton in 1534 after Eyton had been acquitted for causing the death of one of Brereton's retainers by the Star Chamber.

In bringing down Anne for adultery, Cromwell could get rid of Brereton and Norris too.

Cromwell and the Catholic Conservatives

As Cromwell began to work with Chapuys for a reconciliation between Henry VIII and the Emperor, and the restoration of Mary, he came to some kind of agreement with the Catholic conservatives. This group consisted of the Seymours, Sir Nicholas Carew, the Marquis and Marchioness of Exeter, the Countess of Kildare and Baron Montagu. In April 1536, Chapuys[19] reported that the Conservatives had heard, probably from Cromwell himself, of a breach between Anne and Cromwell. They had also heard that Cromwell had been asked by the King to give up his lodgings to Edward Seymour and his wife so that he could visit Edward's sister, Jane, without being seen. I agree with Ives[20] that Chapuys probably brought Cromwell and the Conservatives together when it became apparent that they were both working towards the same purpose.

At the end of the day, Cromwell was a pragmatist. He could see that Anne was going down and could easily take him with her if he didn't join the other side. After Anne's fall, he then worked to free himself from the conservative faction by implicating them in plots concerning Mary.

Cromwell Gained from the Coup

Not only did Cromwell get rid of Anne, her brother, Brereton and Norris, he also gained financially and in prestige. He succeeded to Lord Privy Seal in July 1536, after Thomas Boleyn surrendered it, gained a stewardship from the fall of George Boleyn and the abbey of Lesnes from Brereton for his servant, Ralph Sadler.

Mark Smeaton's Arrest

On 30th April 1536. Mark Smeaton, a court musician and a member of the Boleyn circle, was apprehended and taken to Thomas Cromwell's house in Stepney. Not to the Tower of London, but to Cromwell's own home. According to The Spanish Chronicle, which has to be taken with a large pinch of salt, Cromwell "called two stout young fellows of his, and asked for a rope and a cudgel, and ordered them to put the rope, which was full of knots, round Mark's head, and twisted it with the cudgel until Mark cried out, "Sir Secretary, no more, I will tell the truth, " and then he said, "The Queen gave me the money. " "Ah, Mark, " said Cromwell, "I know the Queen gave you a hundred nobles, but what you have bought has cost over a thousand, and that is a great gift even for a Queen to a servant of low degree such as you. If you do not tell me all the truth I swear by the life of the King I will torture you till you do." Mark replied, "Sir, I tell you truly that she gave it to me". Then Cromwell ordered him a few more twists of the cord, and poor Mark, overcome by the torment, cried out, "No more, Sir, I will tell you everything that has happened". And then he confessed all, and told everything as we have related it, and how it came to pass."[21]

George Constantine, Sir Henry Norris's servant, wrote of how he'd heard that Smeaton was "grevously racked",[22] although he didn't know if it was true. Whatever the truth of the matter, the fact that Smeaton was taken to Cromwell's home shows Cromwell's personal involvement in what was going on, although Greg Walker points out that Cromwell may have simply been acting on allegations made against Smeaton and Anne.

He Kept People Away from the King

Men like Archbishop Cranmer, who may have been able to talk the King around, were barred from seeing the King. Cranmer, who was at his country home in Kent, was called back to Lambeth but it was made plain that he should not try to see the King. Instead, he had to write to the King and try to defend Anne that way, although his letter cannot be seen as much of a defence and was tempered by an added postscript after his meeting with the Star Chamber.

It appears that George Boleyn may have travelled from Greenwich to Whitehall in an attempt to see the King, but was arrested and thrown in the Tower instead. The same is true of Anne's friends Sir Richard Page and Sir Thomas Wyatt, men who may have spoken up for her, given the chance.

Suspect 2 – King Henry VIII

The next suspect is the King himself and those who believe he was ultimately responsible cite the following reasons:

The King was the Master and Cromwell was His Servant

Historian Robert Hutchinson[23] writes that it was natural that Henry VIII would turn to his minister to remove his unwanted second wife. Cromwell would not have dared to risk his life by moving against the Queen without the King's blessing; he was simply there to do the King's bidding. In a letter to Stephen Gardiner and John Wallop in Paris, Cromwell referred to "the King's proceeding", rather than to "my plan".[24]

It was Henry VIII who signed the death warrants and who stood by as his wife went to her death. Historian Derek Wilson writes of how Henry VIII behaved in his usual manner, giving orders to his ministers and then "retiring into the shadows" so that he could feign surprise when presented with the evidence against Anne.[25]

The King Wanted to Take a Third Wife

Chapuys had reported that after Anne's miscarriage in January 1536, the King had told one of his principal courtiers in secret "that he had been seduced and forced into this second marriage by means of sortileges and charms, and that, owing to that, he held it as nul. God (he said) had well shown his displeasure at it by denying him male children. He, therefore, considered that he could take a third wife, which he said he wished much to do."[26] Chapuys also reported that after Catherine of Aragon's death, Anne had "cried and lamented...fearing lest she herself might be brought to the same end".[27]

However, historians like Eric Ives believe that there is no evidence that Henry was looking to replace Anne. He was still referring to Anne as his "most dear and most entirely beloved wife the Queen" and writing of his hope for "heirs male" as late as 25th April 1536.[28] He was also still pushing for Anne to be recognised by Europe as his rightful wife and Queen. As we've hears, he even tricked Chapuys into recognising Anne as Queen, by bowing to her, on 18th April 1536. Why bother if he was about to replace her with Jane?

Henry and Anne were due to leave for Rochester, en route to Calais, on 2nd May, the day after the May Day jousting, but this was not cancelled until 11pm on Sunday 30th April, after the arrest of Mark Smeaton. Surely, if Henry had ordered Anne's fall then he would not have planned this trip?

The King's Behaviour

Chapuys wrote that "the King has shown himself more glad than ever since the arrest of the Concubine, for he has been going about banqueting with ladies, sometimes remaining after midnight, and returning by the river" and that "He supped lately with several ladies in the house of the bishop of Carlisle, and showed an extravagant joy".[29] Chapuys thought this behaviour was odd and was rather cynical, commenting that "You never saw prince nor man who made greater show of his [cuckold's] horns or bore them more pleasantly. I leave you to imagine the cause."[30] Henry VIII was devastated in 1541 when Catherine Howard betrayed him, weeping in front of his privy council when he found out the truth about her. Chapuys commented then that "this king has wonderfully felt the case of the Queen, his wife, and that he has certainly shown greater sorrow and regret at her loss than at the faults, loss, or divorce of his preceding wives", going on to say "In fact, I should say that this king's case resembles very much that of the woman who cried more bitterly at the loss of her tenth husband than she had cried on the death of the other nine put together, though all of them had been equally worthy people and good husbands to her: the reason being that she had never buried one of them without being sure of the next, but that after the tenth husband she had no other one in view, hence her sorrow and her lamentations. Such is the case with the King, who, however, up to this day does not seem to have any plan or female friend to fall back upon."[31] Henry showed no surprise, shock or upset at the investigation into Anne or at her fall.

Henry VIII also became betrothed to Jane Seymour on 20th May, the day after Anne Boleyn's execution, and then married her on 30th May. This ruthless and rather unseemly behaviour does suggest that his love for Anne had dwindled long before her death and that he had been planning marriage to Jane for some time. Of course, you could equally say that the paranoid King was manipulated by Cromwell into believing that Anne was guilty and so felt that she deserved everything that she got; and that Cromwell and the Seymours had been working on him for a while.

Henry's Stamp

John Schofield[32] believes Henry's involvement is proven by the lack of logic in Anne being condemned for adultery even though Henry's marriage to Anne was annulled. Cromwell, as a lawyer, would have wanted a logical, "watertight case", yet the case against Anne made no sense. The blackening of Anne's name and the complexity of the plot bear the stamp of a husband who wanted his wife dead. The plot was down to emotions such as jealousy, fear, resentment and hatred, not Cromwell's rational and legal brain.[33] It would have been far easier for Cromwell to annul the marriage and send Anne to a nunnery. Instead, he had to build a very complicated and nonsensical case.

Henry Involved Himself in the Proceedings at the Start

After receiving news of Mark Smeaton's confession, Henry chose to question Sir Henry Norris on their ride to Whitehall from the May Day joust, offering Norris a pardon if he would confess.

Revenge

Anne and George Boleyn had, allegedly, ridiculed Henry VIII's clothes and his ballads, and had also discussed his sexual problems. George had even joked that Elizabeth may not be Henry's daughter. Their fall could, therefore, be seen as Henry VIII's ultimate revenge. It could also be said that Anne had made a fool of Henry and let him down. He had abandoned his wife of over twenty years for her, broken with his beloved Church, executed former friends and advisers, all to be with Anne and yet she had failed to provide him with a son.

The Gossip

John Hill of Eynsham in Oxfordshire got into trouble for saying "that the King caused Mr. Norrys, Mr. Weston, and such as were put of late unto execution, for to be put to death only of pleasure" and "that the King, for a frawde and a gille, caused Master Norrys, Mr. Weston, and the other Queen to be put to death because he was made sure unto the Queen's grace that now is half a year before."[34] So, the gossip spreading around England was that the King had got rid of Anne and the men so that he could marry Jane. Chapuys had noted on the day of Henry and Jane's betrothal that "everybody begins already to murmur by suspicion, and several affirm that long before the death of the other there was some arrangement which sounds ill in the ears of the people".[35]

Henry's Own Words

Henry later warned Jane Seymour against becoming involved in matters to do with the Kingdom. It was reported that "he had often told her not to meddle with his affairs, referring to the late Queen, which was enough to frighten a woman who is not very secure."[36] In 1546, when the Conservatives were trying to bring down Archbishop Thomas Cranmer, Henry warned Cranmer that "false knaves" could be "procured" to stand as witnesses against him and to bring about his condemnation.[37] It was obviously the done thing!

Suspect 3 – Jane Seymour and the Catholic Conservatives

Some believe that Jane Seymour and the Catholic conservative faction who supported the Lady Mary hold some of the responsibility for Anne Boleyn's fall.

In April 1536, Chapuys reported to Charles V that Jane Seymour was being coached by Sir Nicholas Carew in how to behave towards the King, and that she was also being "advised to tell the King boldly how his marriage is detested by the people, and none consider it lawful".[38] Carew, Courtenay, Montagu and the other Conservatives were evidently hoping that Jane would be the next Anne and that Henry's new flame could be used to bring down the Queen they detested so much. This would pave the way for the restoration of Lady Mary to the succession. The martyrologist, John Foxe, in his "Book of Martyrs", put the King's "assent" to the events of 1536 down to "crafty setters-on"[39] who turned him against his wife and made him disinherit his daughter.

Some say that Jane had learned from Anne's example in her courtship with Henry. When Henry VIII sent Jane a purse full of sovereigns, she sent it back to him with a message saying "that she had no greater riches in the world than her honor, which she would not injure for a thousand deaths" and that if the King wanted to send her gifts then she begged him to do so after she was married. Like Anne before her, Jane was holding out for marriage, perhaps in the hope that Henry would warm to the thrill of the chase. However, this could also have been Jane's natural behaviour. She did appear to be a genuinely humble, virtuous and chaste young woman. Whatever her family and the Conservatives were planning, Jane may not have been a willing participant, and, at the end of the day, she was simply a woman, a chattel and pawn.

Suspect 4 - Anne Boleyn

I've heard it said that Anne Boleyn has to take some responsibility for her fall in 1536 even though she was innocent of the crimes for which she was condemned. In his TV series on Henry VIII, "Henry VIII: Mind of a Tyrant",[40] David Starkey spoke about how Anne's forthright character and ability to say "no" to Henry, when nobody else would, were attractive in a mistress but not what Henry found acceptable in a wife. By 1536, it is said, Henry could no longer tolerate Anne's nagging, her hot temper and her jealousy. One documentary, "Days that Shook the World: Execution of Anne Boleyn",[41] goes as far as to say that there were two reasons for Anne's fall: her refusal to "curb" her "bold manners" and her inability to provide Henry with the longed-for son and heir. However, how could Anne change? Henry had married her for love. He had been attracted to the feisty Anne, a woman who was willing to stand up to him and who was outspoken, if Anne changed her ways then she wouldn't be the woman he'd fallen in love with. It was an impossible situation – become the submissive wife, and lose what attracted Henry in the first place, or stay the same and risk annoying the King and making enemies.

We know that Anne and Henry's marriage was volatile and that the couple argued regularly but even Chapuys put this down to "lovers' quarrels, to which we must not attach too great importance".[42] It was a marriage based on love and passion, a real marriage rather than an arranged or diplomatic one, so it was bound to have its up and downs. Anne's jealousy, which is also sometimes seen as a factor in her fall, was a natural result of this love match. Anne had been a lady-in-waiting when she had caught Henry's eye, so how could she be sure that one of her ladies or another lady at court wouldn't steal Henry away from her? Whereas Catherine of Aragon had been able to turn a blind eye because she had a royal family and Emperor behind her, Anne could not. Anne had to fight for her marriage, she had to keep Henry interested. Although some historians, for example Alison Weir,[43] write of the marriage being in trouble from the start, there is no evidence of that. George Wyatt wrote that the royal couple "lived and loved, tokens of increasing love perpetually increasing between them. Her mind brought him forth the rich treasures of love of piety, love of truth, love of learning. Her body yielded him the fruits of marriage, inestimable pledges of her faith and loyal love"[44] and they were often described as being "merry". Volatile, yes, unhappy, no. Passionate rows, but equally passionate making up.

As Eric Ives and Greg Walker have pointed out, the Queen's household was an "arena" for the courtly love tradition which Anne had learned in the household of Margaret of Austria. The courtly love tradition was a chivalric game where a courtier would choose a "mistress" to woo with poems, songs and gifts. It wasn't about sex, or even having a proper relationship, it was about chivalry and flirtation – a platonic relationship.[45] Courtiers were expected to sigh over the Queen and praise her beauty, it was all part of the game. Unfortunately, courtly love seems to have got out of hand in the case of Anne Boleyn and also became twisted to bring her down.

Mark Smeaton's mooning over Anne was used to force a confession, and her unthinking snub of him may have led him to hit back at her. Anne's reckless words to Norris regarding him looking for "dead men's shoes" were twisted to be evidence of a conspiracy to murder the King and Anne's ramblings in the Tower regarding Weston incriminated him and led to his execution. What started out as harmless courtly love and flirtation ended in six brutal deaths. Some blame Anne for allowing it to go on. Yes, her mention of "dead men's shoes" was reckless, but she was reprimanding Norris, not encouraging him; she was reminding him that she was taken. She may have mentioned the King's death, but it was unintentional and could in no way be seen as encouraging Norris to conspire with her. Anne panicked, realising that these words could be used against her, and went into "damage control" mode, ordering Norris to go to her almoner, John Skip, and swear that she "was a good woman". It also appears that she tried to explain herself to her husband, an argument which Scottish theologian, Alexander Alesius, witnessed. Gossip spread like wildfire at the Tudor court and it is easy to imagine Henry VIII getting wind of Anne and Norris's altercation. Anne was probably trying to explain herself, but perhaps someone beat her to it and gave the story a bit of a twist. As far as Sir Francis Weston was concerned, Anne had spoken to him about "Mistress Shelton", accusing him of loving her rather than his wife, "and he made answer to her again that he loved one in her house better than both. And the queen said, 'Who is that?'. ' It is yourself'." Surely, he was simply playing the chivalrous knight of courtly love, here, and flattering his queen.

Greg Walker[46] writes of how it was "unguarded speech and gossip", rather than adultery or incest, that condemned Anne Boleyn, quoting the words of Anne's aunt, Lady Boleyn, who attended Anne in those final days in the Tower: "such desire as you have ha[d to such tales] has brought you to this".[47] We cannot know what Lady Boleyn was referring to. It may have been the courtly love tradition, or it may have been Anne and her brother, George, laughing at the King's ballads, mocking his dress and discussing his sexual inadequacies – definitely unguarded speech, and words that could easily have turned Henry's love for his wife into bitter resentment and hate. Anne had allowed inappropriate talk and behaviour in her household, she had been reckless and disrespectful regarding the King, and she had let her tongue run away with her in the Tower. Regardless, that's a far cry from being guilty of incest and murder. Anne had provided Henry and Cromwell with ammunition, but she didn't give them the gun.

Historian Retha Warnicke gives another reason for Anne's downfall. Warnicke writes that "the sole reason"[48] for the King turning against his wife was her miscarriage of a monstrously deformed foetus in January 1536. Warnicke believes that this deformed foetus would have been seen as evidence of witchcraft and unnatural sexual acts, acts which the King would obviously not have been involved in. Warnicke cites Nicholas Sander, a Catholic recusant writing in Elizabeth I's reign, as the source to back up the deformed foetus story. Sander wrote of Anne miscarrying "a shapeless mass of flesh", but he is the only source to say that and he wasn't even a contemporary of Anne's. The chronicler Charles Wriothesley recorded that Anne had miscarried a "man child" and that Anne "said that she had reckoned herself at that time but 15 weeks gone with child"[49] and Chapuys backed that up, writing that Anne miscarried "a male child which she had not borne 3½ months".[50] It beggars belief that the deformed foetus would not have been mentioned at Anne's trial, as evidence of sexual sin, if Anne had really miscarried such a foetus.

Anne's miscarriage may have been a factor in her fall, in that it made her vulnerable and may have caused an already paranoid King to doubt his marriage, but it was not the one and only cause.

I have read claims online that Anne Boleyn was a victim of a Papal conspiracy. This is similar to a storyline in "The Tudors" when William Brereton, who is actually a Jesuit priest in the series, is hired to assassinate Anne and then gives his life to bring her down by confessing to adultery with her. There is no truth to this story, or to those which claim that the Papacy caused Anne's miscarriages by poisoning her. However, Anne's religious views would have made her unpopular with the Catholic conservatives at court, people who were just waiting for an opportunity to get rid of her.

Of course, there are those who believe that there is no smoke without a fire and that Anne may have been guilty of at least some of the crimes she was alleged to have committed. Possible reasons include desperation to provide the King with a son, jealousy at Henry's infidelity or just simple lust. However, there would have been no point in providing the King with a son who looked just like one of his courtiers; and would the intelligent Anne have really risked her position and marriage for a roll in the hay? No. Anne's guilt was a foregone conclusion, with her household being broken up and the executioner being ordered in advance of her trial. Anne was no saint, but I find it hard to believe that she was guilty.

A Combination

Some people may consider this sitting on the fence, but I choose to believe that Anne's fall was not down to just one person. In my opinion, there were a number of people who had a hand in it. Pamela Kaputska, on The Anne Boleyn Files Facebook page, describes Cromwell, Henry VIII and the Seymour faction as all coming together to form "the perfect storm" and I think that's spot on.

Ultimately, I believe that the buck has to stop with Henry as he was the one in control. In my opinion, he wanted rid of Anne because he had convinced himself that their marriage, like his previous marriage, was contrary to God's laws and that God was showing him this by not blessing him with a son and heir.

Henry wanted to move on to Jane Seymour, who was of fertile stock, and to have another chance at having a son and happiness. He had tired of Anne, who was too much work, and he felt that she had let him down. He had moved heaven and earth to be with her and she hadn't lived up to her promise. The miscarriage of January 1536 proved to Henry that the marriage just wasn't right; it made his doubts very real. By April 1536, he was open to the Seymours and Catholic conservatives feeding his paranoia, convincing him that the English people were against Anne. He came to believe that everything was all Anne's fault, that he had fallen under her spell and made a huge mistake, so he ordered Cromwell to use the law to extricate him from his marriage to Anne. Henry was the one who made the decision and Cromwell was his servant, the man who provided his master with the machinery to exercise his will. Cromwell was to blame for bringing Anne down so brutally, and for getting the five men involved, but Henry was the one who started it all and the Seymours influenced Henry and took advantage of his vulnerability and anxiety.

I agree with Derek Wilson that the plot against Anne and the men was too complex to be down to Cromwell alone; if this were the case, there would certainly have been easier ways of ending the marriage. Adultery and incest were not even treason, so Anne and the men also had to be charged with conspiring against the King. Why would Cromwell have even bothered to accuse Anne of a charge that wouldn't lead to her death? The charges of adultery and treason were levied in order to blacken Anne's name completely, and they were the result of love turned to hate, the need to annihilate Anne entirely – they were Henry's idea and Cromwell had to make them work. If the adultery and incest bore Henry's mark, the legal machinery and the falls of Norris and Brereton bore Cromwell's.

Conclusion

The Anne Boleyn I have come to know though my research is a far cry from the Anne of popular fiction, but she is certainly no saint, angel or martyr, and does not deserve to be put on a pedestal. Anne was stubborn, ambitious, impatient, hot-tempered, driven, calculating, spiteful at times, and a woman who would not suffer fools gladly. On the other side of the coin, she was also fiercely loyal to her friends and passionate about supporting the arts, poor relief and education. In short, she was not the typical Tudor housewife. She was a "power player"[1] who would have seen herself as Henry's partner, an equal, rather than his submissive consort.

Whatever her faults, Anne Boleyn was not the victim of her own pride, ambition and conceit. Rather, she was the victim of a paranoid and desperate man, and of a political coup. Her personality and the rash things she said made her enemies, but it was her situation that killed her, not her temper. If she had been more submissive to Henry, would it have saved her? Of course not. She still would have miscarried; she would still have been seen as a usurper, the religious divides would still have existed and Henry would still have doubted his marriage. He would probably have got bored of her sooner! I cannot see how Anne could have prevented the events of 1536 in any way.

Anne and her brother, George, were people who enjoyed the limelight. They captivated those around them with their magnetism, their wit and their charm. As my good friend Clare Cherry once said to me, those ten years in the sunlight of the Tudor court would have been preferable to them than a lifetime in the shadows. They died before their time, they died brutally; but, oh, how they lived! Their names and their stories are still being remembered and told nearly 500 years later, and they are captivating generation after generation. Their magnetism, it seems, stretches through the ages and grabs us. I am proud to be telling their story on a daily basis.

The Cast – After May 1536

Henry VIII (1491-1547)

Henry's third marriage was shortlived, with Henry losing Jane Seymour to puerperal fever in October 1537. He went on to marry Anne of Cleves in January 1540, but the marriage was annulled on 7th July of the same year due to an alleged existing pre-contract between Anne and Francis of Lorraine. Other reasons for the annulment included Henry's lack of consent to the marriage and the lack of consummation. On 28th July 1540, Henry VIII married his fifth wife, Catherine Howard, but she was executed on the 13th February after it was found that she had slept with Sir Francis Dereham before her marriage to the King and that she had been having an affair with Thomas Culpeper during her marriage. Henry VIII married his sixth and final wife, the twice-married and -widowed Catherine Parr, on 12th July 1543. Catherine outlived the King, who died on 28th January 1547. He was laid to rest alongside his third wife, Jane Seymour, in St George's Chapel, Windsor Castle. Henry's nine year old son, Edward, became King Edward VI and was crowned at Westminster Abbey on the 20th February 1547.

The Boleyn family

Although Thomas Boleyn fell from favour after the fall and execution of his daughter, he was a survivor and did not give up. He was active in squashing the rebellion of the Pilgrimage of Grace in 1536 and he was present at Edward VI's christening in 1537. Eric Ives talks of how he buttered up Cromwell by lending him his chain and Garter badge at one point.[1] By 1538, Thomas Boleyn was back properly at court and it was even rumoured that he would marry Margaret Douglas, Henry VIII's niece. However, he did not live long after Anne's fall, dying in March 1539, around a year after his wife. The fact that Henry VIII ordered masses to be said for Thomas's soul is clear evidence that Thomas was back in favour by then.

Elizabeth Boleyn died in April 1538 at Baynard's Castle and was laid to rest in the Howard Chapel of St Mary's Church, Lambeth. Elizabeth had been ill at the time of her daughter and son's arrests in 1536 so it may be that her death was due to that long-term illness.

Anne and George's sister Mary had married William Stafford in 1534 and had escaped the fate of her siblings by being away from court in 1536. Their Boleyn connections seem to have had no adverse effect on the Stafford couple, with William Stafford being chosen to receive Anne of Cleves in Calais in December 1539. The Staffords were in England from January 1540, when Stafford was listed as a Gentleman Pensioner and became an Esquire of the Body. Mary's daughter, Catherine Carey, was appointed as a maid-of-honour to the new queen Anne in April 1540, serving alongside her aunt, Jane Boleyn. In that same month she married Francis Knollys, a Gentleman Pensioner of the King's household. After the failure of the Cleves marriage both Catherine and Jane became ladies to the King's new wife, Catherine Howard. Catherine was able to avoid becoming embroiled in Catherine Howard's fall, but her stepfather was named as giving evidence regarding the Queen and her relationship with Francis Dereham.

Mary Boleyn died in July 1543 and it is not known where she was laid to rest. Stafford remarried in 1552, marrying a distant relation, Dorothy Stafford. The couple was forced into exile, along with Catherine and Francis and their family, when the Catholic Mary I came to the throne in 1553.

Thomas Cromwell (1485-1540)

On 2nd July 1536, Cromwell became Lord Privy Seal, after the resignation of Thomas Boleyn. On 8th July he became Baron Cromwell of Wimbledon. Cromwell's injunctions to the clergy caused unrest resulting in the Pilgrimage of Grace risings in

Yorkshire, Lincolnshire and other northern counties. However, these were quickly squashed by the King, and Cromwell continued his programme of evangelical reform.

In 1539, Cromwell negotiated the marriage of Henry VIII and Anne of Cleves, sister of William, Duke of Jülich-Cleves-Berg, in an attempt to form an alliance between England and Schmalkaldic League of Lutheran princes. Unfortunately, the King did not like Anne when he saw her and blamed Cromwell for forcing him to marry her in January 1540. The King's unhappiness and disillusion allowed Cromwell's opponents to rise up against him and push for his fall. They could never have moved against Cromwell when he stood high in royal favour, but he had failed the king and the king was not willing to protect him. At a council meeting on 10th June 1540, a group led by the Duke of Norfolk got Cromwell arrested and he was taken to the Tower of London. An Act of Attainder was used against him, meaning that he had no trial in which to defend himself. Nonetheless, he was kept alive until the Cleves marriage could be annulled on the grounds of non-consummation. He was executed on 28th July 1540 at the Tower of London and suffered an awful end with a botched execution. It is said that it took three blows to finish him.

Charles Brandon, Duke of Suffolk (c1484-1545)

Suffolk was prominent as the King's lieutenant in suppressing the rebels of the Pilgrimage of Grace in late 1536, and in 1537 he moved to Lincolnshire on the orders of the King. In December 1539, he led the party which met Anne of Cleves at Dover and was also involved in sorting out the annulment of the marriage in 1540. In the early 1540s, he was involved in Henry VIII's wars with Scotland and France, serving as the King's lieutenant in the North from 1543-1544 and then leading the siege of Boulogne in 1544. He died on 22nd August 1545 at Guildford. His cause of death is unknown. He was laid to rest in St George's Chapel, Windsor Castle, on 9th September 1545. Unfortunately, his sons, Henry and Charles, died of sweating sickness in July 1551.

Thomas Audley, Lord Chancellor (1487/8 -1544)

On 29th November 1538, Thomas Audley was made Baron Audley of Walden and was elected as a Knight of the Garter in April 1540. The 1539 Parliament's Act of Precedence gave him "precedence over all but dukes of royal blood in parliament, privy council, and Star Chamber."[2] He survived the fall of Thomas Cromwell and was the Privy Council's expert on treason. He was involved in negotiating the annulment of the Cleves marriage and, later, in interrogating Catherine Howard. He was also a commissioner at the trials of Culpeper and Dereham and was Lord High Steward at the trials of Henry Pole, Baron Montagu, and Henry Courtenay, marquess of Exeter, in 1538. In 1541 he performed the same role at the trial of Thomas Fiennes, ninth Baron Dacre. On 21st April 1544 he resigned the great seal due to illness and died on 30th April 1544 at his home in London.

Henry Fitzroy, Duke of Richmond and Somerset (1519-1536)

After the executions of Anne and George Boleyn et al, Richmond was appointed Chamberlain of Chester and North Wales, and Constable of Dover Castle. He was in attendance at the opening of Parliament in June 1536 but became ill in early July 1536. He died on 23rd July 1536 at St James's Palace, probably of a pulmonary infection. He was laid to rest at Thetford Priory but was then moved to St Michael's Church, Framlingham, after the Priory was dissolved.

Eustace Chapuys, Imperial Ambassador (c1491-1556)

Chapuys was responsible for the Lady Mary submitting to her father in 1536 after she was bullied by members of the King's council. In 1536/7, he supported Dom Luis in his bid to be a potential bridegroom for Mary, but the marriage never took place. Chapuys began to suffer with gout in 1539, but this did not stop him being involved in the negotiations which led to Henry VIII and

Charles V declaring war on France in 1543. Chapuys accompanied the King's men to France.

Chapuys wanted to retire in 1544 but had to help his successor, Van der Delft, for some time. He was then sent to Bourbourg, near Gravelines, to negotiate until July 1545 when he was finally released from service. On his retirement, Chapuys lived in Louvain, where he founded a college, as well as a grammar school at Annecy. In 1555 he decided that his English pension should go towards setting up a scholarship for English students at Louvain. He died on 21st January 1556 and was laid to rest in the Chapel of Louvain College.[3]

Jane Seymour (c1508/09 -1537)

In May of 1537, it was announced that Jane Seymour was pregnant. Henry VIII was ecstatic, ordering bonfires to be lit in celebration and showering his Queen with gifts and affection. It is said that Jane had a pregnancy craving for quail, so the King ordered the very best quail for her from Flanders and Calais. On 12th of October, after a long and difficult labour, Jane gave birth to Henry's longed-for son, a boy named Edward, at Hampton Court Palace. Within two days of her son's christening, on 15th, Jane became feverish and delirious. After her fever reached crisis point on 17th June, it looked like Jane would begin to recover. However, she started to go downhill again, passing in and out of consciousness. On 24th October 1537, Jane Seymour died. She was buried at Windsor Castle, in St George's Chapel.

The Lady Mary, formerly Princess Mary (1516-1558)

After submitting to her father, and accepting her illegitimacy in June 1536, Mary was rehabilitated back at court and stood as godmother at Edward's christening in October 1537. Mary was close to her father's sixth wife, Catherine Parr, even though their religious views were very different. During her brother Edward VI's reign, Mary opposed the new religious policies and continued to celebrate the mass. In 1550, she nearly fled England, but had a last minute change of heart.

In July 1553, Mary fought successfully for the Crown after Edward VI's named successor, Lady Jane Grey, was proclaimed Queen. Edward died on 6th July 1553 and Mary was proclaimed Queen Mary I on 19th July. Her first parliament declared her parents' marriage as valid and Mary as legitimate, and Mary quickly set about restoring England's relationship with Rome. She was met with opposition in 1554 when she decided to marry Philip II of Spain and the resulting rebellion, Wyatt's Rebellion, resulted in the executions of Thomas Wyatt the Younger, Lady Jane Grey and Guildford Dudley, amongst others. Mary married Philip on 25th July 1554. Mary suffered two phantom pregnancies but died childless on 17th November 1558. She was laid to rest in Westminster Abbey. Mary is known for being the monarch who lost Calais and for her burning of Protestant martyrs, hence the nickname "Bloody Mary".

Princess Elizabeth (1533-1603)

The annulment of her parents' marriage and her mother's execution saw Elizabeth being demoted to Lady Elizabeth. Elizabeth went from pampered princess, the apple of her father's eye, to ignored bastard. Elizabeth was so forgotten that her governess, Lady Margaret Bryan, had to write a letter to Cromwell begging for him to intercede with the King as Elizabeth had outgrown all of her clothes and her household had no money to buy more. It was Catherine Parr who restored Elizabeth's relationship with her father; and before he died, he added both Mary and Elizabeth back into the line of succession. When Henry VIII died, Elizabeth lived with Catherine Parr and new husband, Thomas Seymour, but Seymour started acting inappropriately with Elizabeth, so she was sent away. Elizabeth lived happily through Edward VI's reign but had problems during Mary I's reign and was actually imprisoned in the Tower of London in March 1554 after Wyatt's Rebellion. She was released on 19th May 1554 but was placed under house arrest in Woodstock until October 1555, when she was allowed to return home to Hatfield.

Elizabeth became Queen Elizabeth I on Mary I's death on 16th November 1558. She reigned until her death on 24th March 1603 and has gone down in history as The Virgin Queen and Gloriana.

Charles V, Holy Roman Emperor (1500-1558)

Charles V was involved in the Council of Trent, an ecumenical council which opened in 1545 and which began the Counter-Reformation. He worked hard to squash Lutheranism and outlawed the League of Schmalkaden. He suffered from epilepsy and gout. In later life, severe gout led to him having to be carried around in a sedan chair. He abdicated the majority of his titles to his son, Philip, in October 1555 and then retreated into seclusion in a monastery, surrounding himself with clocks. He died of malaria on 21st September 1558.

Henry Courtenay, Marquis of Exeter (1498/9-1538) and Henry Pole, Baron Montagu (1492-1539)

On 4th November 1538, Henry Pole, 1st Baron Montagu, was arrested for treason. Arrested alongside him were his brother-in-law, Sir Edward Neville, and Henry Courtenay, Marquis of Exeter. The latter's family (wife Gertrude Blount and son Edward Courtenay) were also arrested.

The three men were accused of conspiring against the King, of seeking to deprive the King of his title of supreme head of the church and of plotting with Cardinal Reginald Pole, the exiled brother of Montagu. Montagu's brother, Geoffrey Pole, had been imprisoned in the Tower of London at the end of August 1539 and had implicated Henry Pole during his interrogation on 26th October. Margaret Pole, Countess of Salisbury and mother of Reginald, Henry and Geoffrey, was interrogated on 12th November by William Fitzwilliam, Earl of Southampton, and Thomas Goodrich, Bishop of Ely.

Neville was beheaded on 9th December 1538 and Geoffrey Pole was pardoned on the 2nd January 1539, after having attempted suicide several times. Montagu and Exeter were beheaded on Tower Hill on 9th January 1539, and Margaret Pole was eventually executed on 27th May 1541. Exeter's wife was released in 1540 and his son in 1553.

Elizabeth Fitzgerald, Countess of Kildare (d.1548)

Elizabeth died on an unknown date in 1548. Her elder son, Gerald, who had been on the run after forming the Kildare rebellion, returned to England after Henry VIII's death and was restored to his lands.

John Skip (d.1552)

Skip did not suffer because of his association with Anne Boleyn. He was made Master of Gonville Hall and Archdeacon of Suffolk in 1536, rector of Newington in Surrey and Archdeacon in Dorset in 1538, and Bishop of Hereford in 1539. In 1549, Archbishop Thomas Cranmer identified Skip as not fully supporting the new prayer book.[4]

Sir Nicholas Carew (c.1496-1539)

Carew was chosen to be in charge of the font at Edward VI's baptism in October 1537 and his wife was one of the ladies at Jane Seymour's funeral in November 1537. He was a royal favourite until his arrest on 31st December 1538. He was implicated in the plot which resulted in the executions of Montagu and Exeter. Carew was tried on 14th February 1539 and executed on 8th March on Tower Hill.

Matthew Parker (1504-1575)

Like John Skip, Matthew Parker did not suffer as a result of Anne Boleyn's fall, and was rewarded with various benefices and ecclesiastical preferments during the reigns of Henry VIII and

Edward VI. In Mary I's reign, he suffered as a married clergyman and was deprived of his prebend of Ely and deanery of Lincoln. It appears that he sought refuge in Cambridge, where he concentrated on his theological writing. In 1559, during the reign of Elizabeth I, he was made Archbishop of Canterbury and was therefore involved in the synod called to work on Elizabeth's religious settlement. His time as archbishop is known for the vestiarian controversy.

He died on 17th May 1575 at Lambeth Palace. Parker is also known for his collection of more than 700 manuscripts which he bequeathed to Corpus Christi College. They are now housed in the Parker Library at Corpus Christi College, Cambridge, and in Cambridge University Library. The collection spans from the 6th century Gospels of St. Augustine to 16th century records relating to the English Reformation.[5]

Thomas Cranmer, Archbishop of Canterbury (1489-1556)

In the summer of 1536, Cranmer published his "Ten Articles". These defined the beliefs of the new Church of England, the Henrician Church which had been established after the break with Rome. This was followed by "The Bishop's Book". In 1541, Cranmer was chosen as the person to tell the King of Catherine Howard's colourful past, and was involved in interrogating her. In 1543, thanks to support from the King, Cranmer managed to survive a plot against him by clergymen. On 27th May 1544, his "Exhortation and Litany" was published.

Cranmer held the hand of the dying King on 28th January 1547, giving him reformed statement of faith instead of the last rites. He was one of the executors of Henry VIII's will and so was an important of the Lord Protector's administration. In 1549, the Act of Uniformity established "The Book of Common Prayer", which set out the new legal form of worship in England. Its being made compulsory in June 1549 led to the Prayer Book Rebellion. Cranmer was unaffected when Protector Somerset fell and was replaced by John Dudley. In 1552, the Act of Uniformity replaced the Book of Common Prayer with a more Protestant Book of Common Prayer.

On 8th August 1553 Cranmer performed the Protestant funeral rites when Edward VI was buried in the Henry VII Chapel at Westminster Abbey. While other reformed clergy fled the country now that the Catholic Mary I was in control, Cranmer chose to stay. Unfortunately, this led to him being imprisoned in the Tower of London and being found guilty of treason. Although he recanted four times, his execution was not cancelled. On the date of his execution he was given the opportunity to publicly recant at the University Church, Oxford. Instead of recanting, Cranmer opened with the expected prayer and exhortation to obey the King and Queen, and then renounced his recantations, saying that the hand he had used to sign them would be the hand that would be punished by the fire first. He was burned at the stake in Oxford on 21st March 1556.

Sir Thomas Wyatt the Elder (1503-1542)

Wyatt escaped Anne Boleyn's fall and the King made him an ambassador to the court of Charles V, the Holy Roman Emperor. However, Wyatt got into trouble again in 1541 when he was charged with treason for making rude comments about the King and for dealing with Cardinal Pole. Wyatt was once again imprisoned in the Tower of London and this time he had no father to secure his release because his father had died in November 1536. This time, it was Catherine Howard, Henry VIII's fifth wife, who secured his pardon and release, but Wyatt had to agree to return to his estranged wife. In 1542, Wyatt was back in favour and had been restored to his office of ambassador. However, his return to favour was shortlived because Wyatt was taken ill after receiving the emperor's envoy at Falmouth. Sir Thomas Wyatt died on 11th October 1542 at Clifton Maybank House, the home of his friend Sir John Horsey, in Sherborne Dorset. He was laid to rest at Sherborne Abbey. His plain tomb can be found in the Wykenham

Chapel of the Abbey.

Sir Thomas Wyatt's son, Thomas Wyatt the Younger, was executed on 11th April 1554 after leading a rebellion, "Wyatt's Rebellion" or "Wyatt's Revolt", against Queen Mary I. Although he was tried and found guilty on 15th March, his execution was postponed in the hope that he would implicate Mary I's half-sister, Elizabeth, in the uprising. Wyatt went to his death protesting Elizabeth's innocence.

Sir Richard Page (d.1548)

Sir Richard Page was released from the Tower of London by 8th July 1536 and in the October was accompanying the King to Welbeck to deal with the Pilgrimage of Grace rebellion. By November that year he had been appointed as Sheriff of Surrey and Sussex. In 1539, 1542 and 1544, he received various grants, showing that he was in the King's favour; by 1540 he was lieutenant of the gentlemen pensioners. When the King went to France in July 1544 and Catherine Parr acted as regent, Page was appointed chamberlain in charge of Prince Edward's household at Hampton Court Palace. Page died in London in 1548. He was related to Edward Seymour's wife, Anne Stanhope, by marriage as he had married her mother sometime before 1534.[6]

Sir Francis Bryan (c.1490-1550)

Bryan had survived the coup against his relative, Anne Boleyn, by allying himself with the Seymours. In 1537 he was sent to Paris to secretly arrange the kidnap or assassination of Cardinal Pole, but it was suspected that instead he actually tipped Pole off. He acted as ambassador to Francis I in 1538 in Nice while Thomas Wyatt acted as ambassador to Charles V but was recalled due to his reckless gambling, drunkenness and all round bad behaviour. He never acted as ambassador to the French king ever again. Bryan sat on the jury which found his brother-in-law, Carew, guilty of treason in 1539. He was appointed vice-admiral in January 1543, but this was revoked in the February after he disobeyed the instructions of John Dudley, Viscount Lisle and lord admiral. In October 1543 he acted as ambassador to Charles V and in October 1546 he was given the freedom of the City of London. He was made knight-banneret in 1547 for his role in the expedition against the Scots as commander of the horse. In 1548, Bryan married Joan Butler, dowager countess of Ormond, and daughter of James fitz Maurice Fitzgerald, tenth earl of Desmond, making him a wealthy and powerful man. He died in Ireland on 2nd February 1550.[7]

Sir William Kingston (c.1476-1540)

In 1537, Sir William Kingston benefited from the dissolution of the monasteries when he was awarded the land and possessions associated with the abbey of Flaxley in Gloucestershire. In 1539, Kingston was appointed comptroller of the King's household and was also elected a Knight of the Garter. In 1540, he was chosen to inform Thomas Cromwell of the charges against him. After Cromwell's execution, he was able to buy Cromwell's property in Gloucestershire. He died at Painswick, in Gloucestershire, on 14 September 1540.[8]

William Latymer (1498/9-1583)

In September 1538, William Latymer became Master of the College of St Laurence Pountney in London. This was followed by him being given various benefices in Suffolk, Kent, London and Nottingham. In 1547, he voted for clerical marriage and then married a widow, Ellen English. He was a principal witness, along with John Hooper, in the case against Bishop Edmund Bonner in 1549. This case led to Bonner being deprived of his bishopric. In Mary I's reign, Latymer was deprived of his living due to his marriage. He survived by separating from his wife, but this was just an outward pretence. When Elizabeth I came to the throne, Latymer was chosen as one of her chaplains, and he went on to write his treatise or "Chronicklle of Anne Bulleyne". Latymer died at around the age of 84 in 1583. He was laid to rest on 28th August 1583 in Peterborough Cathedral. He left his wife, Ellen, and two sons: Edward and Joshua.

Henry Percy, 6th Earl of Northumberland (c.1502-1537)

Henry Percy managed to avoid being caught up in the Pilgrimage of Grace rebellion of 1536. However, his brother, Sir Thomas Percy, was executed in 1537 after being involved in the rebellion and the 1537 Bigod Rebellion. His other brother, Sir Ingram, died in prison in the Tower of London. Percy died on 29th June 1537 in Hackney and was buried in the parish church there.

Thomas Howard, 3rd Duke of Norfolk (1473-1554)

After acting as Lord Steward at the trials of Anne and George Boleyn, Norfolk went on to be godfather to Edward VI at his christening in October 1537 and a commissioner at Queen Jane Seymour's funeral in November 1537. In 1539, he was chosen to go with the Duke of Suffolk to meet Anne of Cleves at her arrival at Dover. In 1540, during Cromwell's arrest in the council chamber, it was said that Norfolk tore the St George from around Cromwell's neck; certainly, he was very much involved in the plot against Cromwell. When the King's anger turned on the Howard family after Catherine Howard's adultery, Norfolk was fortunate in escaping punishment. He went on to serve the King in the war against the Scots in 1542 but his pro-French stance caused him problems when the King became keen to go to war with France. He served the King in France as lieutenant-general of the army, besieging Montreuil, but was rebuked by the King when he withdrew.

On 12th December 1546, Norfolk and his son, Henry Howard, Earl of Surrey, were arrested and imprisoned in the Tower of London after it was alleged that Surrey had displayed the royal arms and insignia in his own heraldry. Surrey was found guilty of treason on 13th January 1547 at a common inquest at Guildhall and Norfolk was attainted on 27th January. Both were sentenced to death and Surrey was executed on 19th January 1547. Norfolk was lucky; the King died before the former's scheduled execution date. As a consequence, in 1553, Norfolk was released and pardoned by Mary I, and died naturally at Kenninghall on 25th August 1554. He was laid to rest in St Michael's Church, Framlingham.

Jane Boleyn (née Parker, d. 1542)

Jane was left in a difficult financial situation after her husband's death and appealed to Cromwell for assistance. Her father-in-law, Thomas Boleyn, was forced to become involved and Cromwell helped her to obtain a position in Jane Seymour's household. After Jane Seymour's death, she served Anne of Cleves and was one of the senior ladies of the bedchamber who was questioned regarding Anne of Cleves's understanding of what constituted consummation. Her testimony obviously helped the King have his marriage annulled so that he could marry the young Catherine Howard. When Catherine Howard fell in 1541, she and Culpeper laid the blame for their transgressions at Jane's feet. Jane was questioned regarding her involvement in their affair. She was executed with Catherine on 13th February 1542 even though she had had a mental breakdown in the Tower. Her name became synonymous with betrayal and scandal, yet she was more likely a scapegoat.

Extras

You can find lots of extras at The Fall of Anne Boleyn: A Countdown website -

http://www.thefallofanneboleyn.com/

These include:-

- Interactive timeline
- Execution poetry
- Further Reading
- Notes and Sources for each chapter, plus full bibliography
- Printable timeline of the events of 1536
- Places – Details on all of the places mention in the book
- Q&A with Claire
- YouTube videos on Anne Boleyn

A favour, please...

Now that you've read The Fall of Anne Boleyn: A Countdown, it would be wonderful if you could spare a moment and leave a review on its Amazon page or on Goodreads. You can also "like" its Amazon page – every little helps! I read every single review and would love to hear your thoughts.

You'll also have the opportunity to rate the book and share your rating with friends on Facebook and Twitter when you get to the last page.

Thank you so much!

Acknowledgements

This book could not have been written without the encouragement of historian Suzannah Lipscomb, the friendship and ongoing support of Clare Cherry, the patience of my family, and the support I receive on a daily basis from visitors to The Anne Boleyn Files.

I want to thank Clare Cherry and Dr Sarah Morris for reading the draft manuscript and giving me their thoughts, Sarah Franklin for her magical copy-editing, David Leppenwell and my husband, Tim, for the fantastic cover, Professor Eric Ives for allowing himself to be grilled by me, members of the Anne Boleyn Fellowship for beta-reading the book, my parents Frank and Davida Brassington for their love and encouragement, Penny Wright and John Harris for picking me up whenever things got on top of me, Jane Sagi for giving me the history bug, and Mr R Taylor for telling me at the age of 11 that I would be a writer one day. Thank you!

Claire Ridgway,

Lúcar, Spain
April, 2012

About the Author

Claire Ridgway is a writer, researcher and Tudor history detective with a deep knowledge and love of everything about the Boleyn family and the time of the Tudors. She is also the best-selling author of The Anne Boleyn Collection which sold over 3000 copies in its first six weeks.

Claire is well known and respected for her Tudor websites:-

- The Anne Boleyn Files – www.TheAnneBoleynFiles.com
- The Elizabeth Files – www.elizabethfiles.com
- Tudor Society - www.TudorSociety.com

These sites contain in-depth research about the Tudor period and promote historical authenticity. Claire currently lives up a mountain in Southern Spain, but grew up near to Stratford-upon-Avon where she was surrounded by Tudor history. Claire is Tudor obsessed, and makes no apologies for it.

She is always happy to hear from readers and history lovers by email or via The Anne Boleyn Files Facebook page or Twitter

- email claire@theanneboleynfiles.com
- https://www.facebook.com/theanneboleynfiles
- https://twitter.com/anneboleynfiles

Other book by Claire Ridgway

The Anne Boleyn Collection
The Anne Boleyn Collection II
The Fall of Anne Boleyn
On This Day in Tudor History
Tudor Places of Britain

Execution Poetry

There are various poems associated with the bloody events of 1536, two written by Thomas Wyatt, who witnessed the executions from his prison in the Bell Tower, and two once attributed to Anne Boleyn.

Defiled is my name full sore

By Anne Boleyn(?)

> Defiled is my name full sore
> Through cruel spite and false report,
> That I may say for evermore,
> Farewell, my joy! Adieu comfort!
> For wrongfully ye judge of me
> Unto my fame a mortal wound,
> Say what ye list, it will not be,
> Ye seek for that can not be found.

O Death, O Death, rock me asleepe

By Anne Boleyn(?)

> O Death, O Death, rock me asleepe,
> Bring me to quiet rest;
> Let pass my weary guiltless ghost
> Out of my careful breast.
> Toll on, thou passing bell;
>
> Ring out my doleful knell;
> Thy sound my death abroad will tell,
> For I must die,
> There is no remedy.

My pains, my pains, who can express?
Alas, they are so strong!
My dolours will not suffer strength
My life for to prolong.
Toll on, thou passing bell;
Ring out my doleful knell;
Thy sound my death abroad will tell,
For I must die,
There is no remedy.

Alone, alone in prison strong
I wail my destiny:
Woe worth this cruel hap that I
Must taste this misery!
Toll on, thou passing bell;
Ring out my doleful knell;
Thy sound my death abroad will tell,
For I must die,
There is no remedy.

Farewell, farewell, my pleasures past!
Welcome, my present pain!
I feel my torment so increase
That life cannot remain.
Cease now, thou passing bell,
Ring out my doleful knoll,
For thou my death dost tell:
Lord, pity thou my soul!
Death doth draw nigh,
Sound dolefully:
For now I die,
I die, I die.

In Mourning Wise Since Daily I Increase

By Sir Thomas Wyatt, the Elder

Thomas Wyatt wrote this poem to honour the five men who were executed for adultery with Anne Boleyn. It implies that Wyatt thought that these men were innocent.

> In Mourning wise since daily I increase,
> Thus should I cloak the cause of all my grief;
> So pensive mind with tongue to hold his peace'
> My reason sayeth there can be no relief:
> Wherefore give ear, I humbly you require,
> The affect to know that thus doth make me moan.
> The cause is great of all my doleful cheer
> For those that were, and now be dead and gone.
> What thought to death desert be now their call.
> As by their faults it doth appear right plain?
> Of force I must lament that such a fall should
> light on those so
> wealthily did reign,
> Though some perchance will say, of cruel heart,
> A traitor's death why should we thus bemoan?
> But I alas, set this offence apart,
> Must needs bewail the death of some be gone.
>
> As for them all I do not thus lament,
> But as of right my reason doth me bind;
> But as the most doth all their deaths repent,
> Even so do I by force of mourning mind.
> Some say, 'Rochford, haddest thou been not
> so proud,
> For thy great wit each man would thee bemoan,
> Since as it is so, many cry aloud
> It is great loss that thou art dead and gone.'
>
> Ah! Norris, Norris, my tears begin to run

To think what hap did thee so lead or guide
Whereby thou hast both thee and thine undone
That is bewailed in court of every side;
In place also where thou hast never been
Both man and child doth piteously thee moan.
They say, 'Alas, thou art far overseen
By thine offences to be thus dead and gone.'

Ah! Weston, Weston, that pleasant was
and young,
In active things who might with thee compare?
All words accept that thou diddest speak with
tongue,
So well esteemed with each where thou
diddest fare.
And we that now in court doth lead our life
Most part in mind doth thee lament and moan;
But that thy faults we daily hear so rife,
All we should weep that thou are dead and gone.

Brereton farewell, as one that least I knew.
Great was thy love with divers as I hear,
But common voice doth not so sore thee rue
As other twain that doth before appear;
But yet no doubt but they friends thee lament
And other hear their piteous cry and moan.
So doth eah heart for thee likewise relent
That thou givest cause thus to be dead and gone.

Ah! Mark, what moan should I for thee
make more,
Since that thy death thou hast deserved best,
Save only that mine eye is forced sore
With piteous plaint to moan thee with the rest?
A time thou haddest above thy poor degree,

The fall whereof thy friends may well bemoan:
A rotten twig upon so high a tree
Hath slipped thy hold, and
thou art dead and gone.

And thus farewell each one in hearty wise!
The axe is home, your heads be in the street;
The trickling tears doth fall so from my eyes
I scarce may write, my paper is so wet.
But what can hope when death hath played
his part,
Though nature's course will thus lament
and moan?
Leave sobs therefore, and every Christian heart
Pray for the souls of those be dead and gone.

V. Innocentia Veritas Viat Fides Circumdederunt me inimici mei

by Sir Thomas Wyatt, the Elder

Who list his wealth and ease retain,
Himself let him unknown contain.
Press not too fast in at that gate
Where the return stands by disdain,
For sure, circa Regna tonat*.

The high mountains are blasted oft
When the low valley is mild and soft.
Fortune with Health stands at debate.
The fall is grievous from aloft.
And sure, circa Regna tonat.

These bloody days have broken my heart.

My lust, my youth did them depart,
And blind desire of estate.
Who hastes to climb seeks to revert.
Of truth, circa Regna tonat.

The bell tower showed me such sight
That in my head sticks day and night.
There did I learn out of a grate,
For all favour, glory, or might,
That yet circa Regna tonat.

By proof, I say, there did I learn:
Wit helpeth not defence too yerne,
Of innocency to plead or prate.
Bear low, therefore, give God the stern,
For sure, circa Regna tonat.

*circa regna tonat means "about the throne the thunder rolls".

Further Reading

If you want to check the sources used then do make use of the references and bibliography. Here are the sources I would recommend:-

Primary Sources

- A Chronicle of England During the Reigns of the Tudors, from A.D. 1485 to 1559, Charles Wriothesley - http://www.archive.org/stream/chronicleengland00wriouoft

- Archaeologia, or, Miscellaneous tracts relating to antiquity, George Constantine

- Calendar of State Papers, Spain - http://www.british-history.ac.uk

- Chronicle of King Henry VIII. of England: Being a contemporary record of some of the principal events of the reigns of Henry VIII. and Edward VI. Written in Spanish by an unknown hand (The Spanish Chronicle) - http://archive.org/stream/chroniclekinghe00humegoog#page/n6/mode/2up

- Hall's Chronicle, Edward Hall - http://www.archive.org/stream/hallschronicleco00halluoft

- Holinshed's Chronicles - http://www.archive.org/stream/chroniclesofengl03holiuoft

- Letters and Papers, Foreign and Domestic, Henry VIII - http://www.british-history.ac.uk

- The Chronicle of Calais - http://www.archive.org/stream/calaischronicle00camduoft

- The life and raigne of King Henry the Eighth by the Right Honourable Edward, lord Herbert of Cherbury - http://www.archive.org/stream/lifeandraigneofk00herbrich

- The life of Cardinal Wolsey, Volume 2, George Cavendish - http://books.google.com/books/reader?id=DE0Q1wDp4rgC&printsec=frontcover&output=reader

Secondary Sources

- A Brief History of Henry VIII: Reformer and Tyrant, Derek Wilson
- Agnes Strickland's Queens of England Volume I - http://www.archive.org/stream/agnesstricklands01striiala
- Anne Boleyn: A Chapter of English History, Paul Friedmann – Original available online at http://archive.org/details/anneboleynachap00unkngoog or modern copy edited by Josephine Wilkinson, Amberley Publishing
- Anne Boleyn: Fatal Attractions, G W Bernard
- In the Lion's Court: Power, Ambition and Sudden Death in the Reign of Henry VIII, Derek Wilson
- Six Wives: The Queens of Henry VIII, David Starkey
- The Lady in The Tower, Alison Weir
- The Life and Death of Anne Boleyn, Eric Ives – My favourite book on Anne Boleyn
- The Rise and Fall of Anne Boleyn: Family politics at the Court of Henry VIII by Retha M. Warnicke
- The Rise and Fall of Thomas Cromwell: Henry VIII's Most Faithful Servant, John Schofield
- The Tower from Within, George Younghusband - http://archive.org/details/towerfromwithin00youngoog
- 1536: The Year that Changed Henry VIII, Suzannah Lipscomb

Notes

The Cast 1535-1536

1   Lehmberg, "Sir William Kingston."
2   "Letters and Papers, Foreign and Domestic, Henry VIII, Volume 10 -
     January-June 1536," note 965.
3   Hume, Chronicle of King Henry VIII. of England, 70.
4   "Letters and Papers, Foreign and Domestic, Henry VIII, Volume 11:
     July-December 1536," note 381.
5   "Letters and Papers, Foreign and Domestic, Henry VIII, Volume 10 -
     January-June 1536," note 902.
6   ed. Gough Nichols, The Chronicle of Calais In the Reigns of
     Henry VII and Henry VIII to the Year 1540, 47.
7   Hume, Chronicle of King Henry VIII. of England, 70.

Anne Boleyn: From
Courtier's Daughter to Queen

1   Ascoli, La Grande-Bretagne Devant L'opinion Française Depuis La
     Guerre De Cent Ans Jusqu'à La Fin Du XVIe Siècle, 236–237, lines
     148–164.

Summer 1535
The Royal Progress and Wolf Hall

1   Starkey, "Acton Court and the Tudors."
2   "Calendar of State Papers, Spain, Volume 5 Part 1: 1534-1535," note
     193.
3   Richardson, "Henry VIII and Travel."
4   Ives, The Life and Death of Anne Boleyn, 291–292.
5   "Letters and Papers, Foreign and Domestic, Henry VIII, Volume 9:
     August-December 1535," notes 271, 326.
6   "Letters and Papers, Foreign and Domestic, Henry VIII, Volume 10 -
     January-June 1536," note 282.
7   Sander, Rise and Growth of the Anglican Schism, 132.

7th January 1536 –
Death of Catherine of Aragon

1   "Letters and Papers, Foreign and Domestic, Henry VIII, Volume 10 - January-June 1536," note 141.

2   Tremlett, Catherine of Aragon: Henry's Spanish Queen.

3   Ibid.

4   "Letters and Papers, Foreign and Domestic, Henry VIII, Volume 10 - January-June 1536," note 59.

5   Crawford, Letters of the Queens of England, 1100-1547, 180.

6   "Letters and Papers, Foreign and Domestic, Henry VIII, Volume 10 - January-June 1536," note 40.

8th January 1536 –
Free from All Suspicion of War!

1   "Letters and Papers, Foreign and Domestic, Henry VIII, Volume 10 - January-June 1536," note 141.

2   Ives, The Life and Death of Anne Boleyn, 295.

3   "Letters and Papers, Foreign and Domestic, Henry VIII, Volume 10 - January-June 1536," note 141.

4   Hall, Hall's Chronicle, 818.

5   Sander, Rise and Growth of the Anglican Schism, 132.

6   "Meaning of Colors in Christian Art."

7   "Letters and Papers, Foreign and Domestic, Henry VIII, Volume 10 - January-June 1536," note 54.

24th January 1536 –
Henry VIII's Jousting Accident

1   "Letters and Papers, Foreign and Domestic, Henry VIII, Volume 10 - January-June 1536," note 200.

2   Ibid., note 427.

3   Ibid., note 282.

4   Neale, Queen Elizabeth I.

5   McCarthy, "The Jousting Accident That Turned Henry VIII into a Tyrant."

6   Ibid.

29th January 1536 –
Burial and Miscarriage

1   Ridgway, "The Pregnancies of Anne Boleyn and Catherine of Ara-
       gon."
2   "Letters and Papers, Foreign and Domestic, Henry VIII, Volume 10 -
       January-June 1536," note 284.
3   Ibid., note 351.
4   Wriothesley, A Chronicle of England During the Reigns of the Tu-
       dors, from A.D. 1485 to 1559, 33.
5   Neale, Queen Elizabeth I.

10th February 1536

1   "Letters and Papers, Foreign and Domestic, Henry VIII, Volume 10 -
       January-June 1536," note 282.
2   Weir, The Lady in the Tower: The Fall of Anne Boleyn, 17.
3   Ives, The Life and Death of Anne Boleyn, 302.
4   "Letters and Papers, Foreign and Domestic, Henry VIII, Volume 10 -
       January-June 1536," note 601.

Jane Seymour

1   Norton, Jane Seymour: Henry VIII's True Love, 7.
2   Ibid., 11.
3   Ibid., 12.
4   Ibid., 13.
5   Ibid., 42–43.

Early 1536 – Foreign Policy

1   "Letters and Papers, Foreign and Domestic, Henry VIII, Volume 9 :
       August-December 1535," note 838.
2   Ibid., notes 964, 980, 987.
3   "Calendar of State Papers, Spain, Volume 5 Part 2: 1536-1538," note
       29.
4   Ibid.
5   Schofield, The Rise and Fall of Thomas Cromwell: Henry VIII's Most
       Faithful Servant, 111.
6   "Calendar of State Papers, Spain, Volume 5 Part 2: 1536-1538," note
       29.
7   "Letters and Papers, Foreign and Domestic, Henry VIII, Volume 10 -

January-June 1536," note 644.

8   Ibid., note 665.

March 1536 – Act for the Suppression of Lesser Monasteries

1   Hunter, An Introduction to the Valor Ecclesiasticus of King Henry VIII, 18.
2   Saini, "The 1536 Dissolution of the Lesser Monasteries: Same Suppression, Different Century," 24.
3   Eagle and Younge, A Collection of the Reports of Cases, the Statutes, and Ecclesiastical Laws, Relating to Tithes, IV:30–31.
4   Hoyle, "The Origins of the Dissolution of the Monasteries," 297.
5   Youings, The Dissolution of the Monasteries, 43.

6th March 1536

1   "Calendar of State Papers, Spain, Volume 5 Part 2: 1536-1538," note 35.

18th March 1536 - Jane in Favour

1   "Letters and Papers, Foreign and Domestic, Henry VIII, Volume 10 - January-June 1536," note 495.

1st April 1536 - Chapuys, Cromwell, Jane Seymour and the Conservatives

1   "Calendar of State Papers, Spain, Volume 5 Part 2: 1536-1538," note 43.
2   Fuller (1608-1661), History of the Worthies of England, III:320.
3   Clifford, The Life of Jane Dormer, Duchess of Feria, 41.

2nd April 1536 – A Controversial Passion Sunday Sermon

1   Ives, The Life and Death of Anne Boleyn, 309.
2   "Letters and Papers, Foreign and Domestic, Henry VIII, Volume 10 - January-June 1536," note 308.
3   Ives, The Life and Death of Anne Boleyn, 309.
4   "Letters and Papers, Foreign and Domestic, Henry VIII, Volume 10 - January-June 1536," note 615.5.

5   Ibid., note 615.
6   Ibid., note 615 (4).
7   Dowling, "William Latymer's Cronickille of Anne Bulleyne," 57.
8   Ibid., 58.

13th April – Maundy Thursday

1   "Letters and Papers, Foreign and Domestic, Henry VIII, Volume 10 -
        January-June 1536," note 772.
2   Dowling, "William Latymer's Cronickille of Anne Bulleyne," 53.

18th April 1536 – The King Tricks Chapuys

1   Ives, The Life and Death of Anne Boleyn, 313.
2   "Letters and Papers, Foreign and Domestic, Henry VIII, Volume 10 -
        January-June 1536," note 699.
3   Ibid., note 115.
4   Ibid.
5   Ibid.
6   Ibid., note 700.
7   "Letters and Papers, Foreign and Domestic, Henry VIII, Volume 8,"
        note 826.
8   "Letters and Papers, Foreign and Domestic, Henry VIII, Volume 9:
        August-December 1535," note 861.
9   "Letters and Papers, Foreign and Domestic, Henry VIII, Volume 10 -
        January-June 1536," note 1069.
10   Schama, A History of Britain - Volume 1: At the Edge of the World?
        3000 BC-AD 1603, 312.

22nd April 1536 – A Strange Letter from Cranmer to Cromwell

1   Jenkyns, The Remains of Thomas Cranmer, I:162.
2   Ibid.
3   Schofield, The Rise and Fall of Thomas Cromwell: Henry VIII's Most
        Faithful Servant, 119.
4   Ives, The Life and Death of Anne Boleyn, 310.
5   MacCulloch, Thomas Cranmer: A Life, 156

23rd April 1536 – A Warning Sign?

1   "Letters and Papers, Foreign and Domestic, Henry VIII, Volume 10 - January-June 1536", 1536, note 715.
2   Ibid., note 752.
3   "Letters and Papers, Foreign and Domestic, Henry VIII, Volume 6 - 1533", 1533, note 555.
4   "Letters and Papers, Foreign and Domestic, Henry VIII, Volume 8 - February 1535, 1-10", 1535, note 174.

24th April 1536 – Legal Machinery

1   Encyclopædia Britannica Eleventh Edition.
2   Wriothesley, A Chronicle of England During the Reigns of the Tudors, from A.D. 1485 to 1559, 190, Baga de Secretis Pouch VIII.
3   Weir, The Lady in the Tower: The Fall of Anne Boleyn, 89.
4   Ibid.
5   Friedmann, Anne Boleyn, 228.
6   Bernard, Anne Boleyn, 134.

25th April 1536 – Most Entirely Beloved Wife

1   "Letters and Papers, Foreign and Domestic, Henry VIII, Volume 10 - January-June 1536," note 726.
2   Ibid., note 725.
3   Ibid., note 726.

26th April 1536 – Anne Boleyn and Matthew Parker

1   ed. Bruce and ed. Perowne, Correspondence of Matthew Parker, 400.
2   Parker, The Correspondence of Matthew Parker, D.D., Archbishop of Canterbury : Comprising Letters Written by and to Him, from A.D. 1535, to His Death, A.D. 1575, 58.
3   Ives, The Life and Death of Anne Boleyn, 267.
4   ed. Bruce and ed. Perowne, Correspondence of Matthew Parker, 391.
5   Wikipedia, "The Thirty-nine Articles."

27th April 1536 – Parliament Summoned

1   "Letters and Papers, Foreign and Domestic, Henry VIII, Volume 10 - January-June 1536," note 736.
2   Ibid., note 752.

28th and 29th April 1536

1   "Letters and Papers, Foreign and Domestic, Henry VIII, Volume 10 - January-June 1536," note 748.
2   Ibid., note 752.
3   Ibid.
4   Ibid., note 753.
5   "Oxford Dictionary of National Biography," chap. Andrew A. Chibi, "Sampson, Richard (d. 1554)."

29th April 1536 - Sir Henry Norris and Dead Men's Shoes

1   Ives, The Life and Death of Anne Boleyn, 325.
2   "Letters and Papers, Foreign and Domestic, Henry VIII, Volume 10 - January-June 1536," note 793.

Sir Henry Norris

1   Ives, "Henry Norris."
2   Wilkinson, The Early Loves of Anne Boleyn, 119.
3   Ibid., 120.
4   Boehrer, "The Privy and Its Double: Scatology and Satire in Shakespeare's Theatre."
5   Ives, "Henry Norris."
6   George Constantine, Archaeologia, or, Miscellaneous Tracts Relating to Antiquity, 23:50.
7   Hall, Hall's Chronicle, 763.
8   George Constantine, Archaeologia, or, Miscellaneous Tracts Relating to Antiquity, 23:51.
9   Ives, "Henry Norris."

30th April 1536 – A Royal Argument and the First Arrest

1   "Letters and Papers, Foreign and Domestic, Henry VIII, Volume 10 - January-June 1536," note 789.
2   "Calendar of State Papers Foreign, Elizabeth, Volume 1 - 1558-1559," note 1303.
3   Hume, Chronicle of King Henry VIII. of England, 57.
4   Ascoli, La Grande-Bretagne Devant L'opinion Française Depuis La Guerre De Cent Ans Jusqu'à La Fin Du XVIe Siècle.

5   Cavendish, The Life of Cardinal Wolsey, Volume 2, 2:37.
6   Strype, Ecclesiastical Memorials Relating Chiefly to Religion, and the
        Reformation of It, and the Emergencies of the Church of England,
        Under King Henry VIII, King Edward VI, and Queen Mary I, 436.
7   Hume, Chronicle of King Henry VIII. of England, 61.
8   George Constantine, Archaeologia, or, Miscellaneous Tracts Relating
        to Antiquity, 23:64.
9   Ascoli, La Grande-Bretagne Devant L'opinion Française Depuis La
        Guerre De Cent Ans Jusqu'à La Fin Du XVIe Siècle.

Mark Smeaton

1   Cavendish, The Life of Cardinal Wolsey, Volume 2.
2   Nicholas, The Privy Purse Expenses of King Henry the Eighth, from
        November 1529, to December 1532, 100.
3   Ibid., 262.
4   Warnicke, The Rise and Fall of Anne Boleyn: Family Politics at the
        Court of Henry VIII.

1st May 1536 The May Day Joust

1   Ascoli, La Grande-Bretagne Devant L'opinion Française Depuis La
        Guerre De Cent Ans Jusqu'à La Fin Du XVIe Siècle, vv. 495–508.
2   Wriothesley, A Chronicle of England During the Reigns of the Tu-
        dors, from A.D. 1485 to 1559, 35.
3   George Constantine, Archaeologia, or, Miscellaneous Tracts Relating
        to Antiquity, 23:64.
4   Burnet, The History of the Reformation of the Church of England,
        206.
5   Hume, Chronicle of King Henry VIII. of England, 62–63.

2nd May 1536 – Arrests

1   "Letters and Papers, Foreign and Domestic, Henry VIII, Volume 10 -
        January-June 1536," note 782.
2   Wriothesley, A Chronicle of England During the Reigns of the Tu-
        dors, from A.D. 1485 to 1559, 36.
3   Ives, The Life and Death of Anne Boleyn, 328.
4   "Letters and Papers, Foreign and Domestic, Henry VIII, Volume 10 -
        January-June 1536," note 784.
5   Parker, The Correspondence of Matthew Parker, D.D., Archbishop of
        Canterbury : Comprising Letters Written by and to Him, from A.D.

1535, to His Death, A.D. 1575, 58.

6   Wriothesley, A Chronicle of England During the Reigns of the Tu-
        dors, from A.D. 1485 to 1559, 36.
7   Stow, Annals of England to 1603, 964.
8   "Letters and Papers, Foreign and Domestic, Henry VIII, Volume 10 -
        January-June 1536," note 793.
9   Ibid., note 669.
10   "Calendar of State Papers, Spain, Volume 5 Part 2: 1536-1538," note
        55.

3rd May 1536 – I Had Never Better Opinion of Woman

1   "Letters and Papers, Foreign and Domestic, Henry VIII, Volume 10 -
        January-June 1536," note 792.
2   MacCulloch, Thomas Cranmer: A Life, 157.
3   Ibid., note 793.
4   Cavendish, The Life of Cardinal Wolsey, Volume 2, 2:219.
5   Ibid.
6   Cavendish, The Life of Cardinal Wolsey, Volume 2, 2:226.
7   Ives, "The Fall of Anne Boleyn Reconsidered," 6.

Sir Francis Weston

1   Weir, The Lady in the Tower: The Fall of Anne Boleyn, 102–103.
2   Hughes, "Francis Weston."
3   Friedmann, Anne Boleyn.
4   Cavendish, The Life of Cardinal Wolsey, Volume 2.
5   Warnicke, The Rise and Fall of Anne Boleyn: Family Politics at the
        Court of Henry VIII, 4.

Sir William Brereton

1   Ives, "William Brereton."
2   Ives, "Court and County Palatine in the Reign of Henry VIII: The
        Career of William Brereton of Malpas," 5.
3   Ives, "William Brereton."
4   Ives, "Court and County Palatine in the Reign of Henry VIII: The
        Career of William Brereton of Malpas," 11.
5   Ibid., 33.

4th May 1536 - Further Arrests

1   George Constantine, Archaeologia, or, Miscellaneous Tracts Relating
         to Antiquity, 23:65.

4th May 1536 – Lady Rochford's Letter

1   "Letters and Papers, Foreign and Domestic, Henry VIII, Volume 10 -
         January-June 1536," note 798

Jane Boleyn – History's Scapegoat

1   Weir, The Lady in the Tower: The Fall of Anne Boleyn, 111.
2   Guy, "The Lady in the Tower: The Fall of Anne Boleyn by Alison
         Weir - Sunday Times Review."
3   Ascoli, La Grande-Bretagne Devant L'opinion Française Depuis La
         Guerre De Cent Ans Jusqu'à La Fin Du XVIe Siècle, 259.
4   "Letters and Papers, Foreign and Domestic, Henry VIII, Volume 10 -
         January-June 1536," note 798.

4th May 1536 Cruelly Handled – Anne Boleyn in the Tower

1   Weir, The Lady in the Tower: The Fall of Anne Boleyn, 138.
2   "Letters and Papers, Foreign and Domestic, Henry VIII, Volume 10 -
         January-June 1536," note 793.
3   Ibid., note 797.
4   Ibid.
5   Ibid.
6   Ibid.
7   Ibid.
8   Cavendish, The Life of Cardinal Wolsey, Volume 2, 2:221.
9   Strype, Ecclesiastical Memorials Relating Chiefly to Religion, and the
         Reformation of It, and the Emergencies of the Church of England,
         Under King Henry VIII, King Edward VI, and Queen Mary I, 435.

5th May 1536 – Sir Thomas Wyatt, Sir Richard Page and Sir Francis Bryan

1   Hume, Chronicle of King Henry VIII. of England, 63–64.
2   "Letters and Papers, Foreign and Domestic, Henry VIII, Volume 10 -
         January-June 1536," note 840.

3   Ibid., note 855.
4   Ibid., note 865.
5   Ibid., note 1131.
6   "Letters and Papers, Foreign and Domestic, Henry VIII, Volume 10 -
         January-June 1536," note 873.

Sir Thomas Wyatt

1   Bruce, "Unpublished Anecdotes of Sir Thomas Wyatt the Poet, and
         of Other Members of That Family."
2   Cavendish, The Life of Cardinal Wolsey, Volume 2, 2:184.
3   Hume, Chronicle of King Henry VIII. of England, 69.
4   Cavendish, The Life of Cardinal Wolsey, Volume 2, 2:187.

Sir Richard Page

1   "Letters and Papers, Foreign and Domestic, Henry VIII, Volume 2:
         1515-1518," note 2735.
2   "Letters and Papers, Foreign and Domestic, Henry VIII, Volume 3:
         1519-1523," notes 2016, 18(A).
3   Davies, "Sir Richard Page."
4   "Letters and Papers, Foreign and Domestic, Henry VIII, Volume 4:
         1524-1530," notes Grants in March 1528, note 17.
5   Ibid., note 6803 (24).
6   Friedmann, Anne Boleyn, 235.
7   Ibid., 236.

Sir Francis Bryan

1   "Letters and Papers, Foreign and Domestic, Henry VIII, Volume 10 -
         January-June 1536," note 873.
2   Sander, Rise and Growth of the Anglican Schism, 24.
3   Brigden, "Sir Francis Bryan (d.1550)."
4   "Letters and Papers, Foreign and Domestic, Henry VIII, Volume 13
         Part 1 - January-July 1538," note 981.

6th May 1536 – From the Lady in the Tower

1   Smeeton, The Life and Death of Anne Bullen, Queen Consort of
         England.
2   Herbert, The Life and Raigne of King Henry the Eighth.
3   Burnet, The History of the Reformation of the Church of England.
4   Froude, The Divorce of Catherine of Aragon.

5   "Letters and Papers, Foreign and Domestic, Henry VIII, Volume 10 -
         January-June 1536," note 808.
6   Weir, The Lady in the Tower: The Fall of Anne Boleyn, 173.
7   Henry VIII, The Love Letters.
8   Ibid.

7th May 1536 – A Chaplain is Searched

1   "Letters and Papers, Foreign and Domestic, Henry VIII, Volume 10 -
         January-June 1536," note 827.
2   Dowling, "Anne Boleyn and Reform."
3   "Oxford Dictionary of National Biography," chap. Andrew Hope,
         "Latymer , William (1498/9–1583)."
4   Russell, "May 7th, 1536: The Faith of the Prisoner."
5   "Letters and Papers, Foreign and Domestic, Henry VIII, Volume 10 -
         January-June 1536," note 797.

8th May 1536 – The Vultures Circle

1   "Letters and Papers, Foreign and Domestic, Henry VIII, Volume 10 -
         January-June 1536," note 829.
2   Ibid., note 791.
3   Ibid., note 891.
4   Ibid., note 804.

9th May 1536 – Meetings

1   "Letters and Papers, Foreign and Domestic, Henry VIII, Volume 10 -
         January-June 1536," note 833.
2   Ibid., note 834.
3   Ibid., note 338.

10th May 1536 – The Middlesex Indictment

1   "Letters and Papers, Foreign and Domestic, Henry VIII, Volume 10 -
         January-June 1536," note 876.
2   Wriothesley, A Chronicle of England During the Reigns of the
         Tudors, from A.D. 1485 to 1559, 201, Appendix, Baga de Secretis
         Pouch VIII.
3   Weir, The Lady in the Tower: The Fall of Anne Boleyn.
4   Ives, The Life and Death of Anne Boleyn.
5   "Letters and Papers, Foreign and Domestic, Henry VIII, Volume 10 -
         January-June 1536," note 837.

11th May 1536 – The Kent Indictment

1   "Letters and Papers, Foreign and Domestic, Henry VIII, Volume 10 - January-June 1536," note 876.
2   Ives, The Life and Death of Anne Boleyn, 344.
3   "Letters and Papers, Foreign and Domestic, Henry VIII, Volume 6 - 1533," note 1500.
4   "Letters and Papers, Foreign and Domestic, Henry VIII, Volume 7," note 556.
5   Ibid., note 958.
6   Ives, The Life and Death of Anne Boleyn, 344.

The Prisoners Interrogated

1   Hume, Chronicle of King Henry VIII. of England, 64.
2   "Letters and Papers, Foreign and Domestic, Henry VIII, Volume 10 - January-June 1536," note 1036.

12th May 1536 – The Trial of
Norris, Weston, Brereton and Smeaton

1   Ives, The Life and Death of Anne Boleyn, 339.
2   Friedmann, Anne Boleyn, 240.
3   Ives, The Life and Death of Anne Boleyn, 340.
4   Friedmann, Anne Boleyn, 240.
5   "Letters and Papers, Foreign and Domestic, Henry VIII, Volume 10 - January-June 1536," note 848.
6   Ibid., note 908.
7   George Constantine, Archaeologia, or, Miscellaneous Tracts Relating to Antiquity, 23:64.
8   "Letters and Papers, Foreign and Domestic, Henry VIII, Volume 10 - January-June 1536," note 848.
9   Ibid.

13th May 1536 – Henry Percy and the Pre-contract

1   "Letters and Papers, Foreign and Domestic, Henry VIII, Volume 10 - January-June 1536," note 764.

13th May 1536 – The Queen's Household is Broken Up

1   Wriothesley, A Chronicle of England During the Reigns of the Tudors, from A.D. 1485 to 1559, 37.

14th May 1536 – Jane Seymour

1   "Letters and Papers, Foreign and Domestic, Henry VIII, Volume 10 - January-June 1536," note 908.
2   Ibid.
3   Ibid.
4   Ibid., note 901.

Henry VIII's Letter to Jane Seymour

1   Halliwell-Phillipps, Letters of the Kings of England, 1:353.
2   Ibid., 1:312.

14th May 1536 - The Queen's Incontinent Living

1   "Letters and Papers, Foreign and Domestic, Henry VIII, Volume 10 - January-June 1536," note 873.

15th May 1536 – The King to Take a New Wife

1   "Letters and Papers, Foreign and Domestic, Henry VIII, Volume 10 - January-June 1536," note 888.

15th May 1536 – The Trial of Anne Boleyn

1   "Letters and Papers, Foreign and Domestic, Henry VIII, Volume 10 - January-June 1536," note 908.
2   Ibid., note 902.
3   Wriothesley, A Chronicle of England During the Reigns of the Tudors, from A.D. 1485 to 1559, 37.
4   "Letters and Papers, Foreign and Domestic, Henry VIII, Volume 10 - January-June 1536," note 876.
5   Ibid., note 1036.
6   Ascoli, La Grande-Bretagne Devant L'opinion Française Depuis La Guerre De Cent Ans Jusqu'à La Fin Du XVIe Siècle, 261.
7   Younghusband, The Tower from Within.
8   Ascoli, La Grande-Bretagne Devant L'opinion Française Depuis La Guerre De Cent Ans Jusqu'à La Fin Du XVIe Siècle, 261.
9   "Letters and Papers, Foreign and Domestic, Henry VIII, Volume 10 - January-June 1536," note 908.
10 Wriothesley, A Chronicle of England During the Reigns of the Tudors, from A.D. 1485 to 1559, 37–38.
11 ed. Williams, English Historical Documents: 1485-1558, 724.

12   ed. Baker, The Reports of Sir John Spelman, note i.71.
13   Weir, The Lady in the Tower: The Fall of Anne Boleyn, 218.
14   "Letters and Papers, Foreign and Domestic, Henry VIII, Volume 10 -
      January-June 1536," note 1036.
15   Ascoli, La Grande-Bretagne Devant L'opinion Française Depuis La
      Guerre De Cent Ans Jusqu'à La Fin Du XVIe Siècle, 263.
16   Guy, "The Lady in the Tower: The Fall of Anne Boleyn by Alison
      Weir - Sunday Times Review."
17   "Letters and Papers, Foreign and Domestic, Henry VIII, Volume 10 -
      January-June 1536," note 876.
18   Wriothesley, A Chronicle of England During the Reigns of the Tu-
      dors, from A.D. 1485 to 1559, 39.
19   Ascoli, La Grande-Bretagne Devant L'opinion Française Depuis La
      Guerre De Cent Ans Jusqu'à La Fin Du XVIe Siècle, 259.
20   Cherry, "George Boleyn."
21   "Letters and Papers, Foreign and Domestic, Henry VIII, Volume 10 -
      January-June 1536," note 908.
22   Ibid.
23   Cavendish, The Life of Cardinal Wolsey, Volume 2, 2:212.
24   "Letters and Papers, Foreign and Domestic, Henry VIII, Volume 10 -
      January-June 1536," note 1036.
25   Wriothesley, A Chronicle of England During the Reigns of the Tu-
      dors, from A.D. 1485 to 1559, 39.
26   "Letters and Papers, Foreign and Domestic, Henry VIII, Volume 10 -
      January-June 1536," note 908.
27   de Lisle, The Sisters Who Would Be Queen.

16th May 1536 – Archbishop Cranmer Visits Anne Boleyn

1   Cavendish, The Life of Cardinal Wolsey, Volume 2, 2:227.
2   "Letters and Papers, Foreign and Domestic, Henry VIII, Volume 10 -
     January-June 1536," note 890.
3   Ibid.
4   Ibid., note 869.
5   Weir, The Lady in the Tower: The Fall of Anne Boleyn, 236.

17th May 1536 – The Executions of 5 Men and a Marriage Destroyed

1   "Letters and Papers, Foreign and Domestic, Henry VIII, Volume 10 -
     January-June 1536," note 890.

2   Ibid., note 902.
3   Ibid., note 911.
4   Hume, Chronicle of King Henry VIII. of England, 67.
5   ed. Gough Nichols, The Chronicle of Calais In the Reigns of Henry VII and Henry VIII to the Year 1540, 46.
6   Ives, The Life and Death of Anne Boleyn, 278.
7   George Constantine, Archaeologia, or, Miscellaneous Tracts Relating to Antiquity, 23:63.
8   Hume, Chronicle of King Henry VIII. of England.
9   "Letters and Papers, Foreign and Domestic, Henry VIII, Volume 10 - January-June 1536," note 909.
10 George Constantine, Archaeologia, or, Miscellaneous Tracts Relating to Antiquity, 23:65.
11 Ibid., 23:69.
12 Cavendish, The Life of Cardinal Wolsey, Volume 2, 2:34.
13 George Constantine, Archaeologia, or, Miscellaneous Tracts Relating to Antiquity, 23:65.
14 Ives, "Court and County Palatine in the Reign of Henry VIII: The Career of William Brereton of Malpas," 31–32.
15 "Cholmondeley of Cholmondeley Estate Records, WILL of Lady Elizabeth Savage."
16 George Constantine, Archaeologia, or, Miscellaneous Tracts Relating to Antiquity, 23:65.
17 "Letters and Papers, Foreign and Domestic, Henry VIII, Volume 10 - January-June 1536," note 1036.
18 Russell, "May 17th 1536 Deaths on Tower Hill."
19 "Letters and Papers, Foreign and Domestic, Henry VIII, Volume 10 - January-June 1536," note 908.
20 Ibid., note 896.
21 Wriothesley, A Chronicle of England During the Reigns of the Tudors, from A.D. 1485 to 1559, 41.
22 Ibid.
23 "Letters and Papers, Foreign and Domestic, Henry VIII, Volume 10 - January-June 1536," note 909.

18th May 1536 – Anne Prepares

1   Younghusband, The Tower from Within, 131.
2   "Letters and Papers, Foreign and Domestic, Henry VIII, Volume 10 - January-June 1536," note 908.
3   Ibid., note 910.
4   Ibid.

5   Ibid.
6   Sergeant, Anne Boleyn: A Study, 269.
7   "Letters and Papers, Foreign and Domestic, Henry VIII, Volume 10 -
        January-June 1536," note 908.
8   Ibid., note 1036.
9   "BL Cotton MS Vitellius B Xiv, Fol. 220B."

19th May 1536 – The Execution of Queen Anne Boleyn

1   "Letters and Papers, Foreign and Domestic, Henry VIII, Volume 10 -
        January-June 1536," note 919.
2   Ibid., note 1036.
3   Ibid.
4   Ibid., note 911.
5   Ibid., note 1036.
6   Younghusband, The Tower from Within, 134.
7   Ives, The Life and Death of Anne Boleyn, 358.
8   "Letters and Papers, Foreign and Domestic, Henry VIII, Volume 10 -
        January-June 1536," note 1036.
9   Younghusband, The Tower from Within, 135.
10   "Letters and Papers, Foreign and Domestic, Henry VIII, Volume 11:
        July-December 1536," note 381.
11   "Calendar of State Papers Foreign, Elizabeth, Volume 1 - 1558-1559,"
        note 1303.

Anne Boleyn's Resting Place

1   Bell, Notices of the Historic Persons Buried in the Chapel of St Peter
        Ad Vincula in the Tower of London, 21.
2   Ibid., 26.
3   Ibid., 30.
4   Freeman-Mitford, Lord Redesdale, A Tragedy in Stone and Other
        Papers, 35.
5   "Red Roses for Anne Boleyn."

20th May 1536 – The Betrothal of Henry VIII and Jane Seymour

1   "Letters and Papers, Foreign and Domestic, Henry VIII, Volume 10 -
        January-June 1536," note 926.

30th May 1536 –
Henry VIII Marries Jane Seymour

1   "Letters and Papers, Foreign and Domestic, Henry VIII, Volume 10 -
     January-June 1536," note 926.
2   Starkey, Six Wives: The Queens of Henry VIII.
3   "Letters and Papers, Foreign and Domestic, Henry VIII, Volume 10 -
     January-June 1536," note 1047.
4   Wriothesley, A Chronicle of England During the Reigns of the Tu-
     dors, from A.D. 1485 to 1559, 44.
5   Kergourlay, "The Execution of Anne Boleyn."

The Reaction

1   "Letters and Papers, Foreign and Domestic, Henry VIII, Volume 10 -
     January-June 1536," note 908.
2   Ibid., note 965.
3   George Constantine, Archaeologia, or, Miscellaneous Tracts Relating
     to Antiquity, 23:64–65.
4   Cavendish, The Life of Cardinal Wolsey, Volume 2, 2:448.
5   Ibid., 2:445.
6   Fox (Foxe), Fox's Book of Martyrs: Acts and Monuments of the
     Church in Three Volumes, II:407.
7   "Letters and Papers, Foreign and Domestic, Henry VIII, Volume 11:
     July-December 1536," note 860.
8   Ives, The Life and Death of Anne Boleyn, 350.
9   Narratives of the Days of the Reformation, Chiefly from the Manu-
     scripts of John Foxe the Martyrologist; with Two Contemporary
     Biographies of Archbishop Cranmer, 255.

A Foregone Conclusion

1   "Letters and Papers, Foreign and Domestic, Henry VIII, Volume 10 -
     January-June 1536," note 820.
2   Ibid., note 819.
3   Ibid., note 793.
4   Ibid.
5   Ibid., note 815.
6   Bernard, Anne Boleyn.
7   "Letters and Papers, Foreign and Domestic, Henry VIII, Volume 10 -
     January-June 1536," note 908.
8   Ibid., note 908.

9   Ibid.
10   Ibid., note 902.
11   "Letters and Papers, Foreign and Domestic, Henry VIII, Volume 11:
       July-December 1536," note 381.

Who was Responsible for
the Fall of Anne Boleyn?

1   Weir, The Lady in the Tower: The Fall of Anne Boleyn, 323.
2   Wilson, A Brief History of Henry VIII: Reformer and Tyrant.
3   "Letters and Papers, Foreign and Domestic, Henry VIII, Volume 10 -
       January-June 1536," note 242.
4   Ibid., note 254.
5   Ives, The Life and Death of Anne Boleyn, 309.
6   Corrie, Sermons by Hugh Latimer, 123.
7   Hoyle, "The Origins of the Dissolution of the Monasteries," 296.
8   "SP6/1 Folio 8 Sermon Preached by John Skip in the King's Chapel
       on Passion Sunday 1536."
9   Schofield, The Rise and Fall of Thomas Cromwell: Henry VIII's Most
       Faithful Servant, 103.
10   Ibid., 114.
11   "Calendar of State Papers, Spain, Volume 5 Part 1: 1534-1535," note
       170.
12   Ibid.
13   "Letters and Papers, Foreign and Domestic, Henry VIII, Volume 7,"
       note 296.
14   "Letters and Papers, Foreign and Domestic, Henry VIII, Volume 5:
       1531-1532," note 24.
15   "Calendar of State Papers, Spain, Volume 5 Part 2: 1536-1538," note
       61.
16   Ibid., note 137.
17   Walker, "Rethinking the Fall of Anne Boleyn," 9.
18   Ives, The Life and Death of Anne Boleyn, 347.
19   "Letters and Papers, Foreign and Domestic, Henry VIII, Volume 10 -
       January-June 1536," note 601.
20   Ives, The Life and Death of Anne Boleyn, 317.
21   Hume, Chronicle of King Henry VIII. of England, 61.
22   George Constantine, Archaeologia, or, Miscellaneous Tracts Relating
       to Antiquity, 23:64.
23   Hutchinson, Thomas Cromwell: The Rise and Fall of Henry VIII's
       Most Notorious Minister, 85.
24   "Letters and Papers, Foreign and Domestic, Henry VIII, Volume 10 -

January-June 1536," note 873.

25   Wilson, In the Lion's Court: Power, Ambition and Sudden Death in the Reign of Henry VIII, 389.

26   "Calendar of State Papers, Spain, Volume 5 Part 2: 1536-1538," note 59.

27   Ibid., note 13.

28   "Letters and Papers, Foreign and Domestic, Henry VIII, Volume 10 - January-June 1536," note 725.

29   Ibid., note 908.

30   Ibid., note 909.

31   "Calendar of State Papers, Spain, Volume 6 Part 1: 1538-1542," note 211.

32   Schofield, The Rise and Fall of Thomas Cromwell: Henry VIII's Most Faithful Servant, 127.

33   Wilson, A Brief History of Henry VIII: Reformer and Tyrant.

34   "Letters and Papers, Foreign and Domestic, Henry VIII, Volume 10 - January-June 1536," note 1205.

35   Ibid., note 926.

36   "Letters and Papers, Foreign and Domestic, Henry VIII, Volume 11: July-December 1536," note 860.

37   Narratives of the Days of the Reformation, Chiefly from the Manuscripts of John Foxe the Martyrologist; with Two Contemporary Biographies of Archbishop Cranmer, 255.

38   "Calendar of State Papers, Spain, Volume 5 Part 2: 1536-1538," note 43.

39   Fox (Foxe), Fox's Book of Martyrs: Acts and Monuments of the Church in Three Volumes, II:407.

40   Starkey, "Henry VIII: Mind of a Tyrant."

41   Cheadle, "Days That Shook the World: Execution of Anne Boleyn."

42   "Letters and Papers, Foreign and Domestic, Henry VIII, Volume 6 - 1533," note 1069.

43   Weir, The Lady in the Tower: The Fall of Anne Boleyn, 10–11.

44   Cavendish, The Life of Cardinal Wolsey, Volume 2, 2:201.

45   Ives, The Life and Death of Anne Boleyn, 70.

46   Walker, "Rethinking the Fall of Anne Boleyn," 26.

47   Cavendish, The Life of Cardinal Wolsey, Volume 2, 2:454.

48   Warnicke, The Rise and Fall of Anne Boleyn: Family Politics at the Court of Henry VIII, 191.

49   Wriothesley, A Chronicle of England During the Reigns of the Tudors, from A.D. 1485 to 1559, 33.

50   "Letters and Papers, Foreign and Domestic, Henry VIII, Volume 10 - January-June 1536," note 284.

Conclusion

1   Ives, The Life and Death of Anne Boleyn, xv.

The Cast – After May 1536

1   Ives, The Life and Death of Anne Boleyn, 353.
2   Ford, "Thomas Audley, Baron Audley of Walden."
3   Davies, "Chapuys, Eustache (1490×92?–1556)."
4   Newcombe, "Skip, John (d. 1552)."
5   Parker Library On the Web.
6   Davies, "Sir Richard Page."
7   Brigden, "Sir Francis Bryan (d.1550)."
8   Lehmberg, "Sir William Kingston."

Bibliography

Primary Sources

A Collection of the Reports of Cases, the Statutes, and Ecclesiastical Laws, Relating to Tithes. Vol. IV, 1826 (ed. Eagle, F K, and E Younge).

Ascoli, Georges. La Grande-Bretagne Devant L'opinion Française Depuis La Guerre De Cent Ans Jusqu'à La Fin Du XVIe Siècle. Paris, 1927.

Bell, Doyne C. Notices of the Historic Persons Buried in the Chapel of St Peter Ad Vincula in the Tower of London, 1877.

BL Cotton MS Vitellius B Xiv, Fol. 220B, British Library.

Burnet, Gilbert. The History of the Reformation of the Church of England. 7 vols. Clarendon Press, Oxford, 1865.

Calendar of State Papers Foreign, Elizabeth, Volume 1: 1558-1559

Calendar of State Papers, Spain, Volume 5 Part 1: 1534-1535

Calendar of State Papers, Spain, Volume 5 Part 2: 1536-1538

Calendar of State Papers, Spain, Volume 6 Part 1: 1538-1542

Cavendish, George. The Life of Cardinal Wolsey, Volume 2. Samuel Weller Singer., 1825.

Cholmondeley of Cholmondeley Estate Records, Will of Lady Elizabeth Savage, 1545. Cheshire Record Office. http://archive.cheshire.gov.uk/.

Clifford, Henry. The Life of Jane Dormer, Duchess of Feria. London: Burns and Oates, 1887.

Constantine, George. Archaeologia, or, Miscellaneous Tracts Relating to Antiquity. Vol. 23. ed. T Amyot, The Society, 1831.

Parker, Matthew. The Correspondence of Matthew Parker, D.D., Archbishop of Canterbury :

Comprising Letters Written by and to Him, from A.D. 1535, to His Death, A.D. 1575 (edited for the Parker Society by John Bruce, and Thomas Thomason Perowne, 1853).

English Historical Documents: 1485-1558. Eyre & Spottiswoode, 1969 (ed. Williams, C H).

Fox (Foxe), John. Fox's Book of Martyrs: Acts and Monuments of the Church in Three Volumes, Vol. II. London: George Virtue, 1851.

Freeman-Mitford, Lord Redesdale, Algernon Bertram. A Tragedy in Stone and Other Papers. London: John Lane, 1913.

Hall, Edward. Hall's Chronicle. London: J Johnson, 1809.

Herbert, Edward. The Life and Raigne of King Henry the Eighth. London, 1649.

Hume, Martin Andrew Sharp. Chronicle of King Henry VIII. of England: Being a Contemporary Record of Some of the Principal Events of the Reigns of Henry VIII. and Edward VI. Written in Spanish by an Unknown Hand. G. Bell and sons, 1889. (The Spanish Chronicle)

Letters and Papers, Foreign and Domestic, Henry VIII, Volume 2: 1515-1518

Letters and Papers, Foreign and Domestic, Henry VIII, Volume 3: 1519-1523

Letters and Papers, Foreign and Domestic, Henry VIII, Volume 4: 1524-1530

Letters and Papers, Foreign and Domestic, Henry VIII, Volume 5: 1531-1532

Letters and Papers, Foreign and Domestic, Henry VIII, Volume 6: 1533

Letters and Papers, Foreign and Domestic, Henry VIII, Volume 7: 1534

Letters and Papers, Foreign and Domestic, Henry VIII,
                                          Volume 8: January-July 1535

Letters and Papers, Foreign and Domestic, Henry VIII,
                                          Volume 9 : August-December 1535

Letters and Papers, Foreign and Domestic, Henry VIII,
                                          Volume 10: January-June 1536

Letters and Papers, Foreign and Domestic, Henry VIII,
                                          Volume 11: July-December 1536

Letters and Papers, Foreign and Domestic, Henry VIII,
                                          Volume 13: Part 1 – January-July 1538

Letters of the Kings of England. Vol. 1. London: H. Colburn, 1848
     (ed. Halliwell-Phillipps, James Orchard).

Letters of the Queens of England, 1100-1547. Sutton Publishing, 1997 (ed. Crawford, Anne).

Narratives of the Days of the Reformation, Chiefly from the Manuscripts of John Foxe the Martyrologist; with Two Contemporary Biographies of Archbishop Cranmer. Camden Society, 1859 (ed. Nichols, John Gough).

Sander, Nicholas. Rise and Growth of the Anglican Schism, 1877.

Sermons by Hugh Latimer. The Parker Society, 1844 (ed. Corrie, Rev. George Elwes).

Skip, John. SP6/1 Folio 8, Sermon Preached by John Skip in the King's Chapel on Passion Sunday 1536, The National Archives.

Stow, John. Annals of England to 1603, 1603.

Strype, John. Ecclesiastical Memorials Relating Chiefly to Religion, and the Reformation of It, and the Emergencies of the Church of England, Under King Henry VIII, King Edward VI, and Queen Mary I. Clarendon Press, Oxford, 1822.

The Chronicle of Calais In the Reigns of Henry VII and Henry VIII to the Year 1540 (ed. Gough Nichols, John).

The Love Letters of Henry VIII (ed. Ridley, Jasper. Weidenfeld Nicolson Illustrated, 1989).

The Remains of Thomas Cranmer. Vol. I. Oxford University Press, 1833 (ed. Jenkyns, Rev. Henry).

Nicholas, Nicholas Harris (ed.). The Privy Purse Expenses of King Henry the Eighth, from November 1529, to December 1532. London: W Pickering, 1827.

The Reports of Sir John Spelman. Selden Society, 1977 (ed. Baker, J A.).

William Latymer's Cronickille of Anne Bulleyne, Camden Miscellany XXX 39 (1990): 23–65 (ed. Dowling, Maria).

Wriothesley, Charles. A Chronicle of England During the Reigns of the Tudors, from A.D. 1485 to 1559. ed. Camden Society 1875.

Secondary Sources

Bernard, G.W. Anne Boleyn: Fatal Attractions. Yale University Press, 2011.

Boehrer, Bruce. The Privy and Its Double: Scatology and Satire in Shakespeare's Theatre, in A Companion to Shakespeare's Works: Poems, Problem Comedies, Late Plays. Vol. IV. Wiley-Blackwell, 2005.

Brigden, Susan. Sir Francis Bryan (d.1550). Oxford Dictionary of National Biography. Oxford University Press, 2004.

Bruce, John. Unpublished Anecdotes of Sir Thomas Wyatt the Poet, and of Other Members of That Family. Gentleman's Magazine, no. XXXIV (1850).

Cheadle, Tanya. Days That Shook the World: Execution of Anne Boleyn. BBC 2, BBC 4, June 17, 2009.

Cherry, Clare. George Boleyn, unpublished manuscript

Davies, C S L. Chapuys, Eustache (1490×92?–1556). Oxford Dictionary of National Biography. Oxford University Press, 2004.

Davies, Catharine. Sir Richard Page. Oxford Dictionary of National Biography. Oxford University Press, 2004.

Dissolution of the Lesser Monasteries Act. Wikipedia

Dowling, Maria. Anne Boleyn and Reform. Journal of Ecclesiastical History 35, no. No. 1 (January 1984).

Encyclopædia Britannica Eleventh Edition. 11th ed. Cambridge University Press, 1911.

Ford, L L. Thomas Audley, Baron Audley of Walden. Oxford Dictionary of National Biography. Oxford University Press, 2004.

Fox, Julia. Jane Boleyn: The Infamous Lady Rochford. Phoenix, 2008.

Friedmann, Paul. Anne Boleyn. 1st ed. Amberley, 2010.

Froude, James Anthony. The Divorce of Catherine of Aragon: The Story as Told by the Imperial Ambassadors Resident at the Court of Henry VIII. Longmans, Green, and co., 1891.

Fuller (1608-1661), Thomas. History of the Worthies of England. Vol. III. London: Thomas Tegg, 1840.

Green Fingers.com. "Red Roses for Anne Boleyn" http://www.greenfingers.com.

Guy, John. The Lady in the Tower: The Fall of Anne Boleyn by Alison Weir –
Sunday Times Review. The Sunday Times, November 1, 2009.

Hoyle, R W. The Origins of the Dissolution of the Monasteries. Historical
Journal 38 (1995):275–305.

Hughes, Jonathan. Francis Weston. Oxford Dictionary of National Biography.
Oxford University Press, 2004.

Hunter, Rev. Joseph. An Introduction to the Valor Ecclesiasticus of King
Henry VIII. The Commissions on the Public Records of the Kingdom, 1834.

Hutchinson, Robert. Thomas Cromwell: The Rise and Fall of Henry VIII's
Most Notorious Minister. Weidenfeld & Nicolson, 2007.

Ives, E W. Court and County Palatine in the Reign of Henry VIII: The
Career of William Brereton of Malpas. Transactions of the Historic Society of
Lancashire and Cheshire 123 (1971): 1–38.

Ives, Eric. Henry Norris. Oxford Dictionary of National Biography. Oxford
University Press, 2004.

Ives, Eric. The Fall of Anne Boleyn Reconsidered. English Historical Review
(1992).

Ives, Eric. The Life and Death of Anne Boleyn. New ed. Wiley-Blackwell, 2005.

Ives, Eric. William Brereton. Oxford Dictionary of National Biography.
Oxford University Press, 2004.

Kergourlay, Yann. The Execution of Anne Boleyn. The Anne Boleyn Files

Knowles, David. The Religious Orders in England: Volume 3 The Tudor Age.
Cambridge University Press, 1979.

Lehmberg, Stanford. Sir William Kingston. Oxford Dictionary of National
Biography. Oxford University Press, 2004.

de Lisle, Leanda. The Sisters Who Would Be Queen. Ballantine Books, 2009.

MacCulloch, Diarmaid. Thomas Cranmer: A Life. Yale University Press, 1998.

McCarthy, Michael. The Jousting Accident That Turned Henry VIII into a
Tyrant. The Independent Newspaper, April 18, 2009.

Meaning of Colors in Christian Art http://www.medieval-life-and-times.info/.

Neale, J E. Queen Elizabeth I. Penguin, 1971.

Newcombe, D G. Skip, John (d. 1552). Oxford Dictionary of National Biography. Oxford University Press, 2004.

Norton, Elizabeth. Jane Seymour: Henry VIII's True Love. Amberley, 2010.

Oxford Dictionary of National Biography. Oxford University Press, no. 2004

Parker Library On the Web http://parkerweb.stanford.edu/.

Richardson, Glenn. Henry VIII and Travel. Historic Royal Palaces.

Ridgway, Claire. The Pregnancies of Anne Boleyn and Catherine of Aragon. The Anne Boleyn Files, February 3, 2010. http://www.theanneboleynfiles.com/.

Russell, Gareth. May 17th 1536 Deaths on Tower Hill. Confessions of a Ci-devant http://garethrussellcidevant.blogspot.com

Russell, Gareth. May 7th, 1536: The Faith of the Prisoner. Confessions of a Ci-devant, May 8, 2010. http://garethrussellcidevant.blogspot.com.

Saini, Raminder K. The 1536 Dissolution of the Lesser Monasteries: Same Suppression, Different Century. University of British Columbia, 2010.

Schama, Simon. A History of Britain – Volume 1: At the Edge of the World? 3000 BC-AD 1603. BBC Books, 2000.

Schofield, John. The Rise and Fall of Thomas Cromwell: Henry VIII's Most Faithful Servant. The 0History Press, 2008.

Sergeant, Philip W. Anne Boleyn: A Study. London: Hutchinson, 1934.

Smeeton, G. The Life and Death of Anne Bullen, Queen Consort of England. Charing Cross, Britain, 1820.

Starkey, David. Acton Court and the Tudors, Tyndall Lecture Theatre, Bristol, March 10, 2011.

Starkey, David. Henry VIII: Mind of a Tyrant. Channel 4, UK, 2009.

Starkey, David. Six Wives: The Queens of Henry VIII. Vintage, 2004.

Strickland, Agnes. Lives of the Queens of England: From the Norman Conquest, Volumes 4-5, 1852.

Thompson, Patricia. Thomas Wyatt: The Critical Heritage. Routledge, 1995.

Tremlett, Giles. Catherine of Aragon: Henry's Spanish Queen. Faber and Faber, 2011.

Walker, Greg. Rethinking the Fall of Anne Boleyn. The Historical Journal, no. 45 (2002): 1–29.

Warnicke, Retha M. The Rise and Fall of Anne Boleyn: Family Politics at the Court of Henry VIII. Cambridge University Press, 1989.

Weir, Alison. The Lady in the Tower: The Fall of Anne Boleyn. Jonathan Cape, 2009.

Wikipedia. The Thirty-nine Articles, 2012.

Wilkinson, Josephine. The Early Loves of Anne Boleyn. Amberley, 2009.

Wilson, Derek. A Brief History of Henry VIII: Reformer and Tyrant. Robinson, 2009.

Wilson, Derek. Hans Holbein: Portrait of an Unknown Man. Pimlico, 2006.

Wilson, Derek. In the Lion's Court: Power, Ambition and Sudden Death in the Reign of Henry VIII. Hutchinson, 2001.

Youings, Joyce A. The Dissolution of the Monasteries. London: Allen and Unwin, 1971.

Younghusband, George. The Tower from Within, 1919.

Index

ISBN: 978-84-94372-1-9-3

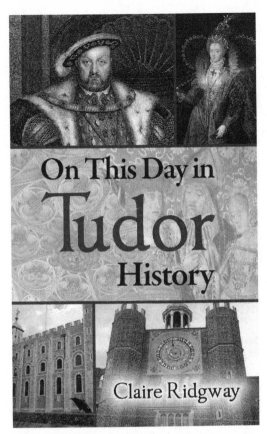

On This Day in
Tudor
History

Claire Ridgway

This book gives a day-by-day look at events from the Tudor era, including births, deaths, baptisms, marriages, battles, arrests, executions and more.

The *must-have* book for Tudor history lovers is perfect for:

- Dipping into daily over your morning coffee
- Using in the classroom
- Trivia nights and quizzes
- Finding out what happened on your birthday or special day
- Wowing friends and family with your Tudor history knowledge
- Researching the Tudor period

Written by best-selling Tudor history author Claire Ridgway, On This Day in Tudor History contains a wealth of information about your favourite Tudor monarchs, their subjects and the times they lived in.

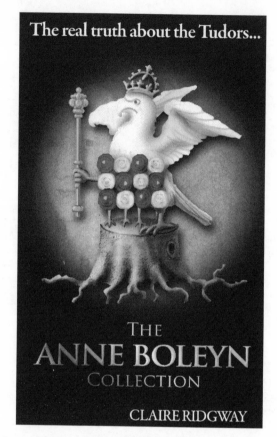

The real truth about the Tudors...

THE
ANNE BOLEYN
COLLECTION

CLAIRE RIDGWAY

ISBN: 978-84-94574-4-9

The Anne Boleyn Collection brings together and revises the most popular articles from top Tudor website The Anne Boleyn Files. Articles which have provoked discussion and debate. Articles that people have found fascinating.

Written in Claire's easy-going style, but with an emphasis on good history and sound research, these articles are perfect reading for Tudor history lovers everywhere. Discover the REAL truth about the Tudors.

- Should Anne Boleyn be pardoned and reburied as Queen?
- Anne Boleyn and "The Other Boleyn Girl".
- Did Anne Boleyn dig her own grave?
- The Six Wives' stereotypes - are they right?
- Did Anne Boleyn commit incest with her brother?

"An absolutely fascinating read. "
- Jeane Westin, Author of His Last Letter

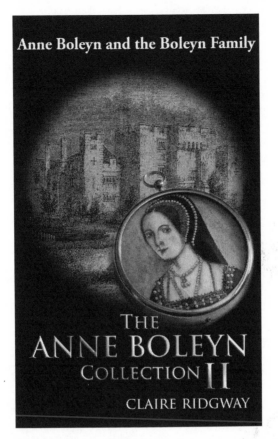

Anne Boleyn and the Boleyn Family

ISBN: 978-84-944574-5-6

THE
ANNE BOLEYN
COLLECTION II
CLAIRE RIDGWAY

Queen Anne Boleyn and her family have gone down in history as ambitious social climbers who stopped at nothing to gain the King's favour, and who paid the ultimate price. But the real Boleyns were very different.

- The origins of the Boleyn family and Anne Boleyn's date of birth
- Anne Boleyn and James Butler
- Anne Boleyn and the accusation of witchcraft
- Anne Boleyn's pregnancies and miscarriages
- Anne and Elizabeth
- Anne Boleyn and the Tower of London
- Thomas and Elizabeth Boleyn, Earl and Countess of Wiltshire
- George Boleyn, Lord Rochford
- Jane Boleyn, Lady Rochford
- Mary Boleyn
- The Boleyns and Religion

INCLUDES OVER 40 ILLUSTRATIONS

MadeGlobal Publishing

Non-fiction History

- Jasper Tudor - **Debra Bayani**
- Tudor Places of Great Britain - **Claire Ridgway**
- On This Day in Tudor History - **Claire Ridgway**
- Illustrated Kings and Queens of England - **Claire Ridgway**
- A History of the English Monarchy - **Gareth Russell**
- The Fall of Anne Boleyn - **Claire Ridgway**
- George Boleyn: Tudor Poet, Courtier & Diplomat
  - **Ridgway & Cherry**
- The Anne Boleyn Collection - **Claire Ridgway**
- The Anne Boleyn Collection II - **Claire Ridgway**
- Two Gentleman Poets at the Court of Henry VIII
  - **Edmond Bapst**
- A Mountain Road - **Douglas Weddell Thompson**

"History in a Nutshell" Series

- Sweating Sickness in a Nutshell - **Claire Ridgway**
- Mary Boleyn in a Nutshell - **Sarah Bryson**
- Thomas Cranmer in a Nutshell - **Beth von Staats**
- Henry VIII's Health in a Nutshell - **Kyra Kramer**
- Catherine Carey in a Nutshell - **Adrienne Dillard**

Historical Fiction

- Between Two Kings: A Novel of Anne Boleyn
  - **Olivia Longueville**
- Phoenix Rising - **Hunter S. Jones**
- Cor Rotto - **Adrienne Dillard**
- The Claimant - **Simon Anderson**
- The Truth of the Line - **Melanie V. Taylor**

Please leave a review

If you enjoyed this book, *please* leave a review with the book seller where you purchased it. There is no better way to thank the author and it really does make a huge difference! *Thank you in advance.*

Made in the USA
Columbia, SC
30 November 2020

25883109R00209